Classical Caledonia

Classical Caledonia
Roman History and Myth in Eighteenth-century Scotland

ALAN MONTGOMERY

EDINBURGH
University Press

Edinburgh University Press is one of the leading university presses in the UK. We publish academic books and journals in our selected subject areas across the humanities and social sciences, combining cutting-edge scholarship with high editorial and production values to produce academic works of lasting importance. For more information visit our website: edinburghuniversitypress.com

© Alan Montgomery, 2020, 2022

First published in hardback by Edinburgh University Press 2020

Edinburgh University Press Ltd
The Tun – Holyrood Road
12(2f) Jackson's Entry
Edinburgh EH8 8PJ

Typeset in 10.5/13 Times New Roman by
Manila Typesetting Company

A CIP record for this book is available from the British Library

ISBN 978 1 4744 4564 1 (hardback)
ISBN 978 1 4744 4565 8 (paperback)
ISBN 978 1 4744 4566 5 (webready PDF)
ISBN 978 1 4744 4567 2 (epub)

The right of Alan Montgomery to be identified as the editor of this work has been asserted in accordance with the Copyright, Designs and Patents Act 1988, and the Copyright and Related Rights Regulations 2003 (SI No. 2498).

Contents

List of figures	viii
Acknowledgements	ix
Introduction	1
Scotland: an indomitable land	2
Inventing a nation	5
Scottish visions of Rome	6
Rediscovering Roman Scotland	11
1 Imagining a classical Caledonia: Sir Robert Sibbald's vision of Scotland's Roman past	15
Education, achievements and antiquarianism	17
Sibbald's vision of Roman Scotland	18
Sources and methodology	20
Influences on Sibbald's Roman Scotland	25
Sibbald's antiquarian reputation and legacy	28
2 Walled out of humanity: Sir John Clerk and his circle	33
Early life and Grand Tour	35
Ancient Rome and modern Union	36
Antiquarian and patron	38
Clerk's response to Roman Scotland	43
A mission to classicise Scotland	46
3 Resisting the 'Conquerors of the Universe': celebrating the Caledonian rejection of Rome	52
Unconquered Caledonia in anti-Union rhetoric	55
Scotland's rejection of Rome in early eighteenth-century historiography	57

	Caledonian indomitability in literary verse	63
	English attitudes towards Caledonian liberty	67
4	'Beyond the Vallum': English interpretations of Scottish history	71
	William Stukeley, antiquarianism and Rome	72
	Stukeley's Roman Scotland	75
	Stukeley's sources and influences	77
	John Horsley and his *Britannia Romana*	79
	Roman Scotland as portrayed in *Britannia Romana*	81
	The reputations and influence of Stukeley and Horsley	84
	Other English views of Roman Scotland	85
5	'Monuments and delights of the arts': rediscovering the material remains of Rome in Scotland	90
	Discovery and excavation	91
	Private collections of Roman antiquities	92
	Institutional collections	95
	Scotland's Roman inscriptions	96
	The artistic merits of Scotland's Roman stones	97
	Misunderstanding and misrepresentation of material remains	99
	Antiquarian interpretations of Scotland's Roman monuments	104
6	Reconquering the Highlands: Hanoverian interpretations of Roman Scotland	112
	Hanoverian 'Romans' versus Highland 'Caledonians'	113
	General Robert Melville and the rediscovery of Agricola's campaigns	115
	The genesis of William Roy's *Military Antiquities of the Romans in Britain*	118
	Roy's interpretation of Scotland's Roman heritage	121
	Alexander Shand and his 'esteemed discoveries of the greatest importance'	126
	Roman Scotland as British history	127
7	The age of 'Agricolamania': early modern uses and abuses of Tacitus' *Agricola*	131
	The rediscovery and early reception of Tacitus' *Agricola*	132
	Agricola the hero	134
	Agricola the enemy	139
	Agricolamania	141

8 Forging a nation: the spurious histories of Charles Bertram and James Macpherson	149
Charles Bertram and the *De Situ Britanniae*	150
The *De Situ Britanniae* and Roman Scotland	153
James Macpherson and Ossian	155
Rome versus Caledonia in the poems of Ossian	158
Filling the void: the motivations of Bertram and Macpherson	163
9 After Ossian: changing interpretations of Roman Scotland	168
Later eighteenth-century Romanist antiquarianism	169
Regional antiquarianism	173
The influence of Ossian	176
New approaches to Scottish history	180
Changing visions of Scotland	182
Conclusion	189
Nineteenth-century approaches to Roman England	192
Classical Caledonia: a study in historical failure	194
Modern attitudes to patriotic Scottish history	197
Bibliography	201
Index	217

Figures

I.1	George Buchanan by Jacobus Houbraken	3
I.2	Colonel William Gordon by Pompeo Batoni	10
1.1	Sir Robert Sibbald by John Alexander or Willem Verelst	16
2.1	Sir John Clerk of Penicuik by Sir John de Medina	34
3.1	Plan of Bar Hill Fort and the Antonine Wall in *Itinerarium Septentrionale*	60
4.1	William Stukeley by J. Smith	73
4.2	Illustration of an Antonine Wall distance slab in *Britannia Romana*	82
5.1	Sculpture of the goddess Brigantia	101
5.2	Ink sketch of the Brigantia sculpture by Sir John Clerk	102
5.3	Illustration of the Brigantia sculpture in *Dissertatio de Monumentis Quibusdam Romanis*	103
5.4	Doocot in the form of Arthur's O'on at Penicuik	107
6.1	Plan and section of Ardoch Fort in *Military Antiquities of the Romans in Britain*	122
7.1	Portrait of Sir John Clerk as 'Agricola' by William Stukeley	138
8.1	James Macpherson by George Romney	156
9.1	George Chalmers by Henry Edridge	171
9.2	'The Roman Wall and Camp near Micklehour' by John McOmie	174

Acknowledgements

My interest in the reception of Scotland's Roman past was first sparked by a master's degree at Birkbeck, University of London, and I am grateful to the many staff members in the Department of History, Classics and Archaeology there who made my studies so rewarding. I owe an enormous debt to Professor Catharine Edwards, my PhD supervisor at Birkbeck who guided me expertly through the writing of my thesis; her vast knowledge of both the ancient world and more recent interpretations of it was truly inspiring. The advice given by my PhD examiners Professor Roey Sweet and Dr David Allan on how to develop and refine my research was also extremely helpful in the formulation of this book.

Over the last four years I have been constantly delighted by the friendship and support offered to me by scholars whose work I greatly admire. Special thanks must go to Iain Gordon Brown, whose lifetime of work and erudite writings on eighteenth-century Scottish antiquarianism inspired much of my own approach. Our discussions on the subject of Sir John Clerk, Sir Walter Scott and others, all fuelled by a bountiful supply of coffee and biscuits, were some of the highlights of this whole project. Similar thanks also go to Professor Lawrence Keppie, both for the time he spent with me at the Hunterian Museum discussing its exceptional collection of Roman distance slabs and for the encouragement and assistance he has offered me since.

Sir Robert Clerk of Penicuik, the descendant of the fascinating Sir John who plays such a major role in this book, has generously allowed me to include quotes from the Clerk family papers and images of his ancestor and his home. My afternoon spent with him at Penicuik as he showed me around his collection and estate as well as the impressive ruins of Penicuik House, recently consolidated thanks to his hard work and determination, is one that I will never forget. I am equally grateful to all of the other institutions and organisations who have allowed me to reproduce their images in the book.

I have travelled many miles during my research, particularly in my hunt for manuscript material and rare books. The assistance that I have received from librarians and archivists has been invaluable, and I am grateful to the staff at the British Library, Institute of Classical Studies, Senate House Library, Bodleian Libraries, Christie's Archive, National Library of Scotland, National Records of Scotland, National Museums Scotland Library, Strathclyde University Library, Edinburgh University Library and Perth Museum for their help and advice over the last six years.

A huge thanks to Susan, Graeme and Gail, whose hospitality made my regular visits to Scotland not only possible but also enjoyable. And finally, my biggest thanks of all go to James for always supporting me in everything that I do.

Introduction

> *L'oubli, et je dirai même l'erreur historique, sont un facteur essentiel de la formation d'une nation . . .*
> (Forgetting, and I would say even historical error, are an essential factor in the formation of a nation . . .)
>
> Ernest Renan, *Qu'est-ce qu'une nation?*, 1882, p. 7

Modern Scotland is a nation that continually struggles with its sense of identity and remains divided over its position within Britain and the wider world. This is not a new phenomenon: in fact, it could be said that Scots have been concerned with such issues ever since they first expressed the symptoms of patriotism, their outward confidence often suggesting an underlying anxiety regarding the status of their homeland. Throughout much of its existence Scotland has been overshadowed by its larger, richer and more populous neighbour to the south. While the two nations often sat in a state of mutual tolerance, this peace was regularly disrupted by political bickering and minor raids that sometimes erupted into full-scale battles and invasions. Although he admits that it is difficult to define, William Ferguson locates early signs of a sense of Scottish identity during the Wars of Independence, a time when English monarchs still believed themselves to be the rightful rulers of Scotland, a claim apparently justified by the spurious histories of Geoffrey of Monmouth that would persist into the Tudor age.[1] Suggestions that the Scottish church should rightly be under English control also threatened religious freedom north of the border. If medieval Scots often found it hard to derive a sense of pride from the current state of their nation, then they naturally turned to the past for nostalgic self-affirmation; for, as Horace Walpole bluntly noted in 1778, 'nations, like private persons, seek lustre from their progenitors, when they have none in themselves'.[2] Although patriotic interpretations of history are hardly unique to Scotland, the nation's status relative to England would only heighten their importance there, and early Scottish historiography often endeavoured to define Scotland's distinctiveness, thereby confirming its right to exist as an autonomous state.

Unfortunately, ancient history cannot always be relied upon to provide the kind of material required for an enriching patriotic narrative. To resolve this issue, early Scottish annalists such as John of Fordun (died c.1384) or Walter Bower (c.1385–1449) were wont to cherry-pick from older texts by Gildas and Bede, combining these elements with fabrications of their own making. The resulting jumble of facts and fictions, legends and half-truths furnished Scotland with its foundation myths, colourful but unlikely tales that began with the arrival in northern Britain of a new people descended from an exiled Egyptian princess named Scota. A similar approach to writing history flourished during the humanist Renaissance, with Hector Boece and George Buchanan both composing works that established the unrivalled antiquity of Scotland and presented her inhabitants as courageous defenders of their liberty.

Scotland: an indomitable land

One of the proudest claims made by Scotland's medieval and Renaissance chroniclers was that their home nation was one of only a handful that had successfully repelled invasions by Rome, the greatest empire that the world had ever known. This, of course, was something that the English had notably failed to do. Indeed, as Scots were not slow to point out, England also later succumbed to the Saxons, the Vikings and the Normans. Scotland's brave repulsion of Roman conquest was repeatedly highlighted in early historiography, these tales of the heroic resistance to foreign attacks from the south obviously reminiscent of their authors' more current concerns.

Writing in the later fourteenth century, John of Fordun made much of the battle to protect ancient Caledonia's integrity. He related an indignant reply sent by the kings of the Scots and Picts to Julius Caesar when the Roman general suggested that they either peacefully submit to his power or face his military might.[3] Fordun was also the first to refer to the Roman wall in Scotland as 'Grymisdyke' (a name which, in various forms, remained in common use until the nineteenth century) whilst describing how the frontier had been breached by Gryme, a mythical Caledonian prince fighting to free southern Scotland from the Romans and their allies, the Britons.[4] Such fantastical stories would only increase in the centuries that followed. The notoriously fabulous *Historia Gentis Scotorum* of Hector Boece, published in Paris in 1527, translated into Scots by John Bellenden at the behest of James V and received with acclaim throughout Europe, makes several references to Caledonia's defeat of Rome. While he cited the recently rediscovered *Agricola* of Tacitus, which includes a detailed account of a first-century invasion of the north that ends in a decisive Roman victory,

Boece also concocted his own glorious sequel in which the Caledonians rose again to reclaim the territory that they had lost.⁵

Humanist scholar, poet and historian George Buchanan (Figure I.1), whose work would remain well-known both at home and abroad well into the eighteenth

Figure I.1 George Buchanan, engraving by Jacobus Houbraken, 1741, after a painting ascribed to Frans Pourbus. (Wellcome Collection, CC BY)

century, expressed some ambivalence towards the early inhabitants of Scotland, praising the austere ancient virtue of the Gaels but criticising their 'rusticity and barbarism'; he was also an admirer of Roman culture and one of the greatest Latinists of his day.[6] His history of Scotland, the *Rerum Scoticarum Historia*, published posthumously in 1582, gives a notably positive spin on the nation's beginnings, following Boece's lead by mixing classical and medieval sources with invented tales of Caledonian triumph. Buchanan's most spirited reference to Scotland's rejection of ancient Rome appears in a 1558 epithalamium composed to celebrate the marriage between Mary Queen of Scots and the dauphin of France. The poem highlights Scotland's long history of unbreached liberty and talks of the nation as a place where Roman conquest was halted (*hic et victoria fixit / Praecipitem Romana gradum*), also noting that this was a feat that many other great nations such as Parthia, Egypt and Germany had failed to achieve.[7] It continues with more imagery of Caledonian bravery, again highlighting Scotland's success in resisting Rome, stating that 'here Rome was satisfied to defend its frontiers / and put up walls to keep out the axe-wielding Scots' (*hic contenta suos defendere fines / Roma securigeris praetendit moenia Scotis*).[8] The paradox of a world-renowned classicist born to a nation that fervently claimed never to have succumbed to Roman conquest was not lost on French scholar Joseph Justus Scaliger (1540–1609), whose epitaph for Buchanan contained the oft-quoted lines:

> *Imperii fuerat Romani Scotia limes*
> *Romani eloquii Scotia finis erit.*
>
> (Scotland formed the frontier of the Roman Empire
> Scotland will be the limit of Roman eloquence.)

By the late seventeenth century, this bold claim to have resisted Rome and all subsequent foreign invasions had become a foundation stone of Scotland's often fragile sense of national pride. But, around the same time, the way in which Scots viewed their past began to change. A new generation of scholars declared the established historiography to be corrupt, even dishonest, and several prefaced their innovative works with condemnations of the 'monkish ignorance' of their predecessors, effectively presenting themselves as the saviours of historical truth.[9]

It is this new breed of antiquarians and historians who will be discussed in *Classical Caledonia*, the men of the long eighteenth century who aimed to lay aside the myths and legends of their forebears and forge a new history for a rapidly evolving nation. During the period covered by this book, from the 1680s, a decade now seen as witnessing the signs of an 'early Enlightenment', through to the beginning of the nineteenth century, interest in Scotland's earliest history was to become more intense than ever before.[10] Some would remain reluctant to delve into the distant past: William Robertson, for example, opened his *History of Scotland* of 1759 with the gloomy assertion that 'the first ages of the Scotch history are dark and fabulous. Nations, as well as men, arrive at maturity by degrees, and the events, which happened during their infancy or early youth, cannot be recollected, and deserve not be remembered'.[11] Others, however, were not to be deterred by such impediments. A new empirical approach and an increase in fieldwork led to a preoccupation with the discovery, study and collection of material remains: 'Amongst the Sciences and Arts much improved in our time, the Archeologie, that is the Explication and Discovery of Ancient Monuments, is one of the greatest use' wrote an optimistic Sir Robert Sibbald in an essay published in 1707, also noting in the same tract the importance of ancient artefacts in attempts to understand early periods for which written evidence was scarce.[12] Travel was becoming easier and faster, while advances in mapping and surveying allowed these antiquarians to more accurately record their finds. As a growing band of Scots involved themselves in the study of the past, so the number of publications on the subject increased exponentially. While the social and political situation in Scotland remained unsettled, history provided not a distraction, but rather a focus, a means, it would be hoped, of bolstering the nation's reputation in an increasingly uncertain world.

Inventing a nation

Before examining in detail the eighteenth-century fascination with Scotland's earliest history, it is worth looking briefly at the wider social and political context in which it emerged. The Regal Union of 1603 had resulted in an absent monarch and an emigration of important and ambitious Scots to London. Battles between Episcopalian and Presbyterian factions of the church moved beyond the theological into all-out violence throughout much of the seventeenth century. The 1690s witnessed terrible famine, while the failure of the Darien Scheme at the end of that decade brought the country to the brink of financial ruin. As a result of civil, religious and political unrest, the later seventeenth century has been identified as one of the most turbulent periods in Scottish history.[13] These various ordeals culminated in the political union of 1707, in which Scotland and England merged to form a new Britain. As even more influential Scots disappeared south to the new British capital, many feared that Scotland was doomed to become a neglected province of this new superstate.[14] Even after the Union, the disdain felt by the English towards their northern neighbours was often tangible: according to Ferguson, this 'Scotophobia' would persist into the later eighteenth century and beyond.[15] In both 1715 and 1745 Britain descended into near chaos in the face of Jacobite rebellion. To complicate matters further, Scotland itself was split in two, the Gaelic-speaking Highlanders viewed with contempt by the Lowlanders, who confidently regarded themselves as more sophisticated, indeed more anglicised than their northern compatriots.[16]

Although, for the sake of clarity, I will describe it throughout this book as a 'nation', eighteenth-century Scotland does not comfortably fit the criteria often used to define that most nebulous of entities. Split into Highlands and Lowlands, it was certainly not unified by a single language or shared cultural traits and, as a state without sovereignty, its status post-1707 was unusually ambiguous. Murray Pittock identifies the eighteenth century as 'the rite of passage for Scotland and Scottishness', with Neil Davidson proposing that, although signs of it can be detected from 1746 onwards, it was only in the early nineteenth century that notions of Highland and Lowland culture were merged to create a single national consciousness.[17] A shared and coherent historical narrative is a crucial element in the development of a nation's self-identity, and it is one important strand of the early modern Scottish efforts to build just such a consolidating narrative that will be examined in *Classical Caledonia*. Pulling Scotland together after a time of trauma and deciding just what 'Scotland' now meant were the tasks at hand, and historiography, particularly attempts to locate the very beginnings of the Scottish nation, was to play an essential role in this process. But, as Ernest Renan proposes in the quote chosen as the epigraph to this Introduction, using history to construct national identity is an inevitably tricky endeavour.

Scottish visions of Rome

As has been much discussed in recent scholarship, a widespread interest in the history, culture and politics of ancient Rome was to flourish amongst Britain's elite during the eighteenth century. Many Scots were swept up in this mania for the classical, and there need be no doubt that what Philip Ayres describes as 'the propensity of the English aristocracy and gentry to image themselves as virtuous Romans in the century following the Revolution settlement of 1688–9' was also to be found north of the border.[18] Indeed, by the early 1770s natural philosopher and antiquarian John Anderson was writing in an essay presented to the Literary Society of Glasgow of 'the high idea which is commonly entertained of Roman greatness'.[19] These Romanist tendencies inevitably came to define much of the literature, scholarship, art and architecture of the period, also influencing attitudes towards history both national and international. For a cultivated early modern Scottish gentleman, be he landed gentry, a member of the clique of virtuosi or one of the many who attended a city high school, a thorough knowledge of Roman language, philosophy and history was the norm. The importance of these subjects was instilled in boys from an early age, and in this way the political and moral ideas that they contained were implanted into impressionable young minds.

The roots of this Scottish fascination with ancient Rome can be traced back to the sixteenth century, when Boece and Buchanan were writing their Latin poetry and histories, also when Gavin Douglas produced a pioneering translation of Virgil's *Aeneid* into Scots. David Allan locates the origins of the Scottish appreciation for ancient Rome in humanist scholarship, noting a particular attachment to the works of Cicero and Livy.[20] Although, as previously mentioned, both Boece and Buchanan were compelled by patriotism to downplay Roman influence in Scotland in their own historical works, they also believed that their fellow Scots would benefit from a revival of the classical tradition; Buchanan concluded, for example, that a total conversion to Latin would mark Scotland's arrival at true civilisation.[21] Similar views were held by David Hume of Godscroft (1558–1630?), another Latin poet and historian much influenced by Livy and admired by Buchanan himself, who held the Roman citizen up as an exemplar for the Renaissance man.[22] A late sixteenth/early seventeenth-century fashion for neo-Stoicism seems to have developed not only thanks to close links with France and the Netherlands, where the movement was already established, but also due to Scotland's political and social instability at this time.[23] Influential Jacobean Scots who studied on the continent included Buchanan, Sir John Scott of Scotstarvit and William Drummond. It was these men, Allan suggests, who brought home with them a new admiration for the Roman state and Roman civil law as well as an appreciation of literary pastoralism inspired by Virgil and his later imitators.[24]

For most educated eighteenth-century Scots, their introduction to the language, literature and culture of ancient Rome took place in the classroom. A review of the curriculum recommended to the teachers at the Edinburgh High School in 1709 demonstrates a heavy reliance on classical texts ranging from Ovid and Cornelius Nepos to Livy, Sallust, Cicero and Florus.[25] Scottish school curricula were generally similar to those in England, with differences including the teaching of Suetonius and Buchanan's psalms; Tacitus' *Agricola* and *Germania* were also studied north of the border, as were the letters of Pliny.[26] English to Latin translation was more common in Scotland than in England, with Thomas Ruddiman's *Rudiments of the Latin Tongue* becoming the standard grammar from 1714 onwards.[27] In a defence of classical learning published in 1769 in which he responded to accusations that education depended too much on Latin, Enlightenment poet and philosopher James Beattie considered its impact to be more than just academic, suggesting that a widespread knowledge of the classics could benefit the Scottish nation as a whole:

> It is however thought by many, who in my opinion are more competent judges, that an early acquaintance with the classics is the only foundation of good learning, and that it is incumbent on all who direct the studies of youth, to have this great object

continually before them, as a matter of the most serious concern; for that a good taste in literature is friendly both to public and to private virtue, and of course tends to promote in no inconsiderable degree the glory of a nation; and that as the ancients are more or less understood, the principles and the spirit of sound erudition will ever be found to flourish or decay.[28]

As well as its language and literature, a demand for instruction on the subject of Roman civilisation can also be detected. *The Edinburgh Evening Courant* of 8 August 1745 includes an advert placed by one James Barclay offering to teach 'mythology, Roman antiquities, geography and Ancient History' in addition to the usual Latin grammar and classical authors.[29] A course on Roman antiquities was also introduced at the Grammar School of South Leith in 1779, and the same topic was being taught at the Canongate High School by 1784.[30] The preface to the internationally popular textbook *Roman Antiquities*, authored by Edinburgh High School rector Alexander Adam and first published in 1791, makes clear the importance of the subject not just for a proper understanding of the ancient past, but also for the training of future statesmen and leaders, providing examples of how (and how not) to organise and rule a world-dominating empire:

> He has endeavoured to give a just view of the constitution of the Roman government, and to point out the principal causes of the various changes which it underwent. This part, it is hoped, will be found calculated to impress on the minds of youth just sentiments of government in general, by shewing on the one hand the pernicious effects of aristocratic domination; and on the other, the still more hurtful consequences of democratic licentiousness, and oligarchic tyranny.[31]

A solid grounding in Latin was expected of anyone who hoped to attend Scotland's universities, where the classics were promoted as a way to introduce young men to what mathematician David Gregory described as 'the Virtue, learning, knowledge of the World and politeness'.[32] Glasgow University professor Andrew Ross, who taught there from 1706 to 1735, held private classes in 'Roman customs', while the 1740s saw the appointment in Edinburgh of a professor dedicated to 'Universal Civil History and Roman Antiquities' who was also one of the last to deliver his lectures in Latin.[33] Many early modern Scots travelled abroad for their education, with Leiden, an institution with a long tradition of fine classical scholarship, the choice of many (particularly Protestant) students.

In their enthusiasm for the classical past, a growing number of wealthy Scots also travelled to Italy to see the wonders of the city of Rome, or perhaps also the impressive remains to be found around the Bay of Naples. Although the Grand Tour is often more associated with the eighteenth century, some Scots made such trips much earlier: Richard Lassels, an English Roman Catholic priest and Royalist exile, wrote an early version of his *Voyage of Italy* to guide Scottish aristocrat David Murray, 2nd Lord Balvaird, on a tour in 1654.[34] Visitors to Rome would come face to face with the magnificent remnants of the culture that they had long studied, and purchasing souvenirs was an important part of any such trip. Douglas Hamilton, 8th Duke of Hamilton returned from a four-year tour in 1776 with acquisitions including a marble Venus and a portrait of himself alongside his tutor and his tutor's son amongst classical ruins by artist and antiquarian Gavin Hamilton. Thomas Dundas, only son of Scottish politician and entrepreneur Sir Lawrence, was painted by Pompeo Batoni surrounded by some of the most famous ancient sculptures at Rome including the Apollo Belvedere, the Belvedere Antinous and the Laocoön. One of the most striking Grand Tour portraits is surely that of William Gordon of Fyvie, depicted by Batoni in front of the Colosseum standing resplendent in his belted plaid, showing himself to be a well-travelled man of taste who was, perhaps most importantly, a proud Scot (Figure I.2).

Several of these tourists, such as Sir James Hall of Dunglass (who was in Italy in the 1780s) and Sir William Forbes (who completed his Grand Tour in 1793), kept exhaustive journals that describe their encounters with relics of the ancient world. As Rosemary Sweet points out, such accounts were sometimes written with the intention that they be shared with family and friends back home.[35] Roger Robertson of Ladykirk wrote to his family in 1751, telling his father about his visits to Pozzuoli, Baiae and Cumae, a later missal also vividly describing (in French) his descent into the subterranean Roman theatre at Herculaneum and discussing the treasures discovered there.[36] Even while surrounded by the imposing classical ruins in Italy, however, memories of Scotland were never far away: Sir James Hall explored the Bay of Naples in 1785 and made notes in his journal about visits to the Roman 'burryed towns' at Herculaneum, Stabiae and Pompeii, noticing at the last of these a hypocaust that he thought similar to one recently uncovered at Inveresk.[37]

As well as admirable civility and exemplary statesmanship, ancient Rome also represented military success, and soldiers were encouraged to emulate its imperialist tactics. In 1753, William Duncan, professor of natural philosophy at Aberdeen University, published his *Commentaries of Caesar Translated into English* that included a 'Discourse Concerning the Roman Art of War'. In the book's dedication to George, Prince of Wales, the author suggests that the prince could learn much from the Roman general even at a time when monarchs no longer led their men into battle, Duncan's belief in the need for a strong monarch in the face of 'dangerous domestic Seditions' no doubt inspired by the Jacobite rebellion that had rocked the nation only seven years previously.

Figure I.2 Colonel William Gordon, oil on canvas by Pompeo Batoni, 1766. (© National Trust for Scotland, Fyvie Castle)

Rediscovering Roman Scotland

Given this admiration for ancient Rome, it is hardly surprising that a significant number of eighteenth-century Scots were eager to identify the Roman heritage of their own nation. A curiosity regarding the physical remains of Rome in Scotland had in fact begun to emerge over the previous century. As early as the 1590s cartographer Timothy Pont was making maps and notes that included details of Roman sites and charted the route of the Antonine Wall across the Forth/Clyde isthmus. During the mid-seventeenth century geographer Robert Gordon of Straloch was mapping and writing about the same Roman frontier and recording the inscriptions found along its length.[38] By the end of the 1600s this interest blossomed and, as we shall see, during the decades that followed it would become something of an obsession for some.

But while certain Scots were intent on discovering Roman remains in their own homeland, their education encouraging high expectations of this most estimable ancient empire, that long-standing tradition of Scotland's repulsion of Rome still strongly influenced approaches to national history. These contradictory pulls made this a historical period that would prove both enticing and problematic for early modern Scots. Many, wary of the idea of foreign conquest, were inclined to celebrate the indigenous people they regarded as their ancestors, namely those courageous Caledonians. Others, anxious to establish links between the modern nation and the classical world, were quick to embrace evidence of Roman power in Scotland: while not quite attempting to re-align the perceived ancestry of themselves and their countrymen, these men were certainly hoping to embellish their worryingly savage origins with a gilding of classical elegance. A few wavered between the two options, unwilling or unable to decide which they preferred, or which showed Scotland in a better light.

The problems and challenges presented by Roman Scotland and the heated eighteenth-century debates that its study inspired are the focus of *Classical Caledonia*. This was a subject that would raise many difficult questions for early modern Scots. How could the prevailing reverence for all things Roman sit with the centuries-old belief that the early inhabitants of Scotland had ferociously battled to remain outside the Roman world? Did the literary sources and the ancient remains north of Hadrian's Wall demonstrate that the Romans had in fact conquered the region, or just that they had repeatedly tried and failed to do so? When it came to formulating a rousing historical narrative for Scotland, was it better to have been conquered and civilised by Rome, or to have repelled it and resolutely remained barbaric? Scholars on both sides of the argument resorted to manipulation of the sources, and both approaches to the past were also mired in myth, misinterpretation and outright fabrication. The Scottish habit of believing the unbelievable if it happened to support pretensions to national supremacy was noted by a cynical Samuel Johnson, who proposed that 'the Scots have something to plead for their easy reception of an improbable fiction: they are seduced by their fondness for their supposed ancestors'.[39] Whoever those supposed ancestors might be, the veracity of Johnson's observation when it came to reconstructing the history of Roman Scotland will be demonstrated in the following chapters.

'I believe that this is the historical Age, and this the historical Nation' proclaimed an ebullient David Hume in 1770.[40] But despite such confidence in Scotland's Enlightenment historiography, eighteenth-century Scots would fail to reach a consensus on the classical heritage of their nation. The early modern reception of Roman Scotland was influenced by various factors, including the widespread admiration for Roman culture among the educated elite, a traditional historiography that proposed the rejection of that culture by Scotland's indigenous people, geographically imprecise literary sources and confusing material remains that suggested repeated Roman invasions of the north, all combined with contemporary anxieties provoked by dramatic changes in the status of the modern nation. None of these factors, apart perhaps from the sheer number of invasions, are unique in themselves. The English and the French both celebrated the refusal of their supposed ancestors to accept Roman domination; neither, however, could deny that this resistance had been ultimately unsuccessful. The inhabitants of the German-speaking states idolised the heroic Arminius/Hermann and, as discussed in Christopher Krebs' *A Most Dangerous Book* of 2011, regularly employed Tacitus' *Germania* to demonstrate their racial purity. What was certainly particular to Scotland was the level of uncertainty regarding the duration and impact of Roman involvement in the region, with the existence of what might be called (to borrow a phrase from later Scottish history) quasi-Roman 'debatable lands' proving endlessly baffling to antiquarians. The conflicting tales of Roman invasion and retreat as well as Caledonian victory and defeat found in ancient literary sources and medieval chronicles proved to be one of the most perplexing aspects of Roman Scotland. Nowhere else presented this level of ambiguity, a landscape dotted with Roman remains that may or may not have been what early modern commentators would have regarded as truly Roman. The eighteenth-century struggle to make sense of this confused and confusing history and the disputes that ensued offer us a fascinating case study in how history can be used and abused in the formulation of a national story.

The antiquarians and historians who wrestled with the subject of Roman Scotland were a diverse group, some researching and writing for pleasure, others for prestige, a small number working for money, each with their own distinct approach to Scotland's early past. Some were set on demonstrating Scotland's natural separateness, while others preferred to highlight its new role as a part of Great Britain. The belief that the Romans had first brought Christianity to these islands was also important to certain commentators. That most were members of the elite and all were male is unsurprising given the nature of scholarship and publishing at the time. Political propaganda and poetry will also be investigated here, revealing the widespread popularity of the imagery of Caledonia's opposition to Rome as a symbol of ongoing battles for national dignity. Employing both manuscript and printed texts, I have frequently quoted the early modern authors' own words, and in doing so have largely retained their erratic orthography, grammar, italicisations and capitalisations, also their arbitrary use of apostrophes, inserting a *sic* only where I believe there is an actual typographical or hand-written error. The identity and provenance of the indigenous peoples inhabiting northern Britain were much debated by these eighteenth-century writers, and indeed still are today. Variously identified in the many texts discussed in this book as Caledonians, Scots and Picts along with other tribal names, to avoid confusion I will generally refer to them using the coverall term 'Caledonians', and similarly use 'Caledonia' to mean the geographical region that later became Scotland.

In the end, following decades of zealous research, Scots realised that the Roman period was not an area of history that could elevate their nation, but rather a historical dead end. A century on from its promising beginnings in the 1680s, the study of Roman Scotland ended up as something of a joke, viewed as the domain of credulous fools and charlatans, and was already being overwhelmed by more romanticised visions of the past. The story of Roman involvement in the north could not provide Scots with the sort of inspiring material that they sought for their national narrative, but the attempts to uncover, record and adapt it, as well as the confusion, disappointment and hostility that it inspired, makes its eighteenth-century reception an area ripe for study, revealing much about the shifting perceptions of both 'Roman-ness' and Scottishness at this pivotal stage in the development of Scotland's identity.

Notes

1. Ferguson, *The Identity of the Scottish Nation*, p. 33; ibid. p. 307.
2. Walpole, *Private Correspondence of Horace Walpole*, p. 131.
3. Fordun, *Chronicle of the Scottish Nation*, pp. 44–5.
4. Ibid. p. 82.
5. Bellenden, *The Works of John Bellenden*, p. 162.
6. Mason, 'Civil Society and the Celts', pp. 105–6.
7. Buchanan, *George Buchanan: The Political Poetry*, p. 137.
8. Ibid. pp. 138–9. The English translation is by McGinnis and Williamson.
9. For example: Gordon, *Itinerarium Septentrionale*, Preface. Also: Sibbald, *Historical Inquiries*, pp. ii–iii. A similar English critique of Scottish historiography can be found in: Stukeley, *An Account of a Roman Temple*, p. 2.
10. On the recent reappraisal of Scottish scholarship pre-1707, see: Bowie, 'New Perspectives on Pre-Union Scotland', pp. 309–13.

11. Robertson, *The History of Scotland*, p. 1.
12. Sibbald, *Historical Inquiries*, p. ii.
13. Withers, 'How Scotland Came to Know Itself', p. 381.
14. On Scottish opposition to the Union both before and after 1707, see: Pittock, *Scottish Nationality*, pp. 55–62.
15. Ferguson, *The Identity of the Scottish Nation*, pp. 227–8.
16. For more on Lowland perceptions of Highland culture, see: Davidson, *The Origins of Scottish Nationhood*, pp. 63–72.
17. Pittock, *Scottish Nationality*, p. 71; Davidson, *The Origins of Scottish Nationhood*, p. 78; ibid. pp. 138–9.
18. Ayres, *Classical Culture and the Idea of Rome in Eighteenth-Century England*, p. xiii.
19. SUL OA/5/5, f. 1: Anderson, 'Of the Roman Wall Between the Forth and Clyde', c.1770.
20. Allan, *Virtue, Learning and the Scottish Enlightenment*, pp. 32–3.
21. Bushnell, 'George Buchanan, James VI and Neoclassicism', p. 95.
22. McGinnis and Williamson, 'Introduction', p. 36.
23. Allan, 'A Commendation of the Private Countrey Life', p. 61.
24. Ibid. pp. 63–4.
25. Law, *Education in Edinburgh in the Eighteenth Century*, p. 74.
26. Clarke, *Classical Education in Britain*, p. 135; ibid. p. 138.
27. Ibid. p. 135.
28. Beattie, *Essays*, p. 493.
29. Law, *Education in Edinburgh in the Eighteenth Century*, p. 76.
30. Ibid. p. 80; ibid. p. 79.
31. Adam, *Roman Antiquities*, p. vi.
32. Gregory quoted in: Ouston, 'Cultural Life from the Restoration to the Union', p. 23.
33. Clarke, *Classical Education in Britain*, p. 143.
34. NLS Adv.MS.15.2.15: Lassels, 'Description of Italy', 1654.
35. Sweet, *Cities and the Grand Tour*, p. 17.
36. NLS Acc.12244, f. 86: Robertson to family, 5 October 1751; NLS Acc.12244, f. 87: Robertson to family, 19 October 1751.
37. NLS MS 6327, f. 19: Hall, travel journal, Rome to Palermo, 1785; ibid. f. 32.
38. Keppie, *The Antiquarian Rediscovery of the Antonine Wall*, p. 41.
39. Johnson, *A Journey to the Western Islands of Scotland*, p. 276. Johnson was referring here to the poems attributed to Ossian that will be discussed in detail in Chapter 8.
40. Hume, *The Letters of David Hume*, p. 230.

1

Imagining a classical Caledonia: Sir Robert Sibbald's vision of Scotland's Roman past

> *Antiquam exquirite matrem*
> (Seek out your ancient mother[land])
> Virgil, *Aeneid* 3.96, quoted on the title page of Robert Sibbald's *Commentarius in Julii Agricolae Expeditiones*, 1711

Born in Edinburgh in 1641 into a wealthy landowning family, Robert Sibbald (Figure 1.1) was to become one of the most noted Scottish scholars of his day. Devoting his life to study, his research covering a wide variety of fields including medicine, geography and history both natural and human, Sibbald was a true virtuoso who was driven by his insatiable curiosity and an ambition to improve the state of learning in Scotland. Demonstrating a fascination with the past and a desire to both stay abreast of and make a contribution to European scholarship, Sibbald's work presents contradictions: while his approach was often old-fashioned, rooted as it was in seventeenth-century traditions, his methodology could be remarkably innovative and the conjectures that he proposed were sometimes radical.

A dedicated Scottish patriot, Sibbald focused largely on his home nation, charting its geography both ancient and modern, and displayed a specific interest in uncovering its Roman past. He scoured the landscape for material evidence of Roman activity north of Hadrian's Wall, studied classical texts, medieval chronicles and more recent writings on the subject and discussed the matter at length with fellow antiquarians in his extensive correspondence. Keen to share the results of his research, Sibbald was the first Scot to publish essays devoted exclusively to the endeavours of the Romans in Scotland. In these texts, particularly his *Historical Inquiries, Concerning the Roman Monuments and Antiquities in the North Part of Britain Called Scotland* of 1707, as well as his *Conjectures Concerning the Roman Ports, Colonies, and Forts, in the Firths* and his *Commentarius in Julii Agricolae Expeditiones*, both published in 1711,

Figure 1.1 Sir Robert Sibbald, oil on wood by John Alexander or Willem Verelst. (© Royal College of Physicians of Edinburgh)

he developed a thorough account of the nation's early history and topography. In doing so, he completely rewrote Scotland's beginnings, for while previous generations of chroniclers and historians had celebrated the region's rebuttal of conquest, Sibbald portrayed its southern reaches as a virtual Roman province, its landscape dotted with Roman towns, ports and forts containing public buildings and monuments, all symbols of an unmistakably classical Caledonia. Although his proposals were to prove influential during his lifetime and for decades after his death, they were also fiercely contested. By looking at his life and times and by surveying his extensive manuscript and published writings, this chapter will reveal the inspiration behind Sibbald's novel portrayal of Roman Scotland. By studying his methodology and motivation, we can come closer to understanding this elaborate construct and gain a clearer picture of how his attitudes towards both ancient Rome and modern Scotland developed during a period of relentless political, social and intellectual change.

Education, achievements and antiquarianism

Sibbald's rather sketchy memoirs, written in the mid-1690s but only relating events up to 1692, reveal an early life dedicated to learning. He began studying Latin aged nine under one James (or possibly Andrew) Crawford of Cupar in Fife and later attended the High School in Edinburgh, where his studiousness earned him the nickname 'Diogenes in Dolio'.[1] His university career began in Edinburgh; later he joined the growing ranks of Scots who were heading to mainland Europe to continue their education, studying at Leiden, Paris and Angers, also visiting London before his return to Scotland in October 1662.[2] This experience opened Sibbald's eyes to the wider intellectual world and inspired an aspiration to establish Scotland's place within it, an attitude that has led Charles Withers to describe him as 'both Scot and European'.[3]

Sibbald trained as a physician and played a key role in the foundation of both Edinburgh's first Physic Garden in 1670 and the Royal College of Physicians in 1682, but he did not restrict himself to the study of medicine alone. A survey of his published works gives a clear indication of the breadth of his scholarship: starting with his *Disputatio Medica de Variis Tabis Speciebus* of 1661 and ending with a *Description of the Isles of Orkney and Zetland* in 1711, the numerous advertisements, proposals, essays and books printed during these five decades cover medicine, antiquarianism, natural history, geography, biography and economics. In 1682 Sibbald was appointed Charles II's 'Geographer of the Kingdome of Scotland, and commanded to publish the naturall History, and the Geographick description yrof'.[4] He began work on what he hoped would become his magnum opus, a two-volume *Scotish Atlas*, one volume dedicated to recalling *Scotia Antiqua*, the other describing *Scotia Moderna*. The *Atlas* would record the nation's flora and fauna (particularly those that offered potential medicinal or financial benefits) and give a 'just and full description . . . of the ancient monuments of the said kingdom, and of the sherrifdoms, royal burghs, towns, rivers, friths, bays, ports, roads, lochs and of his [the King's] castles and forts, the houses of his nobility and gentry'.[5] Scuppered by funding problems, regime change, an overabundance of material and the author's own personal problems, of which more later, this ambitious undertaking would never make it to the press. The content of many of the texts that Sibbald was to publish over the next three decades, however, clearly relates to the research carried out for this unfinished work. An undated manuscript draft of his history of Fife, for example, which features a detailed commentary on the *Agricola* of Tacitus, states that the author had been advised to release it as a 'specimen' to drum up interest in the project, while the preface to the published *History, Ancient and Modern, of the Sheriffdoms of Fife and Kinross*, which includes much material on the Romans, reveals that its text formed part of the *Atlas*.[6]

Despite that fact that he was already heavily involved in his studies of the past by the time he wrote them, Sibbald's memoirs make no direct reference to his antiquarian work. What they do reveal is an interest in classical philosophy, with their author noting that, soon after his return to Scotland, he 'read Seneca and Epictetus, and some other of the stoiks, and affected ym, because of yr contempt of riches and honours'.[7] His fascination with the ancient world is further indicated by the books held in his vast library. The catalogue of sale printed soon after his death in 1722 includes a wealth of volumes pertaining to the language and culture of ancient Rome such as dictionaries, grammars and lexicons, as well as numerous (often multiple) copies of classical texts. More than a third of his books relate to classical literature, substantially outnumbering those dedicated to medicine.[8] A good understanding of classical languages would have been vital for Sibbald's forays into Roman history and, no doubt with an eye to attracting an international readership, he published several works in Latin, despite being advised by peers on at least one occasion to 'write . . . in our own language'.[9] He also used it extensively in his lectures, placing an advert in *The Edinburgh Courant* in 1706 to promote a forthcoming lecture series that warned prospective students they would need to be well-versed in both Latin and Greek.[10] Furthermore, while Sibbald was to mine the classical literary sources for evidence of Roman involvement in Scotland, he also relied on them for his work in other areas, citing Solinus in a discussion of whales and quoting the description of the British coastline included by Tacitus in his *Agricola* (chapter 10) in proposals to improve the state of Scottish fishing.[11] A profound knowledge of Roman learning was, Sibbald believed, crucial for an understanding not just of the past, but also of the present.

By the mid-1690s Sibbald's reputation as an antiquarian had clearly reached beyond the borders of Scotland, as he was invited to contribute new material to Edmund Gibson's 1695 edition of William Camden's iconic *Britannia*. Gibson aimed to include a more accurate translation of Camden's original Latin text, but also recruited a raft of scholars from across the British Isles to improve and expand it. Sibbald had already expressed frustration with the quality of the material relating to Scotland in the original work, criticising Camden for being 'no friend to us in what he writeth', and Gibson clearly felt that Sibbald himself was the best man for the job, describing him as 'master of the affairs of that kingdom'.[12] Sibbald's inclusion in this influential book, the *vade mecum* of many an early eighteenth-century antiquarian, would have significantly raised his profile across Britain and beyond.

Sibbald's vision of Roman Scotland

Although Sibbald studied various periods of Scottish history, it was undoubtedly Roman Scotland that interested him the most. His published texts, most importantly his 1707 *Historical Inquiries*, as well as his many surviving manuscript notes and letters, give an insight into the extent of this fixation, and also allow us to build a coherent picture of his very particular vision of ancient Caledonia. That Sibbald believed Scotland, or at least its southern reaches, to have once been a Roman province is made clear at the opening of *Historical Inquiries*:

> For the Ancients by Triumphal Arches, Temples, Altars, Pyramids, Obelisks and Inscriptions upon them, and Medals, handed down to Posterity, the History, Religion and Policy of their Times, and an Account of the Sciences and Arts which then flourished ... The *Romans* were coming and going here for near four Hundred Years, and they left Monuments of all these sorts mentioned, in this Country ... [13]

Replicating William Camden's late sixteenth-century portrayal of the province of Britannia, Sibbald describes a Roman Scotland traversed by a network of roads lined with country houses, inns, inscribed milestones and places for travellers to rest and change horses.[14] He claimed that the Romans taught the Caledonians to build with stone and also established both *coloniae*, which he identifies as settlements for Romans and their auxiliaries that were governed according to Roman law and custom, and *municipia*, places built by the local tribes and retaining local laws which enjoyed the benefits of Roman civility.[15] Sibbald believed that Latin was also adopted by the indigenous peoples, with Juvenal's claim that '*de conducendo loquitur iam rhetore Thule*' (Thule now speaks of hiring a rhetorician) presented as evidence.[16] He even suggested that traces of Latin had endured and that aspects of 'the language we now use in the North part of *Scotland*' (presumably Gaelic) were descended from it, with certain (unspecified) words deriving from those 'introduced by the *Romans* ... when they were here'.[17]

Sibbald's chronicle of early Scotland begins with the arrival of the Roman general Agricola in the late first century. He apparently discovered a country that was wild, marshy, heavily wooded and difficult to negotiate. As a result, the Romans found it easier to begin their invasion along the coast, constructing forts and 'stations', and later roads and bridges across the marshy hinterland.[18] As will be discussed in more detail in Chapter 7, Sibbald saw Agricola as the man who effectively brought civilisation to Scotland, and in an early manuscript suggested that it was he who had founded a Roman city at Camelon and also built the enigmatic domed structure nearby known as Arthur's O'on.[19] It was also thanks to Agricola, Sibbald proposed, that a fortified frontier was established along the Forth/Clyde isthmus after which 'the Romans indeed made this the outmost limit of their province, and gave the name of Britain to that part of the island within the Roman wall, which was built on this narrow neck of ground'.[20]

The Roman conquest of the north was not a complete success, however, and despite such attempts to subdue and civilise the Caledonians, Sibbald's

Roman Scotland was not a place of continual peace and harmony. He stresses that the Romans 'were not able to make all this country a *Roman* Province', and relates numerous bids by the tribes to reclaim the lands of which they had been 'deprived'.[21] It was due to one such violent uprising that the emperor Hadrian visited the region, building an apparently unfinished wall that Sibbald surprisingly locates in East Lothian.[22] Influenced by George Buchanan, Sibbald's early notes on the Roman wall running between Forth and Clyde attribute it to Septimius Severus, claiming that it was built to protect the 'Roman province' to the south of it; later, having studied the monument and the carved stones found along it, he correctly deduced that it had been built during the reign of Antoninus Pius, proposing that it was constructed in the wake of a Caledonian rebellion.[23] He suggested that Septimius Severus did much to tame the wild and inaccessible terrain of northern Scotland during his early third-century invasion, marching up into the north east and establishing a settlement called Orrea (modern Burntisland) en route.[24] By 1707 he was also attributing the foundation of the supposed city at Camelon to Severus and identifying it as the administrative centre of the province, as well as the residence of the Roman 'Commander in chief'.[25] He now also concluded that Severus had built the stone wall between Solway and Tyne, with the Romans falling back to this frontier after his death.[26] Only during the reign of the late third-century renegade emperor Carausius was the area between the two walls retaken by the Romans, a victory which Sibbald believed was commemorated by the construction of a triumphal arch at Ingliston near Edinburgh.[27] His account of Roman Scotland concludes around the end of the fourth century, when the collapse of the empire forced the Roman troops to retreat to the continent.[28]

Sources and methodology

Sibbald employed various methods in formulating his idiosyncratic portrayal of Roman Scotland, some traditional, some more modern. He frequently cites his sources throughout his work, often referring to classical authors, medieval annals and more recent writings, including those of his contemporaries. He praised recent improvements in 'Archeologie', by which he meant the study of ancient monuments, inscriptions and coins, and made many visits to supposed Roman sites himself, as well as receiving reports on others from friends and acquaintances.[29] In addition, he relied on the (distinctly unreliable, in his case at least) technique of etymology.

Of all of these sources, he viewed the material remains as the most trustworthy and informative. The presence of a Latin inscription could identify a site as unquestionably Roman and Sibbald was particularly interested in the numerous surviving carved stone panels found along the line of the Antonine Wall, valuing the information that they contained on military matters.[30] The find-spots of Roman antiquities large or small could also help to establish the extent of their incursions into Scotland, the existence of supposed Roman camps in Angus and the discovery of what Sibbald believed to be Roman weapons in Moray and Caithness used as evidence for the northern limits of their military activity.[31] Coins were regarded as a useful source, with Sibbald's library containing several books on numismatics such as Charles Patin's *Imperatorum Romanorum Numismata* of 1671.[32] The renowned coin collection put together by the brothers James and Andrew Balfour, as well as the collection of James Sutherland then held in the Advocates Library (which apparently contained numerous Roman coins of Scottish provenance), was also discussed in the antiquarian's works.[33] The imagery and text on coins was particularly valuable: one in the collection of the Advocates Library apparently confirmed the victory of Carausius in southern Scotland, while Sibbald's ideas regarding the appearance of that supposed Roman triumphal arch at Ingliston were based on coins illustrated in Gibson's edition of *Britannia*.[34]

A full investigation of Scotland's Roman remains would have required a great deal of travel, and Sibbald certainly gave the impression that he had covered many miles in search of them. He wrote that, whilst preparing his commentary on Agricola's Caledonian exploits:

> *peragravi omnem fere eam Regionem, quam in suis Expeditionibus hic cum copiis Agricola pervagatus est, & Castra, Castellaque Romana plaeraque, Praetenturas, loca ubi praelia inita, lapides inscriptos, Numismata, aliaque Monumenta illis in locis reperta, inspexi . . .*[35]

> (I covered nearly all of that region, which Agricola travelled through here with his troops during his expeditions, and inspected the camps and many Roman forts, frontier posts, the sites where battles occurred, inscribed stones, coins, and other monuments found in these places . . .)

He visited Arthur's O'on several times, inspecting it carefully with a torch on one occasion, and finding previous descriptions of the Antonine Wall to be confused, he 'viewed some parts of it myself'.[36] When Welsh antiquarian Edward Lhuyd (sometimes spelled 'Llwyd') visited Scotland in 1699, Sibbald wrote an essay for him entitled *Directions for his Honoured Friend Mr Llwyd How to Trace and Remarke the Vestiges of the Roman Wall Betwixt Forth and Clyde* that describes the Roman frontier as well as other historical and natural curiosities to be found along its route. Sibbald's description, however, suggests that the sections of the wall that he had visited himself tended to be in the east, closer to his family home at Kipps near Linlithgow, while the sections west of Falkirk are treated more superficially.[37]

In fact, just as appears to be the case in his geographical writings, Sibbald's claims of extensive fieldwork are somewhat overstated.[38] Much of the information that he published on the material remains of Roman Scotland is derived from the reports he received from various contacts around Scotland and further afield. Sibbald sat at the heart of an influential community of antiquarians, a circle of men similarly dedicated to the study of the past who were eager to share and discuss their discoveries and conjectures with one another. William Nicolson, Archdeacon of Carlisle, himself an avid collector of antiquities, viewed the Roman inscribed stones held at Glasgow University in 1699 and sent news of them to Sibbald, later meeting him in person in Edinburgh.[39] Thanks to his position as assistant librarian and later librarian at the same institution, Robert Wodrow was able to keep Sibbald up to date on the latest Roman artefacts to arrive there.[40] On 28 October 1699, for example, Wodrow wrote to Sibbald of one such addition to the collection, promising to send more details at a later date: 'There is just nou come to my hands a large clear Roman Inscription, rot very curious sculpture about it'.[41] In a letter sent the following year, Sibbald asked Wodrow to 'take notice of all the ancient monuments, the inscriptions, medalls, or other pieces of antiquity found alongst the Roman Wall', while another letter of 1702 begged him for information on any inscriptions that he was aware of, Sibbald adding cryptically 'wee shall have need of them'.[42] Cartographer John Adair, who demonstrated his own interest in the vestiges of Roman Scotland and had planned to publish a map of the Antonine Wall, was employed by Sibbald to conduct surveys for inclusion in the ill-fated *Scotish Atlas*.[43] Although its activities are almost completely unrecorded and even the dates of its foundation and dissolution are unclear, Sibbald also refers to his involvement in a 'Club of Antiquaries' that held weekly meetings in Edinburgh during the first decade of the eighteenth century, at which the history and remains of Roman Scotland would no doubt have been debated at length.[44]

Many of the men who supplied information used in Sibbald's antiquarian tracts were, however, less well-versed in the subject. As was common for such works at this time, much of the material collected for the *Scotish Atlas* was gathered from questionnaires sent out to local gentry and clergyman around Scotland in the early 1680s. Included in the list of queries was one requesting information on any '*vetera Monumenta, inscriptiones, sculpta aut figurata Saxa, Munimenta & Castra antiqua*' (old monuments, inscriptions, sculpted or carved stones, defences or ancient monuments), while a manuscript describing 'Dunbarton' from Sibbald's collection that may be one of the responses mentions the location and current state of the western end of the Antonine Wall.[45] Such an approach to collecting information inevitably risked the inclusion of ideas based more on folklore than historical or physical evidence. Certainly, some of the more unlikely conjectures that appear in the *Historical Inquiries* were derived from such non-specialist contributors, with clergyman William Abercrombie encouraged by local tradition to suggest that a Roman port had once stood at Turnberry and Sibbald's belief that Hadrian had built his wall in East Lothian inspired by reports of a long earthwork there provided by an unnamed landowner.[46]

While Sibbald enjoyed the discovery and study of material remains, regarding them as indisputable records of the distant past, he was ambivalent towards written sources. On the one hand he described the surviving classical texts as 'the best Vouchers of antiquity', on the other he dismissed their accounts of the Roman walls in Britain as 'Lame and perplexed'.[47] Medieval writers were also viewed with suspicion and criticised for further muddling the history of the walls, their works marred by 'Confusion and Incertainty', which was only made worse by later historians, who 'choosed rather to retain the traditions of the First, than to apply themselves to the right way of discovering the Truth of these Matters'.[48] Despite such doubts and criticisms, the expression of which only served to underline the importance of Sibbald's innovative use of material remains, these sources were vital for the formation of the antiquarian's own conjectures. In the preface to the *Historical Inquiries* he relates an extensive list of the classical sources that he had found the most useful, citing:

> *Julius Agricola* by *Cornelius Tacitus* . . . and from what may be gathered from *Herodian* and *Dio*, their Accounts of the Actions of the Emperour *Septimius Severus*, and of his *Son Antoninus Caracalla*, in this Country, and from what *Ammianus Marcellinus* has written of what was done in this country by *Theodosius*.[49]

Also included in the list are 'the poet Claudian', as well as 'the *Tables of Ptolemy*, and the *Peutengerian Tables*, and the *Notitia Imperii Occidentalis*'.[50] The *Historia Augusta* is cited throughout the same essay.[51] These sources were carefully analysed not just for their descriptions of the actions of the Romans in Scotland, but also for the information that they contained on the ancient geography of the region, with Sibbald boldly concluding in his 1710 treatise on Fife that the texts of Tacitus, Dio and Herodian 'say enough to make a just Description of this of the Part Country [*sic*]' in Roman times.[52]

Sibbald's collection of books relating to the classics has already been mentioned, and many of them were editions of the texts that included content relating directly to Scotland. The library that was sold off following the antiquarian's demise included numerous copies of Dio's *Roman History*, one published in Paris in 1548 and another French edition dated 1592, as well as several copies of the *Historia Augusta*, two dated 1603 and 1661 including notes by Isaac Casaubon and another from 1620 with notes by Claude Saumaise.[53] Sibbald's collection also contained several collected works of Tacitus, as well as a 1683 edition of

Tacitus' *Agricola* with notes by German philologist August Buchner and another of 1642 with notes by Dutch scholar Marcus Zuerius van Boxhorn.[54] He also exhibits his knowledge of the various editions of the *Agricola* with notes by other European classical scholars in the preface to his own commentary on Tacitus' text, the publication of which, he surely hoped, would place him amongst their esteemed ranks.[55] Sibbald was seemingly able to put aside his reticence towards the medieval chronicles when it suited his purpose. He refers on several occasions to Bede's descriptions of the Roman walls found in the *Historia Ecclesiastica Gentis Anglorum* and also made use of the *Historia Brittonum* attributed to the ninth-century monk Nennius. The fourteenth-century *Chronica Gentis Scotorum* by John of Fordun is often cited, as is the *Rerum Scoticarum Historia* of George Buchanan, whom Sibbald nominated 'another Livius'.[56]

Sibbald also kept up to date with more recent antiquarian research, referencing the seventeenth-century studies of the Antonine Wall made by Timothy Pont, Christopher Irvine, David Buchanan, Robert Gordon of Straloch and David Drummond; having acquired the personal papers of the first two, he drew heavily on them in his own writings.[57] Indeed, it is largely thanks to Sibbald's reuse of Pont's work (particularly in his contributions to the 1695 *Britannia*) that any of the cartographer's antiquarian discoveries have been preserved for posterity. Scholarship from outside Scotland also played a part in Sibbald's conjectures. Although he was critical of the lack of material on Scotland in early editions of the *Britannia*, he nevertheless cites Camden regularly. It is likely that Sibbald's 1711 *Conjectures Concerning the Roman Ports, Colonies, and Forts, in the Firths*, which describes the landscape around the east coast of southern Scotland during the Roman period, was inspired by English antiquarian William Somner's posthumously published *Treatise on the Roman Ports and Forts in Kent* of 1693, a copy of which was held in Sibbald's library on its dispersal in 1723.[58] Although Sibbald never made it to Rome, he acquired a number of books about the city's classical antiquities. It is surely volumes such as the 1645 *Ritratto di Roma Antica con Figure*, which contains images of ancient architecture by Filipo Rossi, or Andreas Fulvius' similarly illustrated *Antichità di Roma con Figure* of 1588, both of which were in his collection, that informed his own perceptions of ancient Rome and the grandeur of its buildings and monuments.[59]

From time to time Sibbald indulged in etymological conjectures, trying to establish a Roman heritage for Scottish places by analysing their modern names. Aware of its potential pitfalls, William Camden used this method only when no other evidence came to hand, but it was regularly employed by other early antiquarians, often with fanciful results.[60] Sibbald's own ventures into etymology are largely unconvincing. The name of the village of Gullane in East Lothian, for instance, was allegedly derived from its ancient status as a *colonia*, the common Scottish prefix 'Cair' supposedly denoted a former Roman *municipium*, and in the text that he contributed to John Slezer's *Theatrum Scotiae*, Corstorphine near Edinburgh is identified as the Roman Corstopitum.[61]

Influences on Sibbald's Roman Scotland

Sir Robert Sibbald's portrayal of ancient Scotland largely under Roman control, its landscape filled with imposing symbols of Roman civility, was a radical departure from previous historiographies, which were generally more interested in tales of Roman defeat at the hands of heroic Caledonians. What, then, prompted Sibbald to propose such an unconventional view and thus challenge one of the main tenets of Scotland's national pride by calling into question the claim that it had unfailingly maintained its liberty in the face of foreign invasion? Presumably influenced by the publication dates of his treatises that include material on the Romans in Scotland, modern scholars have proposed that Sibbald became preoccupied with the subject in later life and that his notion of Scotland as part of an ancient Britannia was influenced by the context of the British Union.[62] However, as will be demonstrated here, his views on union are difficult to pin down, and in fact his manuscript notes reveal a much earlier interest in the subject than those eighteenth-century publication dates suggest.

Sibbald liked to imagine himself detached from the troubled worlds of politics and religion. Taking inspiration from Robert Leighton, the principal of Edinburgh University during Sibbald's time there, he stated that, as a young man, he preferred 'a quite lyfe, wherein I might not be ingadged in factions of Church or state'.[63] In the early eighteenth century, when debate surrounding the possibilities of British union was reaching its peak, Sibbald's friends and associates varied in their allegiances.[64] In response to English claims that Scotland had historically possessed no sovereignty independent of England, he (anonymously) published a tract using medieval manuscripts to assert *The Liberty and Independency of the Kingdom and Church of Scotland* in 1702, its popularity leading to reprints with additional material in 1703 and 1704.[65] Elsewhere, his stance on union alters according to his audience. On 2 December 1702, writing to anti-unionist Robert Wodrow, he seemed nervous but resigned: 'I ame told the Union goes on a pace, God grant it may be for our good'.[66] Nineteen days later he wrote to Hans Sloane in London sounding enthusiastic and positively impatient: 'I should wish wee were more bent for ane Union and then wee might better advance both learning and trade, and better oppose our foreigne enemies'.[67] Sibbald's attitude towards the Union might be compared with his religious affiliations, which were notoriously indecisive and susceptible to outside influence. Apparently persuaded by his patron the Earl of Perth, he made a brief conversion to Catholicism in 1685, but recanted after a mob attacked his Edinburgh house and he was forced to flee for a time to London, later describing this episode as 'the difficultest passage of my lyfe'.[68] Not for nothing did Sibbald's professional rival Archibald Pitcairn lampoon the antiquarian's wavering political and religious beliefs in verse:

> With each wind he hath steer'd
> And hath often so veered,
> That at last he split on ambition.[69]

Regarding the dating of his antiquarian ideas, that many of his eighteenth-century printed works can be traced back to the seventeenth-century research carried out for the *Scotish Atlas* has already been demonstrated. That its volume dedicated to *Scotia Antica* would depict southern Scotland as a Roman province is indicated by the proposal produced in 1683 (in English and Latin), which reveals that it was to feature a chapter dedicated to the '*Colonia Romana in Scotia*'.[70] Although incomplete, a manuscript of around 1687 apparently related to the same volume lists some of the planned chapters: one section entitled '*De exteris qui Caledoniam Armis Invaderunt*' (Of the outsiders who invaded Caledonia) is dedicated to Roman Scotland, and was to include a chapter on '*Coloniis et Urbibus Romanis*' (Roman colonies and cities) and another describing a Roman temple (presumably Arthur's O'on).[71] These proposed chapters demonstrate that Sibbald's vision of a classical Caledonia was already formulated by the early 1680s, a time when union with England was far from the mind of most Scots. It is in his essay on Thule, first published in 1693 and later included in the 1695 *Britannia*, that he states that all of the land to the south of the Forth/Clyde isthmus was conquered by Agricola and subsequently became part of the province named 'Britain'.[72] Furthermore, the composition of the *Historical Inquiries*, the treatise that most clearly defined the antiquarian's ideas on Roman Scotland, took place long before its 1707 publication. In the preface to his edition of the *Britannia*, Edmund Gibson reveals that it was a 'model he has given us of his intended *Antiquities*' that confirmed Sibbald's suitability as a contributor, implying that a draft of the work was already in circulation before 1695. *Historical Inquiries* was certainly complete by 1703, its publication only held up by the backlog at the presses due to the large quantities of literature relating to the Union that were by then being printed.[73]

Given the difficulty of attributing pro-union tendencies to Sibbald's antiquarian conjectures, it seems that we must look elsewhere in search of the motivations behind his singular vision of Roman Scotland. In fact, his Romanist inclinations are a more likely reason for his radical rewriting of Scotland's historical narrative. That Sibbald was captivated by Roman history and a fervent admirer of Roman culture and civility is evident. For him, that Rome might have played a key role in the development of early Scotland would have been an appealing idea, and a desire to present himself and his fellow Scots as the inheritors of a classical legacy can be detected throughout his writings. In summing up his *Historical Inquiries*, Sibbald makes clear the enduring impact that he believed the Romans had made on the landscape and society of the nation:

> By all which it is clear, that the *Romans* stayed long in this Country: They did introduce Order and Civility where ever they came, and by the Arts and Policy they taught our Ancestors, they tamed their Fierceness, and brought them to affect a civil Life: The Order they established in their Colonies, procured the respect we still have for the Civil Law, and their Colonies and Garrisons, and Ports, gave rise to the building of our best Towns.[74]

Modern Scotland, then, was built on Roman foundations. The civility that the Romans had introduced had survived even after they had left the British Isles and could be traced right up to the present day. In particular, Sibbald proposed that many of the towns and strongholds of medieval Scotland, places that often still remained the major seats of power, were located on the very spots where the Romans had established their forts, ports and colonies.[75]

Although he proudly proclaimed his compatriots 'famous for their learning and inventions', elsewhere Sibbald expressed frustration with the state of scholarship in Scotland, despairing at the lack of research into its history and blaming the limited work on Roman material remains on the fact that 'few in this country have been Curious to Trace them'.[76] For decades Scotland had been riven by religious and constitutional turmoil, yet Sibbald remained optimistic that his own research could improve the lot of the Scottish people. The royal warrant from Charles II that appointed Sibbald to the post of Geographer Royal had, after all, proposed that he should use the role to improve learning and encourage 'the enriching of his said Kingdom'.[77] The years following the Revolution of 1689–90 were to plunge Scotland further into crisis: during the 1690s Scots faced seven years of famine, and by the end of the decade they struggled to contain the financial fallout resulting from the collapse of the Darien Scheme. For Sibbald, identifying and describing a classical past was one way to improve Scotland's standing, aligning it with the other major nations of Europe by establishing its position within the ancient world's most distinguished empire.

The extent of Sibbald's proposed Roman Scotland also reflects early modern ideas of the border between civilisation and savagery. In proposing the existence of ancient towns in Fife, he extended the limits of Roman control far beyond the line of the Antonine Wall and created a frontier remarkably similar to the then boundary between Highland and Lowland culture.[78] He saw clear differences between the two regions, noting that 'the Lowlanders are more civilized and use the language and habit of the English, the Highlanders are more rude and Barb(ruse?) and use that of the Irish'.[79] In Sibbald's mind, the uncivilised inhabitants of the far north had hardly evolved since ancient times: 'the Highlanders retain yett the habit and many of the maners and customs of the Ancient Scots'.[80]

Sibbald's antiquarian reputation and legacy

Sir Robert put considerable effort into promoting his work both at home and abroad. His long correspondence with Sir Hans Sloane indicates that he viewed the English scholar, a fellow physician who had played a major role in the development of the Royal Society, as a useful conduit for the dissemination of his writings south of the border. He sent several proposals for works that he hoped to publish down to London, and Sloane also tried to raise funds for the *Atlas*, although the fact that he found only twelve subscribers by 1709 suggests that his efforts were largely unsuccessful (Sibbald had been hoping for at least 100).[81] When Sibbald's treatises finally made it into print the author sent multiple copies to Sloane to read himself and pass on to members of the Royal Society and other scholars. *Historical Inquiries* was sent soon after publication, his treatise on Fife was dispatched in 1710 and copies of his commentary on the *Agricola* and his *Conjectures Concerning the Roman Ports, Colonies, and Forts, in the Firths* were promised the following year.[82] At times, however, he felt that his work was overlooked and undervalued. Only 200 copies of his *Historical Inquiries* were printed, since 'few here are curious of such matters'.[83] That the *Scotish Atlas* never materialised was surely a huge disappointment to the ageing antiquarian, and references to it in his letters to Sloane dry up after 1710. Hugh Ouston suggests that Sibbald's later years would be overshadowed by a sense of 'isolation and discontinuity'.[84] By then the proposed *Atlas*, its regional approach to Scotland's geography and history inspired by the seventeenth-century taste for chorography, must have already seemed outdated.

In his researches into the past and present of the Scottish nation, Sir Robert Sibbald saw himself as promoting its merits and achievements, presenting Scotland to the rest of the world as a place of learning and polite society. In following Apollo's instructions to seek out his ancient motherland, the words quoted on the title page of his own commentary on Tacitus' *Agricola*, Sibbald aimed to locate a noble heritage for Scotland. For him, this meant classicising Caledonia, filling its southern reaches with evidence of Roman civility. While he saw the ancient Caledonians as the ancestors of early modern Scots, it is evident that he regarded the legacy left by the conquering Romans as a key factor in the evolution of the nation. As a result, any lump of ruined masonry or overgrown earthwork was enthusiastically declared Roman, any place name that contained a syllable faintly reminiscent of Latin pronounced a former Roman settlement. In presenting his new interpretation of Roman Scotland, Sibbald saw himself as a pioneer, and seemingly expected criticism: 'I must intreat Pardon for the Liberty and Boldness I have assumed, having broken the Ice first in this way of writing our Antiquities'.[85] His prediction was to prove correct and, as will be revealed in the next chapter, his proposals were soon to be publicly ridiculed in the writings of aspiring antiquarian Alexander Gordon, a man with his own partisan approach towards Scotland's ancient past.

Despite these disappointments and criticisms, Sibbald's reputation as an esteemed antiquarian was to long outlive the man himself. In 1778, fifty-six years after his death, James Boswell was to describe him as 'the celebrated Scottish antiquary', and when his memoirs were first published in 1837 their editor labelled him an 'indefatigable Antiquary'.[86] Today he is viewed as a key figure in the development of Scotland's proto-Enlightenment, his output playing an important role in the nation's eighteenth-century intellectual revolution.[87] As fanciful as they may seem today, the impact of Sibbald's theories on early modern interpretations of Roman Scotland should not be underestimated. His conjectures would be regularly cited by later antiquarians, not only those determined to demonstrate an enduring Roman impact on northern Britain, but also those more intent on establishing Scotland's long-standing freedom from foreign control. As we shall see, the debate that his ideas ignited would rage for decades, as generation after generation of Scots attempted to establish the racial and cultural roots of their venerable nation.

Notes

1. Paget Hett, *The Memoirs of Sir Robert Sibbald*, p. 55.
2. On early modern Scots studying abroad, see: Emerson, 'Scottish Cultural Change 1610–1710', p. 128.
3. Withers, *Geography, Science and National Identity*, p. 71.
4. Paget Hett, *The Memoirs of Sir Robert Sibbald*, p. 95.
5. Dallas, *A System of Stiles*, Part II, p. 63.
6. A microfilm copy of this manuscript is held at the British Library as BL RP 2417/2. A possible date for it can be found in a letter from Sibbald to Edward Lhuyd dated 10 July 1703 (BL Evelyn Papers Vol. DXVIII Add MS 78685, f. 41), which mentions a recently finished 'History and Description of Fife'.
7. Paget Hett, *The Memoirs of Sir Robert Sibbald*, p. 61.
8. Donaldson, 'The Sale Catalogue of Sir Robert Sibbald's Last Library', p. 87.
9. BL Sloane MS 4039, f. 26: Sibbald to Sloane, 12 September 1702.
10. Paget Hett, *The Memoirs of Sir Robert Sibbald*, p. 9.
11. BL Sloane MS 4029, f. 278: Sibbald to Sloane, 23 March 1703; NLS Adv.MS.33.5.16, f. 37: Sibbald, untitled and undated notes, possibly related to the 'Discourses Anent the Improvements May Be Made in Scotland'.
12. Sibbald, *An Account of the Scotish Atlas*, p. 4; Gibson, *Britannia*, Preface.
13. Sibbald, *Historical Inquiries*, p. ii.
14. Ibid. p. 39. For Edmund Gibson's translation of Camden's original Latin text, see: Gibson, *Britannia*, pp. lxvi–lxvii.

15. Sibbald, *Historical Inquiries*, p. 40.
16. Juvenal, *Satires* 15 quoted in: Sibbald, *Historical Inquiries*, p. 2. The mysterious Thule mentioned by various Roman authors was identified as the north of Scotland by Sibbald in an essay on the subject, published in: Gibson, *Britannia*, pp. 1089–1100.
17. Sibbald, *The History, Ancient and Modern, of the Sheriffdoms of Fife and Kinross*, p. 13.
18. Sibbald, *Conjectures Concerning the Roman Ports, Colonies, and Forts*, pp. 1–2. As with many of the antiquarians discussed in this book, Sibbald's definition of the term 'station' is ambiguous, since he uses it to describe what he believed to be both military and civil Roman sites, as well as some that were apparently a combination of both.
19. NLS Adv.MS.15.1.1, f. 5: Sibbald, 'Atlas Scoticus', c.1682. Camelon is now identified as a military site with evidence of Agricolan and Antonine occupation. For more on Arthur's O'on, see Chapter 5.
20. Gibson, *Britannia*, p. 1094. He is referring to the Antonine Wall, which was later built along a similar route to Agricola's fortified frontier.
21. Sibbald, *Historical Inquiries*, p. 1; ibid. p. 25.
22. Ibid. pp. 6–7.
23. NLS Adv.MS.15.1.1, f. 5: Sibbald, 'Atlas Scoticus', c.1682; Sibbald, *Historical Inquiries*, p. 8.
24. Sibbald, *Historical Inquiries*, p. 16; Sibbald, *Conjectures Concerning the Roman Ports, Colonies, and Forts*, p. 12.
25. Sibbald, *Historical Inquiries*, p. 41.
26. Ibid. pp. 18–19. This is the wall known today as Hadrian's Wall.
27. Ibid. pp. 20–3.
28. Sibbald, *Series Rerum a Romanis . . . Gestarum*, p. 122.
29. Sibbald, *Historical Inquiries*, Preface.
30. For Sibbald's survey of the Antonine Wall distance slabs, see: Sibbald, *Historical Inquiries*, pp. 47–50.
31. Ibid. pp. 15–16.
32. *Bibliotheca Sibbaldiana*, p. 97.
33. Sibbald, *Historical Inquiries*, p. 51.
34. Ibid. pp. 23–4.
35. Sibbald, *Commentarius in Julii Agricolae Expeditiones*, Praefatio.
36. Sibbald, *Historical Inquiries*, p. 44; ibid. p. 27.
37. The original manuscript of this letter is in the Bodleian Library, reference Bodl.Lib.MS Carte 269, ff. 129d–135. It was published in 1910 in: Haverfield, 'Sir Robert Sibbald's "Directions for his honoured friend Mr. Llwyd how to trace and remarke the vestiges of the Roman wall betwixt Forth and Clyde"'.
38. For Sibbald's reliance on the accounts of others in his geographical work, see: Withers, *Geography, Science and National Identity*, pp. 80–1.
39. Keppie, *The Antiquarian Rediscovery of the Antonine Wall*, p. 53.
40. For more on Glasgow University's collection of Roman antiquities, see Chapter 5.
41. EUL MS Laing III.355.19: Wodrow to Sibbald, 28 October 1699.
42. Sibbald, *Memoirs of the Royal College of Physicians*, p. 23; ibid. p. 30.
43. On Adair's work on Roman Scotland, see: Keppie, *The Antiquarian Rediscovery of the Antonine Wall*, pp. 49–50.
44. Sibbald, *Memoirs of the Royal College of Physicians*, p. 34. On the suggested dates for the club, see: Keppie, *The Antiquarian Rediscovery of the Antonine Wall*, p. 47 (where 1703

is proposed as its foundation date); also: Emerson 'Sir Robert Sibbald', p. 47 (where it is suggested that it ran from 1700 until c.1706, perhaps even 1709).
45. Sibbald, *Nuncius Scoto-Britannus*, p. 14; Mitchell, *Geographical Collections Relating to Scotland*, p. 196.
46. Sibbald, *Historical Inquiries*, p. 35; ibid. pp. 6–7.
47. Sibbald, *The History, Ancient and Modern, of the Sheriffdoms of Fife and Kinross*, p. 5; Sibbald, *Historical Inquiries*, p. ii.
48. Sibbald, *The History, Ancient and Modern, of the Sheriffdoms of Fife and Kinross*, p. 5.
49. Sibbald, *Historical Inquiries*, p. ii.
50. Ibid. On the uses of these ancient sources in antiquarian works at this time, particularly various editions of Camden's *Britannia*, see: Hingley, *The Recovery of Roman Britain*, pp. 26–7.
51. For example: Sibbald, *Historical Inquiries*, p. 8.
52. Sibbald, *The History, Ancient and Modern, of the Sheriffdoms of Fife and Kinross*, p. 5.
53. *Bibliotheca Sibbaldiana*, p. 94; ibid. p. 110; ibid, p. 101; ibid. p. 113; ibid. p. 95.
54. Ibid. p. 112; ibid. p. 113.
55. Sibbald, *Commentarius in Julii Agricolae Expeditiones*, Praefatio.
56. NLS Adv.MS.15.1.1, f. 20: Sibbald, 'Atlas Scoticus', c.1682.
57. Sibbald, *Historical Inquiries*, p. iii; Keppie, *The Antiquarian Rediscovery of the Antonine Wall*, p. 47.
58. *Bibliotheca Sibbaldiana*, p. 51.
59. Ibid. p. 43.
60. Parry, *The Trophies of Time*, pp. 29–30.
61. Sibbald, *Historical Inquiries*, pp. 40–1; Slezer, *Theatrum Scotiae*, p. 2. Corstopitum is now known to be Corbridge, Northumberland.
62. Simpson, 'Sir Robert Sibbald – The Founder of the College', p. 78; Hingley, *The Recovery of Roman Britain*, p. 103.
63. Paget Hett, *The Memoirs of Sir Robert Sibbald*, p. 56.
64. Emerson, 'Sir Robert Sibbald', p. 51.
65. Bowie, *Scottish Public Opinion and the Anglo-Scottish Union*, p. 89.
66. Sibbald, *Memoirs of the Royal College of Physicians*, p. 32.
67. BL Sloane MS 4039, f. 53: Sibbald to Sloane, 21 December 1702.
68. Paget Hett, *The Memoirs of Sir Robert Sibbald*, p. 86.
69. Ibid. p. 4.
70. Sibbald, *Nuncius Scoto-Britannus*, p. 5.
71. NLS Adv.MS.15.1.2, f. 2: Sibbald, 'Caledonia seu Scotica Antiqua', c.1687.
72. Gibson, *Britannia*, p. 1094.
73. Keppie, *The Antiquarian Rediscovery of the Antonine Wall*, p. 55.
74. Sibbald, *Historical Inquiries*, p. 51.
75. Sibbald, *Conjectures Concerning the Roman Ports, Colonies, and Forts*, pp. 10–11.
76. NLS Adv.MS.33.5.16, f. 81: Sibbald, 'Discourses Anent the Improvements May Be Made in Scotland', 1698; Sibbald, *Conjectures Concerning the Roman Ports, Colonies, and Forts*, Preface; Sibbald, *Historical Inquiries*, Preface.
77. Dallas, *A System of Stiles*, Part II, p. 63.
78. For a map detailing the extent of Gaelic culture in 1698, see: Dawson, *The Gaidhealtachd and the Emergence of the Scottish Highlands*, p. 282.
79. NLS Adv.MS.33.5.16, f. 81: Sibbald, 'Discourses Anent the Improvements May Be Made in Scotland', 1698.

80. NLS Adv.MS.15.1.1, f. 19: Sibbald, 'Atlas Scoticus', c.1682.
81. BL Sloane MS 4041, f. 300: Sibbald to Sloane, 23 February 1709; BL Sloane MS 4042, f. 22: Sibbald to Sloane, 2 August 1709.
82. BL Sloane MS 4060, f. 354: Sibbald to Sloane, 29 September (1707?): BL Sloane MS 4042, f. 112: Sibbald to Sloane, 16 March 1710; BL Sloane MS 4042, f. 293: Sibbald to Sloane, 2 June 1711.
83. BL Sloane MS 4060, f. 354: Sibbald to Sloane, 29 September (1707?).
84. Ouston, 'Cultural Life from the Restoration to the Union', p. 17.
85. Sibbald, *Historical Inquiries*, Preface.
86. Paget Hett, *The Memoirs of Sir Robert Sibbald*, p. 1; Sibbald, *Memoirs of the Royal College of Physicians*, reverse of title page.
87. Emerson, 'Sir Robert Sibbald', p. 42.

2

Walled out of humanity: Sir John Clerk and his circle

> AMONGST all those of the first Rate
> Our Learned CLERK blest with the Fate
> Of thinking Right can best relate
> These Beauties all,
> Which bear the Marks of ancient Date,
> Be North the Wall.
>
> Allan Ramsay, *A Scots Ode, to the British Antiquarians*, 1726, p. 7

Born in 1676, Sir John Clerk of Penicuik (Figure 2.1) belonged to the generation that followed Sir Robert Sibbald. Renowned during his lifetime as a politician, judge, patron, composer and antiquarian, his reputation faded in the centuries following his death, to the extent that he would be described in the 1970s as 'a figure strangely neglected in the story of the nascent Scottish Enlightenment'.[1] Since then, largely thanks to the pioneering research of Iain Gordon Brown, his importance in the evolution of Scottish learning has become much better understood. Like Sibbald, Clerk was the son of a prosperous landowning family, and both men led lives similarly informed by a love of ancient Rome. An avid reader of classical literature and collector of ancient artefacts, Clerk styled himself as a Roman, even fashioning for himself houses and estates that imitated those of the ancients. Also like Sibbald, Clerk declared himself a Scottish patriot and spent much of his life tracing and discussing the ancient history of his nation. In addition, Clerk was a generous patron of professional antiquarians, most notably Alexander Gordon, also John Horsley, whose extensive fieldwork resulted in two of the most important and influential eighteenth-century books featuring material on Roman Scotland. Unlike Sibbald, however, Clerk only occasionally slipped into Romanist fantasy, generally (but not always) taking a more level-headed approach to his interpretation of Scotland's Roman heritage.

As a result of this pragmatic attitude towards history, Clerk was reluctantly

Figure 2.1 Sir John Clerk of Penicuik, oil on canvas by Sir John de Medina, c.1700. (© Gary Doak Photography, reproduced courtesy of Sir Robert Clerk)

compelled to admit that, rather than the settled province proposed by Sibbald, Caledonia had in fact largely remained outside the sphere of Roman influence. While, at times, Clerk celebrated the courage of the indigenous peoples who had apparently succeeded in repelling Roman conquest, he often expressed disappointment at the absence of a classical heritage in Scotland, and on occasion seemed almost embarrassed to admit that his supposed ancestors were savage tribesman rather than cultured senators, generals and *equites*. As this chapter will demonstrate, a sense that the rejection of Roman culture had been to the detriment of Scotland ancient and modern pervades Clerk's writings. As an educated baronet who grew up admiring ancient Rome, its arts and its order, the fact that the Romans had tried and apparently failed to conquer the north, eventually building a wall to separate it from their empire, presented him with awkward truths regarding the nation's racial and cultural origins. Clerk's roles as antiquarian and patron were undoubtedly vital to the development of Scotland's early modern historiography, but his mixed reactions to the emerging picture tell us much about the complex relationship that eighteenth-century Scots had with their own past.

Early life and Grand Tour

The roots of Sir John Clerk's Romanist tendencies can be found in his youth. He attended the parish school in Penicuik, where he was taught Latin by a master named Alexander Strachan, whom Clerk respected despite his severity.[2] He later matriculated at Glasgow University, but found his studies of 'Logicks and Metaphisicks' there unsatisfactory; it has been speculated, however, that the university's nascent collection of Roman carved stones may have inspired his own passion for collecting antiquities.[3] Next Clerk followed in the footsteps of Sibbald to the university of Leiden, this institution's strong links with Scotland demonstrated by the twelve other Scots who enrolled alongside him in 1694.[4] Although ostensibly there to study law, Leiden saw Clerk further drawn towards ancient history when he attended classes (some of which were delivered in Dutch) given by Perizonius and Jacobus Gronovius: 'I had likeways colleges from the two famous professors of Eloquence on History and on Tacitus and Suetonius'.[5]

Clerk's life experience notably diverges from that of Sibbald in 1697, when he made a formative visit to the city of Rome during his Grand Tour, an endeavour which was still a relative novelty for Scots at this time. Clerk later explained that, although his father had provided only minimal financial assistance, he had experienced a pull towards Italy that he was unable to resist:

> The reasone of this was that my journey was contrary to his inclinations; but the vast desire I had to see a Country so famous for exploits about which all my time had been hitherto spent in reading the classicks, likeways a country so replenished with Antiquities of all kinds . . . I say these things created such a vast desire in me to see it, that I am sure nothing in life had ever made me happy if I had denied my self this great pleasure and satisfaction.[6]

Beginning in the Low Countries, Clerk travelled via Nuremberg and Vienna, finally arriving in Rome in September 1697. He spent time studying law, but his real interests lay elsewhere: 'My two greatest diversions at Rome were Musick and Antiquities'.[7] He attended meetings of virtuosi at the home of antiquarian and philosopher 'Monsignior Chaprigni', who later laid the foundations of Clerk's collection by bequeathing him ancient busts of Cicero and Otto along with a small Diana of Ephesus.[8] He also studied under one Monsignior Caprara, a man who 'might justly be compared to the best of the old Romans . . . and affected to live in Cicero's way at his Villa Tusculana'.[9] Following a trip to Naples with Wriothesley Russell, later Duke of Bedford, he found himself effectively trapped in Italy by his growing debts, and could only return to Scotland following the arrival of funds sent by his father in late 1698.[10] If Clerk had already been enamoured with classical Rome before his Tour, then he left Italy positively enchanted by the place and its history, inspired by its gentleman scholars who modelled their lives on those of the ancients. Such an approach was to inform the rest of his life; as he said himself when describing his return to Scotland, 'I had applied much to Classical Lairning, and had more than an ordinary inclination for the Greek and Roman Antiquities'.[11]

Ancient Rome and modern Union

Largely thanks to the contacts made through his brief first marriage (Margaret Clerk died in childbirth in late 1701), the young Clerk's chosen career in politics developed rapidly. He was elected to parliament for the burgh of Whithorn in 1702 and the following year was appointed to a commission to enquire into public finances and debt. By 1705 he accepted (despite initial reservations) a position on the commission established to negotiate a treaty of union with England.[12] In 1707 he sat in the first British parliament, but it was his appointment as a Baron of the Scottish Court of Exchequer in 1708 that provided both the income and the free time to allow Clerk to indulge himself in what, in a nod to Cicero, he called '*honestum otium*'.[13] Clerk also inherited the family title and estates in 1722, and was often referred to as 'the Baron' amongst his friends and colleagues.

A huge amount of Clerk's manuscript material, including essays, notes and letters, survives in the enormous collection of family papers now held in the National Records of Scotland, with some of his correspondence also published in the *Bibliotheca Topographica Britannica* compiled by John Nichols in the 1780s. His writings reveal that Sir John's admiration for the Romans was all-encompassing, even obsessive. He claimed to have read Horace's *Ars Poetica* at least fifty times, and wrote to English antiquarian Roger Gale in the 1730s on the subject of a recently discovered Roman inscription:

> Every day I look upon such things I cannot but reflect how wonderfully we are obliged to the Romans who left us so much for our entertainment, and have many times wished that we might do more of this kind for the entertainment of our posterity than we commonly do.[14]

This reverence was largely founded on Clerk's belief in the civilising influence of the Roman Empire, a belief that also helped to shape his own attitudes towards British politics. To Clerk, the study of the classics was a patriotic endeavour: 'Those who have the greatest knowledge of Antiquity have, *ceteris paribus*, the best title to be esteemed patriots'.[15] Again to Gale, he wrote of antiquarianism that 'it may be demonstrated that nothing will tend more to promote true British spirits in the love of this country, liberty and glory', adding that 'one must be of a very abject frame of soul who cannot receive any impressions of this kind from the sentiments or valiant actions of the Greeks and Romans'.[16] The same letter reveals that Clerk regarded the ancients as exemplars for the modern citizen: 'What are the heroes of antiquity but so many models by which we may square our lives and actions?'.

An anonymous pamphlet entitled *A Letter to a Friend Giving an Account of How the Treaty of Union Has Been Received Here* and published in 1706, once thought to be by Daniel Defoe but now attributed to Clerk, is perhaps the first indication of the direct influence of Rome on Clerk's attitude towards British union.[17] Clerk here debunks the persistent argument that a union would deprive Scotland of its 'Sovereignty and Antiquity'; although he recognises that Scotland had remained largely unconquered, retaining what some Scots called her 'Chastity', he presents the idea that union benefits all of those involved, quoting Dutch scholar Hugo Grotius, who had written that:

> *Quod si quando uniantur duo Populi non amittentur jura sed communicabuntur, sicut Sabinorum, deinde Albanorum jus in Romanos transfusum est, & una facta republica, ut Livius loquitur.*[18]

> (Even when two people unite, their rights are not lost, just as when the Sabines', then the Albani's rights were transmitted to the Romans, and they became one State, as Livy tells us.)

Further evidence of the classical influences on Clerk's political thinking, and indeed the influence of Clerk's political views on his interpretations of the past, can be found in his *History of the Union*, an ambitious Latin text that he began formulating around 1711 and wrote between 1724 and 1730 which, despite many corrections and revisions over the following years, was left unpublished on his death in 1755.[19] The list of books used by the author during his research features a large classical component, including Caesar, Tacitus, Suetonius, Strabo and Dio amongst many others.[20] The choice to write it in Latin is also intriguing; like Sibbald before him, Clerk no doubt saw the language as a way to engage an international audience, but it also helped to burnish what its modern editor and translator Douglas Duncan describes as the '"Roman" aura with which he liked to surround his private life'.[21] The text promotes the idea that larger nations lead to stability and strength and presents the Roman Empire as the paradigm of such a unified state. Inspired by Giovanni Vincenzo Gravina's *De Romano Imperio*, Clerk proposed that Roman rule was 'introduced for the good of mankind', creating a 'civic bond which had enabled peoples to live charitably together'.[22] In addition, he claimed that the Romans had provided Britain with 'the first government of any name' and suggested that they allowed many of the indigenous Britons to become 'more sociable . . . more civilised . . . more free'.[23] For Clerk, the intention of the invading Roman army was altruistic: 'to unite the British people along with themselves in a single well-grafted society'.[24] His beliefs echo those of Francis Bacon, who expressed similar ideas in his early seventeenth-century *Brief Discourse of the Happy Union in the Kingdoms of Scotland and England* (a parliamentary speech that was published posthumously in London in 1700 and again in 1702 in response to political events), which highlights the success of Rome in combining disparate peoples to create 'the best State of the World' whilst extolling the virtues of British union.[25] Ultimately, Clerk believed, to belong to the Roman Empire was to be part of the civilised world: 'So the fact that Britain was once admitted to that empire is something of which she can be proud'.[26]

Antiquarian and patron

Sir John Clerk's fascination with Rome led him to investigate the ancient history of his home nation, seeking out evidence of Roman exploits and picking up antiquities for his collection along the way. He travelled around Scotland, visiting the Antonine Wall and the Roman forts and camps at Ardoch, Burnswark and Middleby (modern Birrens), and also made a trip south of the border to inspect Hadrian's Wall. Visits further south allowed him to view the celebrated cabinet of Dr Woodward (whose famous 'Roman shield' he correctly dismissed as nothing of the sort) as well as the huge assortment of Roman marbles belonging to the Earl of Pembroke at Wilton House.[27] He made friends in antiquarian circles, and his long correspondence with William Stukeley and Roger Gale in particular feature many references to Roman artefacts discovered across Britain. In an early letter to Clerk, Stukeley describes the Baron as the man capable of reviving classical learning in Scotland, since his 'noble spirit & benign influences strike up a light for the Muses, not seen since the glittering arms of the romans left it'.[28] In 1723 Clerk was invited to join Stukeley's band of *Equites Romani*, a short-lived group of enthusiasts dedicated to the study of Roman antiquities that also numbered the Earls of Pembroke, Hertford and Winchelsea among its esteemed members. Each chose for themselves an appropriate pseudonym, with Clerk deciding on the suitably Whiggish 'Agricola'.[29] In 1725 he was made a member of the Society of Antiquaries in London, with Roger Gale later reading his paper on ancient burial techniques to its Fellows and also facilitating Clerk's election into the Royal Society.[30]

Clerk may have inherited Sir Robert Sibbald's role as the leading authority on Scotland's Roman heritage, but unlike Sibbald he rarely published his antiquarian findings. Despite his 'strong inclination to be a scribler', he preferred to follow Horace's advice to hold back his work for nine years after its composition, and printed only three short essays on Roman antiquities during his lifetime: the

1704 *Enquiry into the Roman Stylus* only recently attributed to him; a *Dissertatio de Stylis Veterum, et Diversis Chartarum Generibus* of 1731, also on the subject of supposed Roman writing tools (actually fibulae) with illustrations of examples found in Scotland; and his *Dissertatio de Monumentis Quibusdam Romanis, in Boreali Magnae Britanniae Parte, Detectis Anno 1731*, in which he described Roman sculptures of a Scottish provenance in his own collection.[31]

The first displays Clerk's wide knowledge of classical literature and the strange object it describes (found near Penicuik and probably not a stylus at all) was later featured in several of the works of Sir Robert Sibbald amongst others.[32] Although he remained unsure of its original purpose, Clerk finally settled on a writing implement, 'since there can be no Question but many of them were brought into *Scotland* by the *Romans*'.[33] The last of these essays took years to complete. Started in 1743, a draft of its introduction was sent to Gale in 1744, Clerk asking him to 'set me right' on any possible errors, with the printed version finally appearing in 1750.[34] Clerk believed that it was important to publish it so 'that these valuable Monuments may be preserved', but also felt a close personal connection with these sculptures that also adorned his home, telling Gale that 'these monuments being some of my Domestick Ornaments I resolve to do them all the honour I can'.[35] Copies of the essay were never sold on the open market, but were distributed to friends and members of the Royal Society.[36] Despite his reticence when it came to publication (all of these works were printed anonymously), Clerk's antiquarian conjectures generally met with a favourable reaction. His *Dissertatio de Stylis Veterum* was praised in Britain, became known in Leiden, with copies received by Herman Boerhaave and Abraham Gronovius there, and was even included in the prestigious *Utriusque Thesauri Antiquitatum Romanarum Graecarumque Nova Supplementa*, an exhaustive survey of the latest classical scholarship compiled by Italian polymath Giovanni Poleni.[37] The *Dissertatio de Stylis Veterum* and the *Dissertatio de Monumentis Quibusdam Romanis* were still read in the 1780s, when Scottish antiquarian George Paton promised to send copies to one Mr Turner and to Richard Gough, editor of Camden's *Britannia*, describing them as 'now both very rare'.[38]

While Clerk was certainly dedicated to the study of ancient Rome and its remains in Scotland, his greatest legacy in this respect was to be his patronage of fellow antiquarians. While he enjoyed visiting supposedly Roman sites, he generally left the hard work of identifying, measuring, recording and publishing such monuments to others. His involvement with English antiquarian John Horsley was important and will be discussed further in Chapter 4, but it is his relationship with Alexander Gordon that would have the greatest impact on the way that Scots would henceforth regard their Roman past. It was thanks to this (sometimes rather strained) friendship that Gordon was able to produce his iconic *Itinerarium Septentrionale* of 1726, a hugely influential tome that was to become, as Iain Gordon Brown describes it, 'the first book on any amateur antiquary's list of desiderata'.[39]

Whether Gordon himself was truly interested in Scotland's Roman heritage or whether he simply regarded it as a means to earn a living and achieve social advancement is debatable. He led a peripatetic life, achieving a Master of Arts degree in his native Aberdeen, later working as a singer and portrait painter. During his professional travels across Europe he seems to have become involved with classical antiquities, and later claimed to have helped preserve the Roman amphitheatre at Capua. On his return to Britain he received patronage from the Earl of Pembroke and headed back to Scotland at the aristocrat's bidding to carry out antiquarian research.[40] It was, Gordon would later suggest, a comment by William Stukeley in his 1720 essay *An Account of a Roman Temple*, which criticised the lack of scholarship on Roman Scotland, or perhaps an encounter with a 'Roman' (actually Bronze Age) sword in the collection of Edinburgh's Advocates Library, that inspired him to turn his attentions towards his chosen subject.[41] A plan for a book on the history and material remains of ancient Scotland was conceived and a friendship with Sir John Clerk was struck up. In 1723 Gordon set off on what he termed an 'antiquary peregrination' bearing a letter of introduction from Clerk that detailed his intentions to 'make an exact survey of all our Roman antiquities'.[42]

In preparation for this not inconsiderable journey, Gordon had borrowed a copy of Sibbald's *Historical Inquiries* from fellow antiquarian James Anderson. Greatly impressed with it and unable to source a copy for himself, he begged for more time with it: 'I have been very much instructed & informed by it . . . this book is absolutely necisary for my designes seeing it directs me to 50 or 60 places which I knew nothing about'.[43] On his return from his 'virtuoso Tuer', however, Gordon's opinion on Sibbald's scholarship had changed. In fact, the *Itinerarium Septentrionale* contains an appendix to its fourth chapter that is dedicated exclusively to the rubbishing of Sibbald's conjectures: 'I was surprized to observe, that he places whole Countries, *Roman* Garrisons, Colonies and Forts in that Country, which I have very good Reason to believe were never there'.[44] The following pages, described by their author as a 'tedious digression', refute many of Sibbald's claims, questioning his identification of several Roman sites and mocking his proposal that Hadrian's Wall was to be found in East Lothian. Overall, the image of Roman Scotland presented in the *Itinerarium* is completely different to that found in Sibbald's *Historical Inquiries*. Rather than a subdued Roman province, Gordon portrays ancient Caledonia as a military zone, the numerous Roman sites that he discovered presented as evidence not of classical civility, but rather of several failed attempts to conquer the region.

While the *Itinerarium* displays, surely with an eye to the tastes of its main patron, a certain respect for 'the great Romans', it is clear that Gordon was more focused on promoting the achievements of the courageous Caledonians who resisted their attacks; the author's attitude towards Scotland's Roman past, which has been described as 'political antiquarianism and patriotic archaeology' indicative of a 'nationalist antiquarian response to the Union', will be analysed more fully in the next chapter.[45] Sir John's reaction to the completed book was decidedly mixed. He wrote to Stukeley that the work 'has faults but what I hope will be overlooked by you & all others who wish well to learning' but added that it 'exceeds my expectation'.[46] Clerk was angry that Gordon had included letters between Clerk and Gale against his instructions and without proper corrections and amendments, and also felt uncomfortable with the implications of the author's more extreme pro-Caledonian polemic. Gordon's patriotic use of the rousing speech placed in the mouth of Caledonian chief Calgacus (known to eighteenth-century antiquarians as 'Galgacus', amended to 'Calgacus' following the discovery of another manuscript version of the text in the early twentieth century) by Tacitus towards the end of the *Agricola* was particularly problematic, Clerk questioning its reliability as a historical source at a time when few other Scots were perceptive or brave enough to do so:

> I once endeavoured to persuade him that it was only a fiction of Tacitus conform[ing] to a liberty usual amongst historians, & that there was no reasoning from any thing contained in it to ye advantage either of Galgacus or his Caledonians, but Mr Gordon's high respect for his countrie hath carried him too far and made him commit a sort of laudable fault.[47]

In his own copy of the *Itinerarium* Clerk wrote in ink next to the offending passage 'Nota. This speech of Galgacus in Tacitus is but a fiction according to a liberty usual amongst all Historians of Antiquity'.[48] He believed that the book had been published too quickly, with Gale revealing that Gordon rushed the printing due to financial pressures.[49] Overall, however, Clerk was willing to overlook the *Itinerarium*'s shortcomings, paraphrasing Horace when he wrote to Gale that '*Ubi plura nitent – non ego paucis offendar maculis*' (where many things shine, I shall not be offended by a few stains), also writing this at the end of his own copy.[50] The fact that the book contains much material related to supposedly 'Danish' antiquities (in fact a mixed bag of brochs, Pictish stones and the like) has often been overlooked, not least by Clerk himself: as Brown points out, the hand-written notes added by Clerk to the *Itinerarium* held in his library at Penicuik all appear in the first (Roman) section, with none at all in the later 'Danish' chapters.[51]

The *Itinerarium* was well received in antiquarian circles and the presentation of a copy to the Prince and Princess of Wales in London by the author himself was reported in *The Caledonian Mercury* on 22 August 1726 (p. 6078); their Royal Highnesses were also pleased to subscribe to a six-foot-long map of the Roman walls that Gordon was now planning. A proposed Latin edition to be printed in Holland, however, never appeared, nor did a French translation that Gordon mentioned to Clerk in 1729, or that map of the walls.[52] Soon the friendship between Gordon and his patron deteriorated. Clerk ridiculed Gordon's plan for a Forth/Clyde canal in 1726, and by 1732, as the increasingly tetchy and defensive Gordon hurried to finish his flimsy and even more dogmatically patriotic *Additions and Corrections . . . to the Itinerarium Septentrionale* (of which more in the following chapter), Clerk declared himself 'out of all patience' with him, later bemoaning 'Sandy Gordon's weakness and want of judgement'.[53] Gordon was prone to arguments, with one letter to the Baron relating his falling out over money matters with the 'rogue my bookseller partner' (bookselling being yet another failed stab at establishing a career) and also expressing bemusement at the news that Roger Gale was feeling 'disobliged' towards him.[54] Clerk was certainly unimpressed with the *Additions and Corrections*, concluding that 'he had done well either not to have printed it at all, or done it with less precipitation'.[55]

Later, Gordon held various professional posts in London, such as secretary to the Society of Antiquaries (1735–41), secretary to the Society for the Encouragement of Learning (1736–9) and briefly secretary to the Egyptian Club. In addition to the *Itinerarium* and its supplement, he published a book on the lives of Rodrigo and Cesare Borgia, translated Francesco Scipione Maffie's Italian text on Roman amphitheatres and spent much time trying (and failing) to comprehend Egyptian hieroglyphics. He became something of a figure of fun, earning himself the nicknames 'Gordonius the Caledonian' (courtesy of Roger Gale), 'poor Itinerarium' and 'poor Caesar Borgia the Heiroglyphician' (both courtesy of classical scholar Thomas Blackwell).[56] In the end, his loss of reputation in Britain, no doubt combined with his penchant for feuds and rumours of financial irregularities at the Society of Antiquaries, led him to emigrate to South Carolina in 1741, where he finally seems to have prospered. Clerk's reservations about Gordon notwithstanding, the two continued to correspond across the Atlantic, with Gordon confirming to the Baron in 1747 that he was still dedicated to antiquity, even in this 'Gothick Region' where he found the locals to be mostly 'proud, ignorant and vindictive'.[57]

In many ways Clerk and Gordon were unlikely associates. One was a staunch Romanist, an established member of the Scottish aristocracy with a keen sense of his own status, the other was chaotic, belligerent, possibly dishonest, and certainly inclined towards patriotic anti-Roman bombast. Their differing approaches to Scotland's past are neatly demonstrated by the pseudonyms each selected on joining Stukeley's *Equites Romani*: while Clerk chose 'Agricola', Gordon named himself after the Roman general's heroic Caledonian opponent 'Galgacus'. But as in all successful partnerships, there were benefits for each, and while Gordon was no doubt glad of the financial and scholarly support offered by Clerk, Clerk's reputation south of the border was also greatly enhanced by Gordon's active promotion of his Scottish patron amongst England's titled and learned gentlemen.[58]

Clerk's response to Roman Scotland

As a proud Scottish patriot who also held the Romans in high esteem, Clerk clearly found himself in something of a quandary when it came to Scotland's early history. Although it is easy to imagine that he would have wished things to be otherwise, the observations made by himself and Alexander Gordon led Clerk to conclude that Sibbald had been wrong, and that Caledonia had almost completely resisted Roman control. In his 1709 *History of the Union of Great Britain*, fellow unionist Daniel Defoe may have declared that early modern Lowland Scots were partly descended from the Romans who had once settled there, but Clerk himself conceded, rather reluctantly we suspect, that his ancestors were instead the barbaric but tenacious tribesmen faced by Agricola, Severus et al. during their unsuccessful attempts to subdue the north.[59] Torn between patriotism and Romanism, his numerous references to Roman Scotland display a noticeable ambivalence: while he sometimes followed tradition in lauding the courageous Caledonians for repelling invasion, in both letters to other (particularly English) antiquarians and his unpublished manuscripts, Clerk demonstrates regret that Scotland had ultimately remained outside the bounds of Roman *imperium*.

A striking example of Clerk's pro-Caledonian patriotism can be found in an essay written for the benefit of the Philosophical Society of Edinburgh after his 1739 visit to Hadrian's Wall.[60] Clerk opens the essay with the bold claim that there is 'no subject, wherin the honour of our forefathers the Ancient Scots & Picts, is more concerned, than what regards the fortified lines made by the Romans, for defending themselves & their subjects of South Brittains against the power of the Northern Brittains'.[61] In this text composed for a learned Scottish audience, Clerk takes a stance that appears startlingly contradictory to his own reverence for the civilising power of Rome:

> Let not here the blind admirers of the Roman power & grandure say that this Praetentura served only to wall out that Barbarity, which the Scots and Picts were endeavouring to spread over the southern parts of Brittain in opposition to that Humanity which the Roman Empire was every where introducing.[62]

He calls upon his readers to recognise the unwillingness of the Caledonians to bow to the rule of the Romans and ends with a display of Scottish patriotism worthy of Alexander Gordon himself, celebrating the enduring Scottish fight for freedom and independence. In doing so, he identifies modern Scots as the successors of these ancient tribes, and locates a spirit in the Scottish nation that had led to it 'being amongst the first in the Cause of British Liberty'.[63] If Clerk wrote this essay with the intention of stirring patriotic zeal in the hearts of his countrymen, then it certainly worked: eminent mathematician John MacLaurin later declared that he had read it 'with equal satisfaction from the learning in it and pleasure from the patriotism'.[64]

When writing to English friends and associates, however, the Baron took a different position, often showing his frustration and embarrassment at Scotland's lack of a Roman heritage and a discomfort with the kind of patriotic antiquarianism with which he himself had regaled the Edinburgh elite. In fact, on occasion he seems distinctly ashamed of the actions of his ancient Caledonian 'ancestors', who, in his mind, had effectively rejected the possibility of civilisation in the defence of their barbaric liberty. In a letter to the Earl of Hertford in which Clerk expresses his delight at being invited to join the Society of Antiquaries in London, he declares himself pleasantly surprised to be granted the honour, since 'perhaps of all mankind those of the Caledonian race have the least reason to expect it, after their Forefathers rejected the society of the Romans themselves & the great advantages that were to be communicated to them'.[65] It was clear to him that Sibbald's claims of numerous Roman towns and monuments across the south of Scotland, many of them supposedly constructed under Agricola, was nothing more than a fantasy. Writing to Roger Gale in 1726, he lamented the dearth of Roman antiquities in Scotland, describing his homeland as 'barren of any thing of this kind' and concluding that those great symbols of Roman power, the elegant porticos and baths mentioned by Tacitus, were built only in England: ''tis more than probable that none of the Caledonian nations had these porticus & balnea & consequently could have very few valuable pieces of Antiquities left amongst them'.[66]

The clearest indication of Sir John's disappointment with the apparent Roman failure to conquer Scotland appears in that aforementioned letter written to Roger Gale in which he criticises Alexander Gordon's belief that Tacitus' account of the speech of Calgacus was a verbatim record of a historical event. Clerk continues with an attack on the short-sightedness of the rejection of classical civilisation: 'I am, I confess, of the opinion of some learned men, that this is a reproach to a nation to have resisted the humanity which the Romans laboured to introduce'.[67] We do not find out who the 'learned men' who shared this view might be, but the reply sent by Gale reveals that he was of a similar mind, proposing that to be invaded was not necessarily a bad thing:

> I think it was no scandall for any People to have been conquered by the Romans, but a great misfortune to them in not submitting to their arms, since their conquests were so farr from enslaving those they vanquisht, that they tended only to the civilizing

and improving them; reducing them under their own laws & Government from their wild and savage way of life, teaching them arts and sciences, and looking upon them as fellow Citizens and Freemen of Rome, which was common mother to all that had the happynesse to fall under her subjection,and every nation that was subdued by her might truly say she was *Faelix adversis, et forte oppressa secunda*.[68]

Clerk's visit to Hadrian's Wall also stirred up mixed emotions. A copy of a letter from him to Gale (in the hand of an amanuensis), which survives in the Clerk family papers, contains a phrase that neatly sums up his ambivalence:

The Romans ['indeed' added in Clerk's own hand] Walled out humanity from us, but 'tis certain they thought the Caledonians a very formidable people when they at so much labour & cost built this Wall as before they had made a Vallum between Forth & Clyde.[69]

Elsewhere he tries to downplay the success of the Caledonians. He proposed to Gale that the Roman invasion was at least a temporary success, writing that 'the best that could have been said for the Caledonians was, that though they had been conquered, yet the Romans could not retain their conquests', adding a note to the same effect in his copy of the *Itinerarium*.[70] That he felt compelled to believe in the reputed valour of ancient Caledonians was due not only to pure patriotism, but also to the fact that admitting otherwise would expose deficiencies in the Romans themselves:

That the Scots & the Picts were so very considerable nations in those days, endowed with high notions of Liberty & great skills in Arms, for if we suppose otherways we must give up our notions of the Roman grandure fortitude & prudence with other vertues that render them venerable to posterity.[71]

Clerk ultimately reveals the reason for his reluctance to entertain the glorification of Caledonian liberty in his *History of the Union*, where he writes of the worrying dilemma that it presents for polite eighteenth-century commentators:

But the descendants of those Caledonians today should take care not to boast of their resistance too much, for to be proud of their refusal of Roman rule means admitting that one's ancestors were barbarians with no claim to civilization whatever.[72]

It is hard to escape Clerk's sense that the oft-eulogised Caledonian repulsion of the invading Romans was the victory of barbarism over polite civilisation and really nothing to celebrate. To make matters worse, his friends seemed intent on reminding him that he lived in a region that had remained outside the bounds of the Roman Empire by highlighting his location north of Hadrian's Wall. This is true of Allan Ramsay's 1726 poem dedicated to the British antiquarians, an extract of which appears as the epigraph to this chapter, and Stukeley too, in one of his more effusively complimentary passages, identifies Clerk as 'the only Atlas & Hercules too, that sustains the cause of polite literature beyond the Vallum'.[73] While both of these writers were certainly aware of Roman remains north of this ancient frontier, the poetic image of Hadrian's Wall not just as the border between England and Scotland, but also as an endpoint to civilisation, was clearly a compelling one. Whether Clerk himself would have agreed is doubtful.

A mission to classicise Scotland

In spite of, or perhaps because of, this disappointment at the lack of a glorious classical legacy for Scotland, Sir John Clerk never gave up on locating evidence of Roman civilisation in his homeland, even where none existed. He witnessed the opening of a tumulus near his home at Penicuik and, having inspected its contents, declared it the final resting place of three 'remarkable' Romans (in fact his description suggests that it was probably a more common Bronze Age burial).[74] He believed that the Roman fort at Middleby, where many of his most treasured antiquities had been unearthed, was once adjoined by a 'fortifyed little city', and claimed to have seen the foundations of many Roman houses there in *lapide quadrato*.[75] In 1741 he optimistically proposed that a recently demolished arch in Edinburgh must have been Roman, since an urn apparently containing Roman coins was found near it.[76] He also identified a (probably sixteenth-century) sculpture of two heads in profile found on the side of a building in Edinburgh's Netherbow as the remains of a sarcophagus, proclaiming it to be the finest Roman sculpture north of the border.[77] From all of this it can be deduced that Clerk was determined to drag Scotland into the boundaries of the classical world and find some signs that the Romans had left their mark there, no matter how fleeting their incursions.

It could also be suggested that Clerk's building and landscaping projects, in which he took inspiration from Rome when furnishing and transforming his own properties, were further evidence of this mission to classicise Scotland. He was a subscriber to Robert Castell's *Villas of the Ancients*, in which the author intended to establish the rules of design of a typical Roman villa with a view to inspiring modern architects and patrons. In the 1720s Clerk composed a poem entitled *The Country Seat*, a text laden with classical references that similarly aimed to enlighten those wishing to design a country house and park; its introduction informs the reader that 'the antient Greek and Roman structures, or the Designs of them by Palladio and others ought to be Standards fit for the Imitation of our modern Architects'.[78]

Although not classical in its design, Clerk's first home at Cammo near Edinburgh happened to be situated close to the remains of a Roman fort at Cramond, allowing him to befriend the site's owner, Sir John Inglis, and thus expand his collection with numerous coins and other antiquities found there.[79]

On inheriting his baronetcy in 1722, Clerk promptly sold Cammo and moved to Penicuik. Not long after he also began work on his architectural masterpiece, the house and gardens at Mavisbank, a small but perfectly formed classical extravaganza that is now identified as the first Palladian villa in Scotland. Such was Clerk's success at creating a classical paradise on the banks of the River Esk that, on visiting it in 1739, Roger Gale wrote to William Stukeley that 'you would there think yourself rather in a valley near Tivoli than Edenborough'.[80] With his typical Romanist enthusiasm, Clerk pronounced the raised (probably medieval) earthworks at the back of the house a 'Roman station', an idea repeated in the notes to the 1892 publication of his memoirs, where it is supposed that the site 'must have been dear to the Baron's reverently antiquarian soul'.[81] Roger Gale, however, decided that it was too small to be a camp and suggested it was a 'place of Druid worship', also recording how Clerk had created a landscaped path leading up to the summit.[82]

Although the old house at Penicuik was to remain unaltered due to the prohibitively high costs of rebuilding it, Clerk decorated its interior and garden with Roman antiquities, while the grounds in which it stood were refashioned in a huge project that began in the late 1720s.[83] Labelling the house a 'villa' in an undated letter to Dutch physician Herman Boerhaave, Clerk described its estate as a place of repose and isolation: 'For as Pliny the younger says of his Tuscan home, here is the most profound and undisturbed ease, there is no need to sport fine clothes, no neighbour calls, and all things give rest and quiet'.[84] Over many years Penicuik was to be developed into Clerk's classical idyll, a place of recreation where he could enjoy his leisure and inhabit his very own vision of a Roman landscape.

That letter from Clerk to Boerhaave gives many details of the house and garden and is filled with references to Rome. Most captivating is Clerk's description of the Hurley Cave, a forty-metre-long rock-cut tunnel constructed in 1742/3 and modelled on the cave of Posillipo near Naples, a place traditionally linked with both Virgil (whose supposed tomb stood nearby) and the Cumean Sibyl (whose underground lair is described in book six of the *Aeneid*) that Clerk had visited on his Grand Tour. Clerk's vivid portrayal of his 'frightful cave' proposes that it recalled the 'memory of the cave of the Cumean Sibyl', adding that it caused visitors to 'shudder, as they stand in doubt whether they are among the living or the dead'. At the finale of this 'mournful' journey, the voyager met with blinding light, as 'suddenly the darkness disappears, as it were at the creation of a new world'.[85] Inside could be found a Latin inscription reading *tenebrosa occultaque cave* (beware of dark and hidden things), the pun no doubt intended. In that same letter Clerk also writes of the 'fountain called Scobea', known locally as Scobie's Well, describing it as 'more lustrous than glass, or even the Horatian fountain of Blandusia itself . . . and so umbrageous that Diana herself with her nymphs might use it for a bath'.[86] Decorated in classical style in 1748, the fountain features an extensive Latin inscription on its pediment explaining the refreshing benefits of the water.

Sir John Clerk lived at a time when signs of Roman civility were being regularly discovered and recorded in England, and his contacts there kept him up to date on the latest finds. In 1732 he visited the site of a villa near Tickencote in Rutland with Stukeley; two years later he commented on the description sent to him by Gale of a villa at Weldon with a mosaic floor and, Clerk speculated, signs of a 'cupola roof'.[87] At other times he learned of a fine silver 'table' from Corbridge and a bronze head of 'Apollo' from Bath.[88] How he must have wished that similar treasures could be dug up closer to home. As a founding member of the new British state, Clerk would have been satisfied to unearth an ancient Britannia that mirrored modern Britain. Instead he found evidence of an island divided by a wall, sophisticated civilisation to the south and unconquerable barbarians to the north. As a proud Scot, he was sometimes compelled to praise the indomitable Caledonians, but often he seemed to find their resistance to Rome more than a little disappointing. Nevertheless, he spent much of his life locating and collecting the remains of Rome in Scotland, sometimes taking his conjectures too far in this respect, also dedicating much effort and expense to classicising his own properties, where he saw himself as living in the manner of Horace or Pliny. In doing so, the Baron Clerk finally brought a touch of classical civility to a region that the Romans had so frustratingly failed to conquer.

Notes

1. Levine, *Dr Woodward's Shield*, p. 261.
2. Clerk, *Memoirs of the Life of Sir John Clerk of Penicuik*, pp. 10–11.
3. Ibid. p. 12; Keppie, *Roman Inscribed and Sculptured Stones in the Hunterian Museum*, pp. 13–14.
4. For a list of his fellow Scottish students, see: Clerk, *Memoirs of the Life of Sir John Clerk of Penicuik*, p. 14 n. 1.
5. Ibid. pp. 15–16.
6. Ibid. p. 19.
7. Ibid. p. 28.
8. Iain Gordon Brown identifies 'Chaprigni' as Monsignor Champini, director of the Academia Physico-Mathematica in Rome, in: Brown, *Sir John Clerk of Penicuik (1676–1755)*, p. 80 and p. 322 n. 148.
9. Clerk, *Memoirs of the Life of Sir John Clerk of Penicuik*, p. 27 n. 1.
10. NRS GD18/5207/4: Clerk to his father, 16 August 1698; NRS GD18/5207/6: Clerk to his father, 4 December 1698.
11. Clerk, *Memoirs of the Life of Sir John Clerk of Penicuik*, p. 36 n. 1.
12. Duncan, 'Introduction', pp. 3–4.
13. NRS GD18/5029: Clerk to Stukeley, 2 June 1726.

14. Clerk, *Memoirs of the Life of Sir John Clerk of Penicuik*, p. 215; Nichols, *Bibliotheca Topographica Britannica*, Vol. 3, p. 449.
15. NRS GD18/5027/2: Clerk to Stukeley, 22 March 1725.
16. Nichols, *Bibliotheca Topographica Britannica*, Vol. 3, p. 239.
17. For a discussion of its attribution, see: Clerk, *Memoirs of the Life of Sir John Clerk of Penicuik*, p. 244 n. G.
18. Clerk, *A Letter to a Friend*, p. 9; ibid. p. 10, quoting Grotius' 1625 *De Jure Belli ac Pacis*, 2.9.9.
19. Duncan, 'Introduction', pp. 5–6.
20. Clerk, *History of the Union of Scotland and England*, pp. 179–80.
21. Duncan, 'Introduction', p. 7.
22. Clerk, *History of the Union of Scotland and England*, p. 33.
23. Ibid. p. 34.
24. Ibid. p. 38.
25. Bacon, *A Brief Discourse of the Happy Union in the Kingdoms of Scotland and England*, p. 6. Although we cannot be sure that Clerk read the speech, he does mention Bacon's model for union in: Clerk, *History of the Union of Scotland and England*, p. 67.
26. Clerk, *History of the Union of Scotland and England*, p. 34.
27. Levine, *Dr Woodward's Shield*, pp. 265–6.
28. NRS GD18/5027/1: Stukeley to Clerk, 21 March 1725.
29. For more on the *Equites Romani*, see: Ayres, *Classical Culture and the Idea of Rome in Eighteenth-Century England*, pp. 91–105.
30. Levine, *Dr Woodward's Shield*, p. 264.
31. Clerk, *Memoirs of the Life of Sir John Clerk of Penicuik*, p. 214.
32. Brown, 'Archaeological Publication in the First Half of the Eighteenth Century', p. 522.
33. Clerk, *An Enquiry into the Roman Stylus*, p. 4.
34. Clerk, *Memoirs of the Life of Sir John Clerk of Penicuik*, p. 166; NRS GD/5031/11: Clerk to Gale, 22 April 1744.
35. NRS GD/5031/11: Clerk to Gale, 22 April 1744.
36. Clerk, *Memoirs of the Life of Sir John Clerk of Penicuik*, p. 166; ibid. p. 222.
37. Brown, 'Archaeological Publication in the First Half of the Eighteenth Century', p. 523.
38. NLS Adv.MS.29.5.7 (iv), f. 73: Paton to Gough, 17 September 1787.
39. Brown, 'Archaeological Publication in the First Half of the Eighteenth Century', p. 510.
40. Brown, 'Alexander Gordon', p. 852.
41. Gordon, *Itinerarium Septentrionale*, Preface; Keppie, *The Antiquarian Rediscovery of the Antonine Wall*, p. 71.
42. NLS MS 1252, f. 1: Clerk, 2 October 1723.
43. NLS Adv.MS.29.1.2 (iv), f. 75: Gordon to Anderson, 19 August 1723.
44. Gordon, *Itinerarium Septentrionale*, p. 43.
45. Ibid. Preface; Brown, 'Modern Rome and Ancient Caledonia', p. 34; ibid. p. 37.
46. NRS GD18/5029: Clerk to Stukeley, 2 June 1726.
47. NRS GD18/5029: Clerk to Gale, 2 June 1726. The speech can be found in: Tacitus, *Agricola* 30–2.
48. NLS MS.Acc.12965, p. 37. For a detailed analysis of Clerk's annotations in his personal copy of *Itinerarium Septentrionale*, rediscovered by Iain Gordon Brown in 2008, see: Brown, 'The Penicuik copy of Alexander Gordon's Itinerarium Septentrionale'.
49. NRS GD18/5030/4: Gale to Clerk, 24 June 1726.

50. NRS GD18/5029: Clerk to Gale, 2 June 1726; NLS MS.Acc.12965, p. 187. Clerk is (mis) quoting Horace, *Ars Poetica* 351–2.
51. Brown, 'The Penicuik copy of Alexander Gordon's Itinerarium Septentrionale', p. 69.
52. Brown, 'Archaeological Publication in the First Half of the Eighteenth Century', p. 518; NRS GD18/5023/3/45: Gordon to Clerk, 11 February 1729.
53. NRS GD18/5029: Clerk to Gale, 29 August 1726; Nichols, *Bibliotheca Topographica Britannica*, Vol. 3, p. 296; ibid. p. 449.
54. NRS GD18/5023/3/57: Gordon to Clerk, June 1732.
55. Nichols, *Bibliotheca Topographica Britannica*, Vol. 3, p. 295.
56. Brown, 'Alexander Gordon', p. 853.
57. NRS GD18/5023/3/95: Gordon to Clerk, 5 July 1747.
58. Sweet, *Antiquaries*, p. 60.
59. Defoe, *The History of the Union of Great Britain*, p. 2.
60. Brown, 'Modern Rome and Ancient Caledonia', p. 36. Several copies of the essay in the hand of an amanuensis survive in the Clerk of Penicuik Muniments, reference NRS GD18/5051.
61. NRS GD18/5051/5, f. 1: Clerk, 'Ane Account of Some Roman Antiquities Observed at Bulness . . .', 1739.
62. Ibid. f. 13.
63. Ibid. f. 14.
64. NRS GD18/5097/4: MacLaurin to Clerk, 9 October 1739.
65. NRS GD18/5028/4: Clerk to Hertford, 17 April 1725.
66. NRS GD18/5029: Clerk to Gale, 6 March 1726.
67. NRS GD18/5029: Clerk to Gale, 2 June 1726.
68. NRS GD18/5030/4: Gale to Clerk, 24 June 1726. The Latin, which can be translated as 'flourishing in adversity but overcome by favourable fortune', is from an unattributed poem about the Claudian conquest of Britain that appears in various early modern anthologies, including those compiled by Pierre Pithou, Joseph Justus Scaliger and Peter Burman.
69. NRS GD18/5031/14: Clerk to Gale, 19 August 1739.
70. NRS GD18/5029: Clerk to Gale, 2 June 1726; NLS MS.Acc.12965, p. 137.
71. NRS GD18/5023/4: Clerk to Gordon, 6 April 1724.
72. Clerk, *History of the Union of Scotland and England*, pp. 38–9.
73. NRS GD18/5027/3: Stukeley to Clerk, 7 June 1725.
74. Gordon, *Itinerarium Septentrionale*, pp. 170–1.
75. NRS GD18/5033: Clerk to Gale, 10 September 1729.
76. Lukis, *The Family Memoirs of the Rev. William Stukeley*, Vol. 3, p. 420.
77. For a discussion of the early modern interpretations of this sculpture, see: Brown and Montgomery, 'The "Roman Heads" at the Netherbow in Edinburgh'.
78. NRS GD18/4404/1, f. 1: Clerk, 'The Country Seat', 1727.
79. Clerk, *Memoirs of the Life of Sir John Clerk of Penicuik*, p. 247.
80. Lukis, *The Family Memoirs of the Rev. William Stukeley*, Vol. 1, p. 317.
81. Tait, *The Landscape Garden in Scotland*, p. 23; Clerk, *Memoirs of the Life of Sir John Clerk of Penicuik*, p. 249.
82. Lukis, *The Family Memoirs of the Rev. William Stukeley*, Vol. 1, p. 317.
83. For more on Clerk's antiquities collection see Chapter 5. A discussion of Clerk's landscaping of the estate at Penicuik can be found in: Cooper, 'Sir John Clerk's Garden at Penicuik'.

84. Clerk, *Memoirs of the Life of Sir John Clerk of Penicuik*, p. 236. Clerk is referring here to Pliny, *Epistulae* 5.6.
85. Clerk, *Memoirs of the Life of Sir John Clerk of Penicuik*, p. 239.
86. Ibid. The *fons Bandusiae* is mentioned in Horace, *Odes* 3.13.
87. Lukis, *The Family Memoirs of the Rev. William Stukeley*, Vol. 3, p. 32; ibid. p. 45.
88. Ibid. p. 109; ibid. p. 181. The first is the Corbridge Lanx, a silver platter now in the collection of the British Museum, while the second, now identified as Minerva, can be found in the museum of the Roman Baths at Bath.

3

Resisting the 'Conquerors of the Universe': celebrating the Caledonian rejection of Rome

> Their Great Fore-fathers sought the Field,
> Not doubting of their Arm's Success;
> They made insulting Foes to yield,
> Who, lab'ring to be great, grew less,
> The Roman *Eagle towring to the skies,*
> *Pierc'd by their* ARROWS, *reeling sinks and dies.*
>
> Alexander Robertson, *A Poem on the Royal Company of Archers*, published in *The Caledonian Mercury*, 12 July 1726, p. 6009

That the eighteenth-century English elite were enthralled by the glories of ancient Rome and were often eager to both emulate its culture and discover physical evidence of its civilising effects on their homeland has been widely recorded in recent scholarship.[1] As has been demonstrated in the first two chapters of this book, such an approach also spread north of the border, leading some notable Scots to search for traces of Roman civilisation in their own nation. But while Sir Robert Sibbald may have hoped to classicise ancient Caledonia in his publications on the subject of Roman Scotland and Sir John Clerk expressed frustration at the nation's lack of classical antiquities, mourning his supposed ancestors' rejection of Roman domination and the civility that it would have brought, it is worth remembering that such men would have been in the minority in Scotland at this time. In fact, a survey of various aspects of Scottish writing in the first decades of the eighteenth century reveals that ancient Caledonia's repulsion of Roman invasion was repeatedly celebrated not only in antiquarian texts, but also in political tracts and patriotic poetry. While, as we shall see in later chapters, the idea that the Romans had left their mark on Scotland was to persist amongst some scholars and historians, for other such men, and for the wider early modern Scottish population, the idea that their nation had been one of the few to successfully resist Roman conquest was amongst their proudest boasts. During a period of political uncertainty and social change, this claim was to become even more vociferous. As the current status of Scotland and its people became less clear, so Scots turned to their past in search of reassurance and honour.

As indicated in the Introduction, this idea of Scotland's ancient integrity was established by the fourteenth century and was repeated and further developed in the Renaissance histories of Hector Boece and George Buchanan. Although doubts regarding the reliability of these early chronicles were beginning to emerge by the eighteenth century, they were still read and regularly cited. Buchanan's *Rerum Scoticarum Historia* was taught in Scottish schools, translated into English and published in London in 1690 as *The History of Scotland*. As a result, it would survive into the eighteenth century as probably the most familiar version of the nation's history. Sir Robert Sibbald wrote his own biography of the sixteenth-century historian and Latinist, and Buchanan's description of the Caledonian repulsion of Roman invasion in his epithalamium for Mary Stuart (quoted in the Introduction) was particularly highly regarded, with an essay on his poetical works published in *The Bee* in November 1791 stating 'Of this passage, which has been often quoted, one need only say that it has hardly ever been excelled, even by our author himself'.[2]

While it was clear that Scotland could never compete with England when it came to wealth or international influence, the northern nation's antiquity and hard-fought liberty appeared unrivalled. At a time when the provenance and precedence of Caledonia's indigenous tribes were being hotly debated, to establish a link with the warriors who faced and seemingly defeated Rome was key to bolstering early modern Scottish self-esteem. Writing the dedication to the king that prefaces his 1681 *Institutions of the Law of Scotland*, the statesman and lawyer James Dalrymple, Viscount Stair, highlights the racial purity and indomitability of the Scottish nation:

> We do not pretend to be amongst the Great and Rich Kingdoms of the Earth, yet we know not who can claim preference in Antiquity and Integrity, being of one Blood and Lineage, without mixture of any other people, and have so continued above two thousand years; during all which, no forreign Power was ever able to setle the Dominion of a Strange Lord over us . . .[3]

Implicit in this statement is the fact that England could make no such claims. For while the English had their own anti-Roman freedom fighters to admire, both the textual and material evidence left no doubt that Caratacus and Boudica had ultimately failed in their struggles to break free from the yoke of Rome, just as later inhabitants of the south had yielded to the Saxons, the Vikings and the Normans.[4]

As a nation that had supposedly never been conquered by outsiders, Scotland could also boast an unbroken line of (mostly mythical) kings allegedly dating back to 330 BCE, a distinction commemorated in the 111 portraits of Scottish monarchs (including Calgacus in his Boecian guise of 'Galdus') painted by Dutch artist Jacob de Wet II in 1684–6 and installed in the Great Gallery of the Palace of Holyroodhouse. This, together with claims that the Scottish church was more ancient than the church in England and had developed largely free from papal influence, allowed Dalrymple to underline Charles II's position as the latest in a long line of great Christian monarchs, also conflating here the rejection of ancient Rome with a repudiation of the modern Church of Rome:

> It is yet a greater glorie to Your Royal Familie, that You have been Christian Kings before any other Familie in Christendom were Kings: And that You and Your Subjects of Scotland have been least under the Yoak of Rome, in your Sacred or Civil Interest, their Arms could never subdue You, but they turned on the Defensive; and to exclude Your Valour, two of their most famous Emperors, Severus and Hadrian, were at an Incredible Coast to Build two Walls, from Sea to Sea . . . [5]

By the end of the seventeenth century, the international reputation of the Scots as a race of fierce warriors was entrenched. While Keith Brown identifies both positive and negative aspects of this bellicose image, it seems that many Scots, particularly in the Highlands, were happy to play up to and promote such an idea.[6] As the eighteenth century began and a union with England became increasingly likely, the assertion that Scotland had remained free of foreign influence due to the formidable bravery and martial supremacy of her people became more insistent, the ancient rejection of oppressive forces from the south gaining new resonance. This chapter will reveal that proclamations of Caledonian liberty were to appear in various forms and forums. As well as being opposed to British union, several of the key figures who glorified Caledonia's rejection of Rome had Jacobite affiliations, and some were distinctly sentimental in their approach to Scottish history. In difficult times, many looked back to an imaginary past, recalling a Golden Age when the inhabitants of Scotland were more heroic, more principled and steadfast; as Iain Gordon Brown points out, 'the Union was responsible for making nostalgia the most characteristic emotion in the Scottish national psyche'.[7] While some of the men who focused on this aspect of Scotland's history were esteemed antiquarians, many of those who wrote about it were less well-versed in the historical evidence and more reliant on the mythical aspects of their national narrative. All of them, however, were obviously influenced by current early modern concerns regarding Scottish sovereignty. While the identity of the ancient inhabitants of the north remained a highly contentious subject, the idea that Scotland's indigenous tribes had displayed great fortitude in the face of hostile Roman legions, and that it was these very tribesmen who were the ancestors of the modern population, was almost beyond question. The strength and ubiquity of this belief, as well as its importance for propping up Scotland's battered sense of national dignity in the years leading up to and following the Union, were to cast a long shadow over early modern attitudes towards the history and material remains of Roman Scotland. As we shall see, in unsettling times, traditional tales that shed an unmistakably rosy glow on Scotland past and present were hard to let go.

Unconquered Caledonia in anti-Union rhetoric

The fact that Caledonia's successful defence of her liberty against Roman oppression was heavy with patriotic potential was recognised by Scottish political agitators, particularly around the time of the Union. Murray Pittock identifies the importance of early Scottish history in the 'pamphlet wars' of the early eighteenth century, noting that arguments concerning English suzerainty over Scotland were 'deeply infused with the legendary or half-legendary matter of the Scottish and English foundation myths'.[8] While much of this rhetoric was inspired by Geoffrey of Monmouth's fabulous account of Brutus, also by the medieval Wars of Independence, Scotland's defence of her liberty against Rome also played its part in establishing the nation's separateness from and superiority over England.

In 1703, for example, prolific pamphleteer James Hodges referred to Scotland's long battle for independence in a text that was to be widely read, also prompting several responses from Daniel Defoe. In it, Hodges laments the decline of Scotland's powers in the preceding century, and pushes for a federal rather than incorporating union:

> That the Scots have done and suffered more for maintaining their National Freedom and Indepedency, than any of the mention'd Kingdoms and Dominions, or than any other in *Europe*, as the Histories of both Kingdoms compared with those of other Nations do abundantly Testifie ... That, whereas England hath been four times conquer'd, to wit, by the *Romans*, the *Saxons*, the *Danes*, and the *Normans*; the *Scots* are the only people of *Europe*, whom, tho' none more violently assaulted, yet neither *Romans*, who conquer'd all the rest, nor any other Nation, have ever been able to conquer; since the first Setling of their Government.[9]

Three years later, Hodges published another pamphlet on a similar theme warning that Scotland risked being swallowed up in a union, thus ending up as nothing more than a powerless satellite state of England. Again the reader is reminded, in a rather whimsical digression, that Caledonia was the only part of the world to successfully resist the 'Great, Strongest and IRON-like Monarchy' of Rome:

> All other Nations were unto it as Gold, Silver, Brass, Clay, and Brick, whom the Iron, a Harder Metal, Subdued and Broke into Pieces. Only the *Romans*, the Conquerors of the World, Found the *Scots*, amongst all other Nations, of a Metal, such as STEEL is to IRON yet Harder, than Themselves ... Therefore is it that *Scaliger*,

a Disinterested Author, Affirms, *That* Scotland *did set the Bounds and Limits to the* Roman *Empire*.[10]

Calls for the preservation of Scotland's 2000-year-old independence, which had supposedly lasted since the rule of mythical King Fergus I, appeared in many of the petitions sent to parliament from Scotland's towns and presbyteries.[11] A similar sense of patriotism inspired several pieces of political doggerel, including *The True Scots Genius Reviving*, published by committed pamphleteer William Forbes of Disblair, written, its subtitle informs us, 'upon occasion of the RESOLVE past in PARLIAMENT, the 17th of July 1704'. Imagining a nation emerging from a century of apathy to regain her liberty, the poem presents a Caledonia enchained by England but determined to win her freedom:

> Was it for this I bore the fiercest shock
> Of *Roman* Legions? And with fury brock
> Through all the Glittering Squadrons, who amaz'd
> To find Me fix them Limits wondering gaz'd!
> The forward Legions with their Thundring train,
> Strove oft to leap the Adrian wall in vain;
> Were still Repulsed, still beat back again.
> In midst of all their Eagles I did Grasp
> My Freedom, and retain'd it to the last.

A 1706 tract, published anonymously but generally attributed to Glasgow minister James Clark, bears the title *Scotland's Speech to her Sons* and again cites Scaliger whilst bemoaning the fact that the English were about to succeed where the Romans had failed, also blaming the Scots themselves for their impending loss of sovereignty:

> You may secure me against such Intollerable Incroachments and Injuries, as have spoiled the Glory of my INDEPENDENT SOVEREIGNTY in Times past. *Roman* Arms could never do, what *English* Craft and *Scots* Silliness have done, to call it worse:
>
> > *Imperii fuerat Romani Scotia Limes*
> > SCOTLAND of Old *Rome*'s Arms did Bound
> > None but Scots-men can SCOTLAND Wound.

As the Union came into force, many Scots mourned the demise of their once mighty nation. One anonymous poem, entitled *An Elegye Upon the Never Enough to be Lamented Decease of that Antient Illustrious and Venerable Lady Princess Scocia* and produced as a pamphlet in 1707, recalls the legend that Scotland had been founded by the descendants of an exiled Egyptian princess named Scota. It remembers the past greatness of the Scots, remarking that 'The Roman conquest they did stop also / Who o're their Land could never half way go', but admits that those days are surely gone for ever.[12]

Scotland's rejection of Rome in early eighteenth-century historiography

The first decade of the eighteenth century witnessed an increased interest in the Picts, as Scottish antiquarians and historians attempted to establish their national ancestry. Medieval chroniclers had tended to sideline the Picts, whose very existence had proved problematic for ideas of racial continuity, challenging the popular belief that it was the people known as the Scots who were indigenous to the region and thus the forefathers of the modern nation.[13] A lack of written sources, aside from a handful of mentions in Roman texts, hampered research (even today they are often described as an 'enigmatic' people), and Kidd notes that the Picts were of 'little ideological importance' before the eighteenth century.[14]

In 1706, however, a text was published on the subject that would prove highly influential, although its authorship and date remain almost as mysterious as the Picts themselves. Entitled *The History of the Picts*, the original manuscript had been held for decades in the collection of the Edinburgh Advocates Library and was probably written around the beginning of the seventeenth century. Attributed to Henry Maule of Melgum when published, the name of James Balfour has also been suggested as a possible author.[15] The publication proved a great success in antiquarian circles, its popularity and rarity leading to it changing hands for significant sums in the eighteenth century and also prompting an early nineteenth-century reprint.[16]

In its portrayal of the Picts, this work conforms to the traditional image of Caledonian bravery and resistance. Its eighth chapter focuses on the Picts' interactions with the Romans and bears the suitably bombastic title 'Of the Most Memorable Battles Fought by the Picts, and Victories by Them Obtained Against the Romans'. While earlier chapters, particularly that which deals with Pictish manners and habits, heavily cite classical sources such as Caesar, Pliny and Strabo, the sections that relate Pictish victories tend to look elsewhere, since the Roman authors who deal directly with events in northern Britain tell only of defeats of the indigenous tribes. Here the histories of Fordun and Boece, with all their fanciful tales of ancient kings battling and defeating Roman legions, provide the inspiration for a rousingly patriotic text.

Maule, if he was indeed the author, describes seven battles between the Picts and the 'tyrannical and bellicose Romans', adding that these are only the most memorable, as such altercations were 'many in number and great in atchievement'.[17] Each of these battles ends, of course, in Pictish victory. The most dramatic successes over the invading armies are won thanks to the Pictish king Thetargus, the Romans losing almost 40,000 men in one encounter, and also to the troops of King Drustus, a battle near Camelon in which the Picts fought side by side with King Fergus II of the Scots resulting in a spectacular

60,000 Roman deaths.[18] The final chapter also includes a list of Pictish kings, as well as a list of the Roman commanders that they faced. The picture painted by this *History of the Picts* is unequivocal: the period of Roman involvement in Scotland saw constant conflict, with the Picts, despite some losses, almost always coming out on top. Such portrayals had an inevitable impact on Scottish interpretations of the past. By 1719 Irish antiquarian John Toland (who had studied at Edinburgh and Glasgow three decades previously) would comment drily that 'they are apt all over Scotland, to make everything Pictish, whose origin they do not know'.[19]

Perhaps one of the last Scottish histories to rely heavily on Hector Boece and his increasingly mistrusted *Historia Gentis Scotorum* was Patrick Abercromby's *Martial Atchievements of the Scots Nation*. Although the title of this 1711 publication was inspired by the aforementioned warlike reputation of the Scottish people, and as such is another example of the Scots' own desire to encourage such an image, the book itself charts the general history of the Scottish nation from its legendary beginnings right up until the reign of James IV. Born into a Catholic family, Abercromby had lost his prestigious role as royal physician after the Glorious Revolution and remained a confirmed Jacobite for the rest of his days.[20] He was also a fervent opponent of union with England. Abercromby was well aware of the classical texts that refer to the north (in particular the *Agricola* and Dio's *Roman History*) and references them when detailing the early incursions of the Romans into Scotland, but he turned to the fantastical tales of Boece and Buchanan for descriptions of later invasions. He was also intent on proving that the race known as the Scots was already established in north Britain when the Romans arrived, suggesting that 'Reason and Conjecture' supported this idea, while claims that they later emigrated from Ireland were based rather on 'Tradition and History'.[21]

Viewing himself as a direct descendent of the ancient Scots, Abercromby praises their courage and endurance in the face of the Roman threat:

> I mean the *North*-Britains, who had so often withstood, and so bravely repel'd the *Roman* Attacks; against whom two Emperors came over and fought in person, whom even *Julius Agricola* could not beat out of the Island, and who in fine, after an almost continu'd Strugle, of very nigh 200 years, from the Reign of Claudius, to that of Severus, had compel'd the Conquerors of the Universe to set Boundaries to their Ambition.[22]

Abercromby's Caledonians were admirable even in defeat, with the mythical King Eugene and his army of both men and women taking their own lives to avoid submission to the victorious Romans, who were helped on this occasion by the Picts.[23] Oblivious to George Buchanan's complaint that Hector Boece 'attributes Matters, acted by others against the *Romans* in *Britanny* [Britain], to his

Country-Men, the Scots', Abercromby also lifted several tales from the *Historia Gentis Scotorum* that transpose southern heroes to Scotland.[24] The famous Caratacus described by Tacitus in his *Annals* 12.33–8 is said to be the Caratak mentioned in the Scottish King Lists, with Abercromby repeating Boece's claim that he was actually a Caledonian monarch who travelled down to England to help the Britons fight the Romans.[25] Caratak is also presented as the uncle of Calgacus, who also happened to be the nephew of '*Scots* Heroine' Boudica, thus creating an impressive dynasty of Caledonian freedom-fighters.[26] Abercromby writes extensively on the character and exploits of the valiant Calgacus, identified here as Corbredus Galdus, twenty-first king of the Scots who, Abercromby asserts, had been raised in the court of Boudica, from whom he learnt the 'Rudiments of Heroism'.[27] Thanks to the fact that he grew up in such close proximity to the Roman province, he was also influenced by the Roman way of life: indeed, although Abercromby admits to being sceptical that Calgacus' speech would have been delivered in the polite and elegant prose related by Tacitus, he does suggest that the Caledonian chieftain was 'Polish'd by his Education, almost *Roman*'.[28] Like both Boece and Buchanan before him, Abercromby allowed Calgacus a glorious comeback following his defeat at the hands of Agricola. Overall, although he reveals himself to be well-read, Abercromby's interpretation of Roman Scotland relies on a highly selective approach to the ancient, medieval and Renaissance sources, with aspects of each employed to create a satisfying collage of Caledonian glory.

If Alexander Gordon, author of the *Itinerarium Septentrionale*, the genesis and reception of which were discussed in the previous chapter, was less reliant on centuries-old history books and more thorough in his researches into the material remains of Rome in Scotland, the end result of his work was similarly patriotic. Despite depending on the patronage of one of Scotland's preeminent unionists and most dedicated Romanists, Sir John Clerk of Penicuik, Gordon wrote a book that was largely anti-Roman, and by implication anti-English. For him, the impressive military remains of Rome described and illustrated in his *Itinerarium* (Figure 3.1) were evidence of the failed attempts of Rome to conquer the north. An entire chapter is dedicated to proving that Scotland had never succumbed to Roman invasion, this diatribe opening with a spirited cry for Scottish independence:

> If Scotland boasts being numbered among the Nations which never bowed their Necks to the Yoak of *Roman* Bondage, I think from the foregoing Sheets, it appears plain, that their Pretence is not built upon a wrong Foundation: For, from the Tenor of the whole *Roman* History in *Britain*, it cannot be shewn, that the *Scots* and *Picts* ever suffered the least Part of their Country to lie under Subjection, any considerable Time, without re-possessing themselves thereof, and taking a just Revenge upon their Enemies and Invaders.[29]

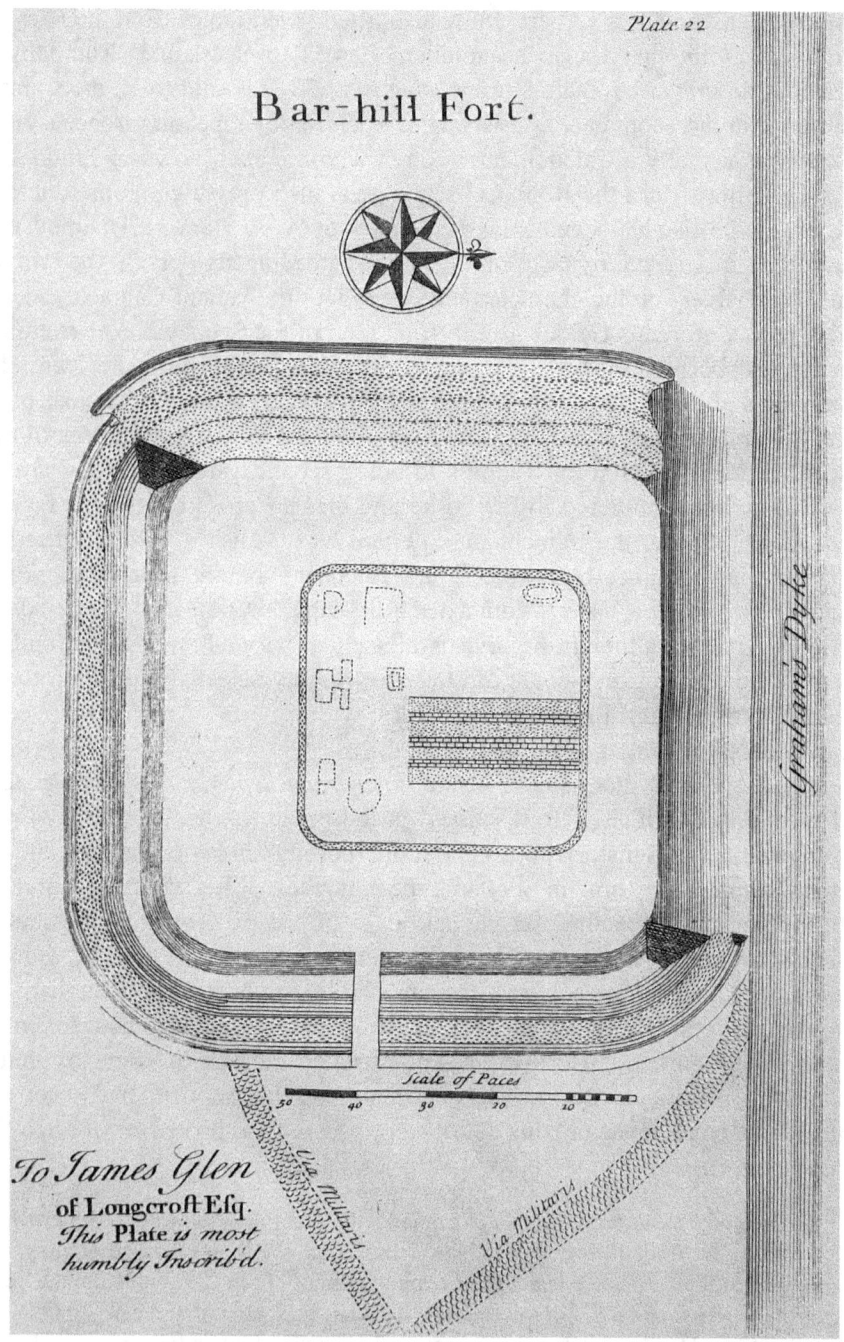

Figure 3.1 Plan of Bar Hill Fort and the Antonine Wall, Plate 22 in Alexander Gordon's *Itinerarium Septentrionale*, 1726.

In the chapter that follows, Gordon highlights the repeated failure of the Romans in their various attempts to colonise the region. He proposes that it was only thanks to the ingenuity of Agricola himself that the Romans made any headway in their first-century incursion, adding rather pedantically that Tacitus' account of the invasion mentions no great Roman victories in the north besides the famous battle of Mons Graupius.[30] The existence of a Roman wall in Scotland and its brief period of occupation are also presented as evidence of the persistent threat from the Caledonians to the north.[31] Gordon refutes claims that a gap in the list of Scottish kings implied a period when the Scots were banished from their homeland by a Roman/Pictish alliance and was particularly surprised that such a notion could be proposed by other Scots, naming sixteenth-century historians Bishop John Leslie and John Major as the culprits.[32]

The *Itinerarium* is filled with calls for liberty, with the speech of Calgacus from Tacitus' *Agricola* mined for references to the rejection of slavery and the battle for Caledonian freedom. That its author saw this as an ongoing battle is made plain:

> I therefore wish, that the Sons of *Scotland* would, in all Ages, follow the excellent advice of their valiant countryman *Galgacus*; *Et majores vestros & Posteros cogitate*. "Remember your Ancestors great Actions, and have an Eye to Posterity." By which he certainly meant, That, above all Things, they should be careful to maintain their Liberty; which, the better to preserve, 'tis my humble Opinion, that they ought as effectually to resist the Invasions of Modern *Rome*, as their Fore-fathers did those of the Ancient.[33]

Whether the 'Modern Rome' mentioned here should be taken literally as the Church of Rome, or more metaphorically as the English, remains open to question. Although Alexander Gordon was critical of previous Scottish efforts to record the early history of the nation and saw his own work as plugging the gaps in the flawed historical record and correcting the mistakes of his predecessors, in its patriotic pro-Caledonian stance his *Itinerarium* follows closely in the footsteps of Fordun, Boece and Buchanan. While we have already heard of Sir John Clerk's discomfort with these elements of the book, we can only wonder what the many English subscribers, who included the Bishop of Bristol, the Earl of Stafford and the Bursar of King's College, Cambridge among their ranks, made of such jingoistic, anti-English posturing.

Three years after the publication of Gordon's *Itinerarium Septentrionale*, a book appeared that was to have a profound impact on Scottish historiography, calling into question some of its most fundamental tenets. Written by Father Thomas Innes, a Roman Catholic priest with Jacobite sympathies who was born in Aberdeenshire but spent much of his life in Paris, the 1729 *Critical Essay on the Ancient Inhabitants of the Northern Parts of Britain, or Scotland* includes a scholarly debunking of the myth of an unbroken line of Scottish monarchs, artfully deconstructing the works of both Boece and Buchanan that had had such an influence on previous generations. While he is often regarded as a careful and dedicated scholar who relied more on manuscript evidence than patriotic tradition, Innes' work was not without its own agenda: as Robert Wodrow noted in 1728, Innes' intention was to establish the antiquity of Scottish Christianity, 'to sheu that Scotland was Christianized at first from Rome'.[34] Innes claimed, like others before him, that the Scots were relative latecomers, arriving in the north of Britain from Ireland long after the Romans had left the region. The author admitted the importance of the Romans in the formative history of Scotland; although he was aware of current scholarship (including the *Itinerarium*), he stated that the content of his own book was based on an unpublished account written by himself many years previously that he believed to be consistent with the more recent published works on Britain's Roman antiquities.[35] Innes also reinterpreted the ancestry of early modern Scots, proposing a hybrid nation descended from the Romans, the Britons, the Picts, the ancient Scots and the Saxons. Apparently aware of the negative reaction that such an idea would provoke amongst his countrymen, Innes added that, since most modern nations, including Italy, France, Spain and England, were formed in this way, ''tis no disparagement to the present inhabitants of *Scotland* to be in this like to other nations, originally descended of different people'.[36] He suggested that some of the country submitted to Roman rule, at least for a while, and also states, like Sibbald, that the Romans 'left their language' in Scotland.[37] Based on these ideas, he proposed three groups of ancient Britons: 'provincials' who inhabited the region south of Hadrian's Wall; unconquered 'extra-provincials' north of the Antonine Wall; and the 'Midland Britains' who lived in the lands in between, sometimes under Roman control, sometimes 'over-run by the northern inhabitants of *Britain*'.[38]

Aware of an impending threat to his reputation in the form of John Horsley (of whom more in the next chapter), Alexander Gordon returned to the fray in 1732 with his *Additions and Corrections, By Way of Supplement, to the Itinerarium Septentrionale*. This slender volume displays a nationalist antiquarianism even stronger than that of the original book, a large part of it dedicated to refuting Innes' claims regarding the origins of the Scots. In its dedication to Scottish seaman James Macrae, the Caledonians' fight for their territory is compared to Macrae's own daring defence of his boat, the Cassandra, against pirates (whose captain was, rather appropriately, surnamed England) in the Indian Ocean in 1720. Gordon's association of the marauding pirates with the ancient Romans is explicit, and with the modern English implicit:

> The Bravery of our Heroic Ancestors against those whom *Tacitus* calls *Raptores Orbis*, The *Plunderers of the World*, has too near a Resemblance to your own, not to affect you; since the same Man who defended the *Cassandra* with so much Resolution, against Pyrates of a still worse Nature, must with equal Courage have defended his country, had he lived in those Days.[39]

Although he generously described Innes as 'very ingenious and learned', Gordon proclaimed the Catholic clergyman's idea that the Scots were late arrivals in the north of Britain as a 'Chymera... and Hypothesis without any Foundation'. The belief that the courageous Caledonians who had faced the Romans were the true ancestors of the modern Scot was, Gordon stated, never in doubt:

> So that the Scots ought not (without better Evidence than what has been shewn to the contrary) ever to give up that just Pretence which they have, of being the Offspring of those very Heroes and real inhabitants of *Britain*, whom the Romans never could conquer; and who, unmix'd with any other Nations, the *Picts* excepted, never suffere'd their Liberties to be wrested by Force out of their Hands.[40]

He declared himself 'extreamly glad' that his patron Sir John Clerk of Penicuik shared this opinion; but while Gordon remained full of praise for the ancient Caledonians, he was less impressed by their modern counterparts, describing his fellow Scots despairingly to Clerk as 'a degenerate & worthless Pack for the most part, considering their inveterate Silly Superstition, Pride & faction'.[41]

Caledonian indomitability in literary verse

Further evidence of the popularity of tales of Caledonia's brave repulsion of Rome amongst eighteenth-century Scots can be found in the work of the nation's poets. In the years after the Union, some Scots revived the long tradition of vernacular poetry as they tried to preserve and promote a distinct cultural heritage.[42] Poets, like antiquarians, often wrote of a glorious past, a valiant and free nation now under threat or even lost. While it is hard to know how aware the wider early modern Scottish population were of their own nation's ancient history, the number of references to the Caledonian rejection of Roman invaders in popular poetry of the time suggests that it was a well-known and much-loved story. That this historical tale of a battle for liberty also held a more contemporary resonance at a time when Scottish national identity was perceived as compromised and the nation's independence lost for ever also seems to have been generally understood. As with the antiquarians already discussed, the poets who employed such imagery of a Caledonian resistance also tended to display Jacobite sympathies. Paradoxically, some poets expressed their jubilation at Caledonia's rejection of Roman influence in verses evidently inspired by classical literature.

Representing the tail end of a long Scottish tradition of writing Latin poetry, which had reached its zenith during the Renaissance and Reformation, *The Grameid* of James Philp (or sometimes Philip) of Almerieclose has been described as the last Neo-Latin epic to be written in Britain and also the first great work of Jacobite literature.[43] The unfinished poem dates from the final years of the seventeenth century and relates the gallant endeavours of the Jacobite hero John Graham of Claverhouse in the run up to his victory at the Battle of Killiecrankie in 1689. Acting as a standard bearer to the Jacobite army during the ill-fated campaign, Philp was an eyewitness to the events that he described. Although it is difficult to assess the impact of the text (which remained unpublished until 1888) in the decades after its composition, the survival of five manuscript copies suggests that it would have been circulated amongst Jacobite sympathisers. Showing the influence of Lucan and Virgil, *The Grameid* makes allusions to the greatness of ancient Rome, comparing its protagonist Graham with the revered military leaders of classical history, the poet also likening himself to the Roman writer Ennius who accompanied Scipio into battle.[44] Despite his ingenious attempts to render Scottish names into idiomatic Latin (Falkirk becomes *Varium Sacellum*, Montrose is *Mons Rosarum*), Philp was determined to remind readers that Scotland had remained free of Roman control:

> *Haec loca Martigenae nunquam videre Quirites*
> *Non Cimbri furor, aut rabiosi Saxonis arma*
> *Attigerant;*[45]

(These places [near Lochaber] never saw the Mars-begotten
Romans, nor did they come into contact with the fury of the
Cimbri, or the weapons of the wild Saxons;)

Philp saw the defeat and exile of the Stuarts as a loss for Scotland, its long-held reputation for remaining free of foreign domination now lost thanks to the recent ascent of William of Orange:

> *Scotia plebeios nec gesserat inclyta fasces,*
> *Nullius aut duras sub leges venerat hostis:*
> *Substitit hic domito Romana potentia mundo;*
> *Atque triumphatis utroque a cardine terris*
> *Scotia limes erat, Romanaque repulit arma.*[46]

(Scotland the illustrious had never obeyed democratic rule, nor
come under the law of an enemy. Here Roman power stayed
her course over a conquered world; and Scotland was the limit
of her triumph, which stretched from every corner of the world,
and repelled Roman arms.)

The Caledonian defiance of Roman conquest as a synecdoche for Scottish national liberty appears regularly in the verse of Scotland's most popular early eighteenth-century poet, Allan Ramsay. Father of the portrait painter and antiquarian of the same name, Ramsay senior was born in the mid-1680s and came from relatively humble origins. As a result, he was denied a classical education and later lamented his ignorance of Latin, although a manuscript biography in the hand of his son suggests that he picked up enough of the ancient language to 'catch the spirit of the Odes of Horace'.[47] Instead, suggests his biographer Alexander Kinghorn, Ramsay was raised on 'historical tales, legends of Scots heroes and the living oral tradition of popular balladry, all of which caught the developing national consciousness of this talented child and laid the foundations of his antiquarian interests'.[48]

Originally trained as a wigmaker, Ramsay later found success as a bookseller and publisher. It was this, together with his growing fame as a poet, that allowed him access to Edinburgh's literary circles, and in 1712 he helped to found the Easy Club, a group that has often been labelled as displaying Jacobite and nationalist sentiments during whose meetings verse would be discussed and performed in an atmosphere of polite conviviality.[49] Ramsay's political beliefs were complex and at times contradictory, and although he was certainly fiercely patriotic and sceptical to some extent of the benefits of British union, many of his friends and associates were staunch Whigs, among them his patron Sir John Clerk of Penicuik.[50] Marshall Walker notes that Ramsay played no role in the 1715 Jacobite uprising, and also managed to be 'judiciously absent' from Edinburgh during the 1745 occupation by the army of Charles Edward Stuart.[51] What cannot be denied are the poet's success and popular appeal: by 1720 he was Edinburgh's best-loved poet, his works circulated and enjoyed throughout Scottish society.

Ramsay first employs the imagery of Caledonian resistance in his 1718 poem *Tartana: or the Plaid*. This wistful verse opens by highlighting the antiquity of Scotland's national dress, then moves on to the impressive mettle of its (tartan clad) ancient inhabitants:

> 'Twas they could boast their Freedom with proud *Rome*,
> And, arm'd in Steel, despise that Senate's Doom;
> Whilst o'er the GLOBE their *Eagle* they display'd,
> And conquer'd Nations to them Homage pay'd,
> We only then unconquer'd, stood our Ground,
> And to the mighty *Empire* fixt the Bound.[52]

In 1724 he published an anthology entitled *The Ever Green*, which contained old vernacular Scots poems; one, *The Vision*, claimed to be a translation of a medieval text but was actually authored by Ramsay himself. Supposedly written at the time of the Wars of Independence, it proposes that the English are about to conquer Scotland, thus achieving 'Quhat *Romans* or no Mans / Pith culd eir do befoir' (What neither the Romans nor any man's strength could ever do before).[53] Similar ideas are contained in *On Seeing the Archers Diverting Themselves at the Buts and Rovers,* published six years later and inspired by the Royal Company of Archers. Founded in 1676, this private club was granted a Royal Charter by Queen Anne in 1704, although its militaristic nature and close links to the Stuarts later led to it being viewed with suspicion by the Hanoverian regime. Appearing in a 1726 anthology of verse in both English and Latin dedicated to the society, Ramsay's poem describes the archers in action, a rousing sight that 'Brings Bygane Ages to our View / when burnish'd Swords and whizzing Flanes / Forbade the Nerwegens and Danes / Romans and Saxons to invade'.[54] Towards the end of the same book, *The Archers March* (which would later appear in Ramsay's famous anthology *The Tea-table Miscellany*) also recalls Scotland's past excellence in martial matters:

> Our own true Records tell us,
> That none cou'd e'er excell us,
> That none cou'd e'er excell us,
> In martial Archery.
> With Shafts our Sires engaging,
> Oppos' the Romans Raging,
> Defeat the Fierce Norwegian,
> And spared few Danes to flee.[55]

In such poems, Ramsay displays his nostalgic pride in the strength of Caledonia and her admirable rejection of Roman invasion. However, his oeuvre also makes regular reference to the glory of ancient Rome and its culture. His *Epistle to a Friend at Florence, in His Way to Rome*, written for the painter John Smibert, prepares the artist for the wonders that he will find in the city, listing 'Amphitheatres, Columns, Royal Tombs / Triumphal Arches, Ruines of vast Domes / Old aerial Aqueducts, and strong pav'd Roads / which seem to've been not wrought by Men, but Gods'.[56] The preface of his 1721 collected works draws attention to the inspiration that Ramsay found in the writings of Horace, and included in the same volume are five of his ten 'imitations' of the Roman poet's verse. One in particular, entitled *To the Phiz*, features what has been described as 'a complex set of images which brings Edinburgh and Rome into conjunction', stating that the towering Pentland hills near the Scottish capital are 'as high as ony Roman wa'' (As high as any Roman wall).[57] Although he never visited Rome, Ramsay was surely aware of its reputation and recognised that an understanding of classical culture was commonly regarded as a sign of learning and good taste. Ramsay senior passed his admiration for Horatian verse, as well as other aspects of Roman culture, down to his son, who would later spend much time and effort searching for the remains of Horace's Sabine villa.[58] Both Philp and Ramsay, then, were admirers of Roman culture and imitators of the great Roman authors, and yet both revelled in the fact that their supposed ancestors had soundly rebuffed Roman invasion. Perhaps these poets saw no contradiction in such an approach, or perhaps they recognised that to admit the greatness of Rome was to show that the Caledonians who resisted them were even greater.

Rather than poems of melancholy, failure or regret, these verses sing of reviving past glories. If Scotland was now accepting Roman culture and civility, it was on her own terms, not as a conquered province of Rome, but rather as its equal.

Ramsay certainly realised that such notions would stir the hearts of his fellow Scots, and in this he was not alone. An excerpt from another poem dedicated to the Archers, but not included in the 1726 anthology, appears as the epigraph to this chapter. Printed anonymously in *The Caledonian Mercury* (attributed only to 'a worthy Patriot'), it accompanied a report on a procession from Edinburgh to Leith the previous day, the cavalcade preceding an archery contest won by 'that Mars-like Hero the Earl of Wigton'. The author was zealous Jacobite Alexander Robertson of Struan, the chief of clan Robertson who was actively involved in the uprisings of 1689, 1715 and 1745 and as a consequence spent much of his life in exile. He was also a respected poet during his lifetime, although his body of 'good, dutiful verse in the cavalier mode' has been largely neglected since, perhaps due to its political content.[59] The fact that this poem was published in one of Scotland's most popular newspapers of the period suggests not only that it would have been widely circulated, but also that its references to that reeling and sinking Roman eagle would have (in the opinion of its author, at least) been understood and appreciated by a broad Scottish audience.[60]

Caledonian heroics were also memorialised in other works by Ramsay's contemporaries, particularly in other verses included in that 1726 collection of *Poems in English and Latin, on the Archers, and Royal Company of Archers*. The volume's opening poem, which appears in both Latin and English and is initialled 'T.K.' (Thomas Kincaid, an active member of the club who won its Edinburgh Arrow contest in 1711), makes reference to Roman frontiers built to keep out fearsome Caledonian warriors:

> Who can with so much Envy be possest,
> Not frankly to rejoyce to see at last
> The Scottish Archers now again reviv'd;
> Whose martial Deeds can hardly be believ'd?
> These made great Rome her conquering Pride let fall,
> And here defend her Friends with Ditch and Wall.[61]

English attitudes towards Caledonian liberty

As these political pamphlets, antiquarian books and patriotic poems have demonstrated, Caledonia's ability to withstand Roman invasion, a veritable 'David and Goliath' tale of the noble savage defeating the 'Conquerors of the Universe', was a source of much bravado, used to boost the flagging self-esteem of many early eighteenth-century Scots. Indeed, this ancient success was trumpeted even where it was hardly relevant: a description of Corsica printed in *The Caledonian*

Mercury on 18 October 1731 (p. 9308), for example, refers to the island's subjection by the 'all conquering (*Scotland excepted*) Romans'. This was, after all, one way in which the Scots, brave defenders of their national liberty, appeared to outshine the English.

South of the border, however, English antiquarians were more sceptical of such claims, offering alternative, less ennobling explanations for the lack of Roman involvement in the north. The worrying suggestion that the Romans had not failed to conquer Scotland, but rather had seen no purpose in doing so was one that was proposed on several occasions. Scots were predictably scornful of such ideas. In his *Itinerarium Septentrionale*, Alexander Gordon reveals that such an opinion was common, without identifying any specific sources, and puts much energy into refuting it:

> I am therefore much surprized, that some, who never omit any Opportunity of lessening the Honour of that People [the Scots], should vent their Prejudices by giving out, That the *Romans* never thought it worth their while, either to conquer *Scotland*, or stay in that Country, not being able (as they say) to subsist in so barren a Soil; but I must, in common Justice, assure these Gentlemen, that by such a partial (though fashionable Way of speaking nowadays) they are not aware how manifestly they betray their own Ignorance.[62]

If Scotland was such an unattractive place, Gordon argued, why would the Romans under both Agricola and Severus have put so much effort into trying to subdue it? Furthermore, the very scale of these two Roman incursions disproved claims that Scotland was too barren to support a large invading army. Rather than desolate wastelands, he described the mountains of the Highlands as a natural defence against attack, 'preserving them from the griping Tallons of the grand Plunderers of the World'.[63]

The two most prominent Romanist antiquarians in England at this time, William Stukeley and John Horsley, remained less than convinced by Scotland's claims of ancient valour. In his essay entitled *Iter Boreale*, which records a 1725 visit to Hadrian's Wall and was published posthumously in the second of edition of his *Itinerarium Curiosum*, Stukeley presented the frontier as evidence that the Romans considered the region beyond it 'not worth while wholly to conquer' and instead 'resolved to quit their strengths northwards, and content themselves with the desirable part of Britain'.[64] Horsley offered a similarly dismissive view of Caledonia in his 1732 *Britannia Romana*, implying that Rome's failure to conquer the north was more due to apathy than defeat: 'The Romans seem to have been indifferent about keeping possession of any part of this island beyond the walls', he wrote, citing Appian of Alexandria's suggestion that, in the time of Antoninus Pius, the Romans controlled 'more than half of *Britain*, and the best of it too, and had no occasion for the rest'.[65] Nevertheless, both Stukeley and

Horsley demonstrated an extensive interest in the history and remains of Rome in Scotland, and both wrote extensively on the subject. It is to them that we now turn in order to assess English interpretations of Scotland's ancient past, to consider the view from the other side of Hadrian's Wall.

Notes

1. For the influence of Rome on England's eighteenth-century elite, see: Ayres, *Classical Culture and the Idea of Rome in Eighteenth-Century England*. On the 'civil interpretations' of England's Roman heritage at this time, see: Hingley, *The Recovery of Roman Britain*, pp. 169–201.
2. *The Bee*, Vol. 6, pp. 52–3.
3. Dalrymple, *The Institutions of the Law of Scotland*, Dedication.
4. For examples of attitudes towards England's anti-Roman freedom fighters, see: Smiles, *The Image of Antiquity*, pp. 135–40.
5. Dalrymple, *The Institutions of the Law of Scotland*, Dedication. On pre-eighteenth-century attitudes towards the history of Scottish religion, see: Ferguson, *The Identity of the Scottish Nation*, pp. 98–116.
6. Brown, 'Scottish Identity in the Seventeenth Century', pp. 245–6.
7. Brown, 'Modern Rome and Ancient Caledonia', p. 34.
8. Pittock, *Inventing and Resisting Britain*, p. 141.
9. Hodges, *The Rights and Interests of the Two British Monarchies Inquir'd Into . . . Treatise I*, pp. 9–10.
10. Hodges, *The Rights and Interests of the Two British Monarchies Inquir'd Into . . . Treatise III*, pp. 114–15.
11. Kidd, *Subverting Scotland's Past*, p. 41.
12. *An Elegye Upon the Never Enough to be Lamented Decease of that Antient Illustrious and Venerable Lady Princess Scocia*, p. 2.
13. Broun, 'The Picts' Place in Kingship's Past Before John of Fordun', pp. 16–17.
14. Kidd, 'The Ideological Uses of the Picts', p. 170.
15. Webster, *Miscellanea Pictica*, Advertisement.
16. Ibid. p. iii.
17. Maule, 'The History of the Picts', p. 30.
18. Ibid. pp. 31–2.
19. Toland, *A Collection of Several Pieces of John Toland*, p. 111.
20. du Toit, 'Patrick Abercromby', p. 89.
21. Abercromby, *The Martial Atchievements of the Scots Nation*, p. 28.
22. Ibid. p. 25.
23. Ibid. p. 27.
24. Buchanan, *The History of Scotland*, p. 80.
25. Abercromby, *The Martial Atchievements of the Scots Nation*, p. 39.
26. Ibid. p. 45–6.
27. For Abercromby's discussion of Calgacus/Galdus, see: *The Martial Atchievements of the Scots Nation*, pp. 45–55.
28. Ibid. p. 51.
29. Gordon, *Itinerarium Septentrionale*, p. 135.

30. Ibid.
31. Ibid. p. 136.
32. Ibid. pp. 139–40.
33. Ibid. p. 138, quoting Tacitus, *Agricola* 32.4.
34. Wodrow, *Analecta*, pp. 516–17. For an extensive discussion of Innes' scholarship, see: Kidd, *Subverting Scotland's Past*, pp. 101–7.
35. Innes, *A Critical Essay on the Ancient Inhabitants of the Northern Parts of Britain*, pp. xx–xxi.
36. Ibid. p. 2.
37. Ibid.
38. Ibid. pp. 9–10.
39. Gordon, *Additions and Corrections*, p. ii.
40. Ibid. p. 10.
41. NRS GD18/5023/3/57: Gordon to Clerk, ? June 1732.
42. Brown, 'Modern Rome and Ancient Caledonia', p. 34.
43. Houghton, 'Lucan in the Highlands', p. 190.
44. Ibid. p. 202.
45. Philip, *The Grameid*, p. 78. For more on Philp's Latinisation of Scottish names, see: Houghton, 'Lucan in the Highlands', p. 195.
46. Philip, *The Grameid*, p. 23.
47. Kinghorn, 'Biographical and Critical Introduction', p. 5.
48. Ibid. p. 6.
49. For a discussion of the political affiliations of the Easy Club, see: Andrews, *Literary Nationalism in Eighteenth-Century Scottish Club Poetry*, pp. 32–7.
50. On Ramsay's politics, see: Kinghorn, 'Biographical and Critical Introduction', pp. 12–19.
51. Walker, *Scottish Literature Since 1707*, p. 69.
52. Ramsay, *Tartana*, p. 10.
53. Ramsay, *The Ever Green*, p. 212.
54. *Poems in English and Latin, on the Archers, and Royal Company of Archers*, p. 34.
55. Ibid. p. 49. Although the poem is unattributed in the 1726 anthology, it is included in: Ramsay, *The Works of Allan Ramsay*, pp. 101–4.
56. Ramsay, *Poems*, p. 344.
57. Kinghorn and Law, 'Allan Ramsay and Literary Life in the First Half of the Eighteenth Century', p. 69.
58. For the importance of Horace in the life and work of both Allan Ramsays, see: Brown, *Poet and Painter*, pp. 25–7 and pp. 41–6.
59. Pittock, 'Alexander Robertson of Struan', p. 202.
60. A slightly different version of the poem can also be found in the posthumously published: Robertson, *Poems, on Various Subjects and Occasions*, pp. 31–3. It is (apparently incorrectly) included by Kinghorn and Law in: Ramsay, *The Work of Allan Ramsay*, p. 105.
61. *Poems in English and Latin, on the Archers, and Royal Company of Archers*, p. 4.
62. Gordon, *Itinerarium Septentrionale*, p. 137.
63. Ibid. p. 138.
64. Stukeley, *Itinerarium Curiosum*, Centuria II, p. 56.
65. Horsley, *Britannia Romana*, p. 65. He is citing Appian, *Roman History* Preface.5.

4

'Beyond the Vallum': English interpretations of Scottish history

> Upon the Main, I am of Opinion, that no Historian should offer to write the Transactions of his own Nation, without consulting the Accounts given of them by Foreigners.
>
> Patrick Abercromby, *The Martial Atchievements of the Scots Nation*, 1711, Preface

Although it comes as no surprise that Scottish antiquarians of the eighteenth century were fascinated by Roman Scotland, it is important to note that the subject also attracted attention south of the border. An analysis of the changing English perceptions of Scotland's early history confirms that there was more than just Scottish patriotism at play in the nation's developing historiography. The first half of the eighteenth century saw the publication of two key works featuring Roman Scotland written by arguably the most renowned English antiquarians of the period, namely William Stukeley and John Horsley. These two publications presented startlingly different depictions of ancient Caledonia and its relations with Rome.

Stukeley's *An Account of a Roman Temple, and Other Antiquities, Near Graham's Dike in Scotland* appeared in 1720; although he had already established himself as an esteemed member of London's intelligentsia by this time, this essay was the first of his works to be published. As well as including a description of the 'Temple' of its title, the mysterious, probably Roman structure in central Scotland known as Arthur's O'on, Stukeley's *Account* also expounds the antiquarian's vision of the Roman landscape that surrounded it, presenting southern Scotland as a virtual Roman province filled with evidence of classical civilisation. Although it is not dedicated solely to Scotland, Horsley's *Britannia Romana*, printed in 1732 soon after its author's untimely death, also contains much information on the Roman heritage of the northern nation. Its description of ancient Caledonia is, however, starkly at odds with that of Stukeley. Following his own lengthy travels in Scotland and much careful study of the sites and artefacts that he saw there, Horsley described the region as troublesome and barren, filled with material remains that provided evidence not of Roman civility, but rather of brief military campaigns.

Although it is difficult to ascertain how aware they were of Scottish scholarship on the subject, it seems that many of the conclusions reached by English antiquarians were formulated with little or no knowledge of the work published by their northern counterparts. But it was no coincidence that this shift from the idea of a civil Roman Scotland to that of a largely unconquered Caledonia closely resembles the contradictory beliefs held by early modern Scottish antiquarians. Just as in Scotland, changes in the way that information was collected played its part, as a reliance on conjecture based on the reports of others gave way to more careful personal investigations and fieldwork. The reception of Roman Scotland amongst the English certainly illustrates how evidence was interpreted by men with no patriotic bias towards the Caledonians, or indeed any vested interest in demonstrating Scottish supremacy. It also mirrors evolving attitudes towards Roman endeavours in the region south of Hadrian's Wall, with many English antiquarians also turning their attention to the military aspects of the Roman conquest and occupation of their own nation.

Evidence that early eighteenth-century English antiquarians were interested in Scotland's history, or evidence at least that they felt they should be, can be found in Humfry Wanley's 1707 draft for the founding charter of a short-lived early incarnation of the Society of Antiquaries of London. Capturing the political spirit of the moment, Wanley proclaimed that the society would 'promote the Ends of the Union, since a Communication & Correspondence with the Scotch will ensue, which begets mutual Love'.[1] The fact that this charter was formulated partly with the intention of procuring royal endorsement for the project may have inspired such an overt unionist stance, but as the first two chapters of this book have already demonstrated, close relations between English and Scottish antiquarians and intellectuals (Sibbald with Sloane, Clerk and Gordon with Gale and Stukeley) were to become the norm in the years that followed. Ideas and conjectures were exchanged in letters and visits were made between the two countries, each nation's scholars expressing an interest in the most recent discoveries of their neighbours. Driven by the eighteenth-century taste for all things Roman, English antiquarians were soon drawn into discussions on and investigations into the much debated and largely unrecorded material remains in the land that William Stukeley described poetically as lying 'beyond the Vallum'.[2]

William Stukeley, antiquarianism and Rome

Born in 1687 in Holbeach, William Stukeley (Figure 4.1) was to become a man of varied interests. Following his degree at Cambridge, completed in 1708, he went on to study medicine at St Thomas's in Southwark, following which he practised

Figure 4.1 William Stukeley, mezzotint by J. Smith, 1721, after Sir Godfrey Kneller. (Wellcome Collection. CC BY)

as a physician for several years in Boston, Lincolnshire. For reasons that are not clear, he returned to London in 1717, where his reputation as a virtuoso of some merit began to grow. He was to remain in the capital for almost a decade and during that time he became friends with many of the period's most eminent thinkers, including Isaac Newton and Hans Sloane, as well as aristocratic antiquarians such as the Earls of Pembroke and Winchelsea. Stukeley was nominated a Fellow of the Royal Society in 1718 and was one of the founding members of the new Society of Antiquaries established in London that same year, also taking up the role of secretary. In 1719 he graduated M.D. at Cambridge and in 1720 he became a Fellow of the Royal College of Physicians.

Stukeley himself identified the stirrings of antiquarianism in his childhood. He impressed his father with a hand-done copy of a medieval manuscript, and was later inspired by the discovery of a Roman hoard near his home to take 'a fancy for old Coyns and Medals'.[3] As a young man he developed a talent for writing Latin verse and he expressed a 'passionate love for Antiquitys' during his time at Cambridge; since his lowly income would not allow foreign travel, he decided to concentrate on the history of his own country.[4] Although better known (even notorious) today for his fantastical portrayals of the druids, Stukeley's interest in Britain's Roman past was extensive and enduring. In 1714 he received advice from fellow antiquarian Maurice Johnson that he should read the works of Caesar as well as Tacitus' *Agricola* and the third book of his *Histories* (particularly Henry Savile's 1591 translation) in order to learn more about early British history.[5] In 1716 Stukeley wrote an account of the Roman remains at Richborough in Kent. Following the publication of his *Account of a Roman Temple*, he produced a short essay giving a description *Of the Roman Amphitheater at Dorchester*, published in 1723. The first edition of his *Itinerarium Curiosum* of the following year includes much material on Roman sites, including 'numerous plates ... of ground-plots and prospects of Roman cities' and descriptions of the routes of Roman roads across England, as well as information on various prehistoric and medieval monuments.[6] His other published works on Roman Britain include the 1728 *Description of a Roman Pavement Found Near Grantham in Lincolnshire* and a text about a Roman silver plate discovered in Derbyshire of 1736. Even in later life, when Stukeley's fascination for standing stones and 'Druid temples' had become something of an obsession, he published a book on *The Medallic History of Marcus Aurelius Valerius Carausius* and an *Account of Richard of Cirencester*, which, as will be discussed in Chapter 8, described the revelations contained in a recently identified (but completely spurious) source on Roman Britain.

Although less obviously Romanist in his daily life than his friend Sir John Clerk of Penicuik, Stukeley's writings on Roman history reveal no small amount of veneration for the ancient civilisation. For him, the Romans were a 'brave and wise people' who possessed a 'noble and great genius'; Stukeley also claimed that the Romans who settled in Britain 'were for elegance and politeness much upon the level with those of the continent'.[7] Summing up the two aspects of Roman civilisation that perhaps most impressed eighteenth-century gentlemen, he saw them as a race 'equally renowned for Arts and Arms'.[8] Just like his brother-in-law Roger Gale, who wrote to Sir John Clerk of the benefits of Roman conquest (see Chapter 2), Stukeley viewed Roman invasion as something to be welcomed rather than resisted. In an unpublished manuscript treatise of 1726 on Caesar's expeditions to Britain, Stukeley not only described the Roman general in glowing terms ('a tall handsome man', 'very courteous & affable', 'a most excellent horseman') but also proclaimed his incursions as the beginning of 'the auspicious era of our happiness, when the bright rays of polite arts flew over on the wings of Roman Eagles'.[9] A devout man who served as the vicar of All Saints church in Stamford between 1730 and 1747, Stukeley also argued that the Romans had played an important role in spreading Christianity, believing that they had replaced the Jews as God's chosen people, their empire created by him for the purpose of disseminating his word.[10] Thanks to the Roman occupation of Britain, he claimed, 'the clouds of barbarism were broke by the Roman eagles, & made pervious to the meek rays of the Gospel'.[11]

Stukeley found inspiration in the culture and habits of the Romans and, although he was wary of the excesses that had brought down the empire, seemed to desire a revival of Roman ideals. A visit to Hadrian's Wall in 1725 undoubtedly stimulated such feelings, the antiquarian later summing his approach as follows:

> I hold myself obliged to preserve, as well as I can, the memory of such things as I saw; which, added to what future times will discover, will revive the Roman glory among us, and may serve to invite noble minds to endeavour to that merit and public spiritedness which shine through all their actions.[12]

Perhaps more than any of the other antiquarians discussed so far, Stukeley believed that emulating the Romans could benefit not just the individual, but also society as a whole. He also recognised the importance of saving and studying the physical remains of the past and, in an attitude shared by Sir John Clerk, viewed such an act as ensuring his own posterity.[13] In his *Account of a Roman Temple*, Stukeley describes the vestiges left by the Romans in Scotland as the legacy of the ancients, confirming their glorious achievements and surviving to be admired by later generations. 'They deserve it at our hands, to preserve their remains', he later wrote.[14]

Stukeley's Roman Scotland

William Stukeley was determined to demonstrate that Roman Britain had been just as sophisticated as the rest of the empire and came to believe that Roman civilisation had been established beyond Hadrian's Wall into the region now known as southern Scotland, even briefly extending beyond that into the far north. Writing before 1720, he viewed the history and antiquities of Roman Scotland as an area ripe for research:

> But I am sorry to confess the Scantiness of Materials and Helps for this Purpose, from the meagre Surveys and Accounts of these parts. I cannot but wonder That Nation, where are many good Scholars, should be so deficient herein; that their

> Historians should content themselves to compile their Works from Invention and fabulous Reports, rather than from searching into real Remains and undoubted Evidences of former Times.[15]

His *Account of a Roman Temple* gives a comprehensive description of the ancient landscape between the Roman walls as he imagined it and includes a detailed map of the Antonine frontier that the author claimed to have designed himself. Although he acknowledges that the main focus of the essay is to be the structure known as Arthur's O'on, Stukeley begins by establishing its position in a region replete with Roman monuments:

> But first will be convenient, to give a general View of the State of the country hereabouts, which many hundred Years ago was so throng'd with the Illustrious *Romans*, who have left there, so many noble Trophies of their Footsteps to eternize their Memory, and for future Ages to admire.[16]

Stukeley traced the origins of Roman civility in Scotland back to the arrival of Agricola, noting that the Roman general constructed a line of 'stations' between the firths of Forth and Clyde in order to 'separate the barbarous and rugged Regions of the Island, from the Southern, of greater Pleasure and Fertility, whose Inhabitants had submitted to their Manners and Government'.[17] He also concluded that the limited time spent by Agricola in the region would have led to only a minimal amount of Roman intervention, suggesting that, although he may have begun the construction of cities in southern Scotland, he was not there long enough to build 'Temples and more publick Buildings of Elegance and Magnificence'.[18] This area, Stukeley believed, was lost after the Agricolan forces retired, but was regained during the reign of Antoninus Pius, when Lollius Urbicus restored both the military installations and the cities and built his mighty wall.[19] The wall was refortified by Carausius, but the region was then let go once again by Constantine the Great, only to be retaken by 'Theodosius, Father of the Emperor of that Name'.[20]

A number of supposed Roman settlements in the area surrounding the Antonine Wall are listed in the *Account of a Roman Temple*, including a town at Abercorn and another called Itucoden near modern Bonnybridge, a city near Linlithgow called Lindum Caledonum as well as 'the Roman City *Simetria* at *Simerston*, *Dunblissis* at *Dunbass*, *Oliclavis* at *Over Kilvyn*; *Glascow* was *Dareoglassis*; *Renfrow, Ranafrovium*; *Paisley Praesidium*' amongst others.[21] It is notable that most of these conjectured Roman towns mentioned by Stukeley coincide with the locations of modern towns and cities. In fact, it was the later development of these sites that Stukeley blamed for the lack of surviving material evidence, particularly towards the eastern end of the Roman wall. Their loss, he believed, 'may be attributed to that Part being more frequented, the Court of the *Scots* Kings having been divers times kept at *Linlithgo*, *Calendar* Castle &c. So that these valuable Remains of Antiquity have been destroyed or put into new Buildings'.[22]

Stukeley also mentions that most famous Roman 'city' at Camelon, revealing that it was still possible to 'discern the Tracks of the Streets, Foundation of Buildings and subterraneous Vaults'.[23] He was certain that the Romans had built many cities linked by a network of roads beyond the Antonine frontier, and in the top right hand corner of his map of the Roman wall he identifies the fort at Ardoch as a *civitas* named Victoria.[24] He also indicated that much of the splendour of Roman Scotland had been lost during regular attacks from the northern barbarians, and surmised that Arthur's O'on itself was only spared due to its resemblance to 'Celtic' temples.[25] Ultimately, he believed, it was largely because of these troublesome natives that the Romans decided to leave Scotland, 'tired out by the untractable disposition of these people'.[26]

Stukeley's sources and influences

Although he made numerous trips across England in search of antiquities between 1710 and 1725, including a journey along Hadrian's Wall with Roger Gale, and certainly intended to travel further north, William Stukeley never actually made it to Scotland.[27] As a result, his elaborate descriptions of the nation ancient and modern were based on the reports of others. His information on the dimensions of Arthur's O'on, for example, was supplied by English architect Andrew Jelfe, who was sent to Scotland by the Board of Ordnance to repair and build military infrastructure after the 1715 Jacobite rebellion. The main source for the images of the carved slabs found along the line of the Antonine Wall included in the *Account of a Roman Temple* was a collection of drawings made by Edward Lhuyd, with transcriptions of two of them also supplied by scientist and physician James Jurin, a Fellow (and later Secretary) of the Royal Society.[28] For the names and locations of the Roman 'cities' in Scotland, Stukeley relied on the work of his friend William Baxter, whose *Glossarium Antiquitatum Britannicarum* of 1719 lists the ancient Latin names of modern places. Although it cites ancient sources such as the Ravenna Cosmography, the Antonine Itinerary and the works of Bede and Nennius, the book, to which Stukeley was a subscriber, is of little merit, its proposals, often based on improbable etymology, dismissed by Stuart Piggott as 'speculative and unreliable'.[29]

Like Sir Robert Sibbald, Stukeley also never travelled to Rome itself. A planned trip to the city in order to see at first hand 'the Pantheon, the Pillars, the Obelisks, the Gates, the Amphitheaters, & all that Art has to boast of Great & Venerable' was cancelled due to financial problems following the death of both his father and his uncle.[30] He later turned this loss to his advantage, making the patriotic claim that he had turned down the possibility of foreign travel in favour of touring his native land.[31] In building his own impressions of Rome, Stukeley had to make do with 'imagination alone & prints', and he often spent his time making drawings of the city's ancient and modern architecture.[32] He no doubt also heard glowing accounts from friends who did visit the Eternal City, such as architect Daniel Lock, who wrote to their mutual friend Samuel Gale on 21 November 1711 listing some of the antique 'wonders' he had seen there, describing them as 'lively instances of the Old Roman Greatness'.[33]

The similarities between Stukeley's account of Roman Scotland and those published by Robert Sibbald around a decade previously are numerous. Both imagined large swathes of ancient Caledonia as a Roman province, its landscape furnished with towns and classical monuments; both present Tacitus' *Agricola* as evidence for this Roman civility in the north; both also propose that many of Scotland's existing towns were constructed on the sites of Roman settlements. Despite these apparent correlations, it appears that Stukeley had little or no direct knowledge of Sibbald's antiquarian work. Stukeley does cite Sibbald in his *Account of a Roman Temple*, referencing a Roman inscription mentioned in the Scot's 1684 volume on natural history, the *Scotia Illustrata*.[34] The fact that he references this text rather than Sibbald's *Historical Inquiries*, which also features the same inscription, suggests that Stukeley had not read the 1707 essay on Roman Scotland in which Sibbald presented his own detailed vision of a classical Caledonia. In fact, it is likely that Stukeley only knew of Sibbald's discussion of the inscription in the *Scotia Illustrata* due to the fact that it is referenced in Baxter's *Glossarium Antiquitatum Britannicarum*.[35] Although he also cites Sibbald's additions to the 1695 *Britannia*, Stukeley apparently believed that this material on Scotland was written by the book's editor, Edmund Gibson.[36] So, although the Scottish antiquarian's ideas may have reached him indirectly, it is distinctly possible that Stukeley had not read any of Sibbald's published works on Scotland's Roman heritage.

Stukeley's description of Scotland as a Roman province, then, is for the most part based on the author's own beliefs and expectations and was largely a figment of his vivid imagination. He viewed the Romans as a benevolent force who established stable society wherever they went, later bringing Christianity to previously heathen lands. The evidence showed that the Romans had spent time in Scotland, so for an avowed Romanist like Stukeley, that they conquered and civilised it was the obvious conclusion. Although his *Account of a Roman Temple* was to be Stukeley's only book dedicated to Roman Scotland, the author's own annotated and interleaved copy of the essay, now held in the Sackler Library, Oxford, reveals that he continued to keep abreast of the latest scholarship on the subject in the years following its publication.[37] The hand-written notations in the book are undated, but their content, as well as variations in the ink and handwriting, suggests that they were added over many years. Stukeley added several notes based on information received from Somerset geologist and antiquarian John Strachey (who visited sites along the Antonine Wall while travelling across Scotland in the employ of the York Buildings Company in 1721), corrected the orientation of the door of Arthur's O'on and also altered one of the illustrations of the structure by adding a stone base. He was visited by Alexander Gordon in 1723, noting after their meeting that 'He had been to view Arthur's O'on & the Antiquity's thereabouts'.[38] This encounter may have inspired some of Stukeley's annotations in his copy of the *Account*, in particular one on the front flyleaf that includes the content of two Roman inscriptions as well as reports of two 'circuses' and a 'sort of circus' in southern Scotland, information that came via the Scottish antiquarian: 'Mr Gordon had this information from Mr Cambel. Mr Cambel informed him likewise of an earthen tube of reddish clay bakd, which is lett into the [Antonine] wall all the way, for communicating an alarm from one tower to another'.[39] Stukeley's annotations also include several references to Gordon's *Itinerarium Septentrionale* of 1726. Others certainly date to the 1750s, as they relate to the 'discovery' of the *De Situ Britanniae*, a source that would dramatically alter Stukeley's views on the extent of Roman power in the north.[40] It was during the same decade that Stukeley developed a fascination for Carausius, with one note in his *Account of a Roman Temple* proposing that the construction of the city of Camelon by the Roman usurper was commemorated on a coin no doubt inspired by the research for his 1757 book on the subject.[41]

Influenced by his great admiration for Rome, Stukeley constructed a Caledonian landscape filled with signs of Roman splendour. For him, wherever the Romans went they brought with them the shining light of civilisation and, less concerned by the long tradition that suggested otherwise, he proposed that Scotland had been no exception. Although he clearly spent much time researching and discussing its content, Stukeley viewed his essay on Roman Scotland as 'only a sketch and an imperfect attempt' and hoped that others would look into the matter more fully in order to correct his mistakes and 'handle the subject as it deserves', later scribbling in his own copy that they could 'add to the History'.[42] But while he extensively annotated and altered his book, presumably with a view to republishing it himself, another English antiquarian was indeed exploring the subject, this time with more dedication to investigating the surviving remains of Rome in Scotland in person, while also maintaining a more level-headed approach to analysing them.

John Horsley and his *Britannia Romana*

Little is known about the early life of John Horsley. Rumours that he hailed from East Lothian led to him being included in the 1855 *Biographical Dictionary of Eminent Scots*, but today it is generally agreed that he was probably born in Northumberland around 1685.[43] His parentage remains obscure and attempts to locate family links rely largely on guesswork. We do know for sure that the Horsleys were Nonconformists, also that John was educated at Newcastle Grammar School and the University of Edinburgh, where records show that he was exempted from first year studies due to his proficiency in Latin and Greek.[44] He also demonstrated abilities in mathematics and science, and would later make use of these in publishing an essay on mechanics, hydrostatics and pneumatics.[45] By 1709 he was living in Morpeth and employed as a dissenting minister and school teacher. It has been suggested that his taste for antiquity was inspired by the nearby remains of Hadrian's Wall, and a meeting with antiquarian John Warburton around 1712–16 seems to have further encouraged his enthusiasm.[46] What started as a hobby became more serious, and by 1727 he had embarked on the composition of a book dedicated to the material remains of Rome in Britain, namely his celebrated *Britannia Romana*.

Horsley quickly made contacts within antiquarian circles. He began a correspondence with Roger Gale, and in late 1728 he arrived at Penicuik House carrying a letter of introduction to Sir John Clerk from William Hamilton, Professor of Divinity at Edinburgh University, which stated that the bearer was 'very desirous of the honour of being admitted to converse with you and to see your pieces of antiquity'.[47] Clerk was impressed by Horsley's classical learning and was to become involved in the formulation of the *Britannia Romana*; he seems to have proofed the illustrations of the Roman inscribed stones from Scotland in 1729.[48] He also realised that Horsley's work might expose errors in Gordon's *Itinerarium Septentrionale* and expressed his hope to ecclesiastical historian Matthew Crawford that this new book would not be too critical of the fragile and defensive Scottish antiquarian.[49] Gordon's own reaction was entirely predictable. Viewing Horsley as competition for Clerk's favour and a threat to his own reputation, he questioned the originality of the Englishman's research, writing to William Stukeley in a rage: 'I verily believe the Poor Priest is crasey . . . I laugh at his second gleanings of the harvest I've reapt . . . I take Mr Horsley's antiquarian affairs to be like the crackling of thorns under a pot *vox et praeterea nihil*'.[50] The frequency with which friends and acquaintances such as Clerk and Thomas Blackwell refer to him as 'Poor Gordon' during this period is notable.[51] On its publication, Gordon was highly critical of Horsley's book, finding faults in many of the plates and accusing the author of plagiarism. He was particularly annoyed at Horsley's inclusion of an image of Sir John Clerk's sculpture of the goddess Brigantia and claimed that it was copied from his own 1732 *Additions and Corrections*, prompting an exasperated Roger Gale to point out that Gordon's supplement had in fact been published several weeks after Horsley's death.[52]

John Horsley left relatively little in the way of published or manuscript material, and as a result the man himself remains something of an enigma. His mighty *Britannia Romana* stands as his greatest legacy: four years in the making, it was self-financed without subscription, Horsley presumably hoping to make back his expenses on publication. The idea of carrying out antiquarian research for financial gain rather shocked Sir John Clerk, who wrote to Roger Gale that 'the poor man writes for bread'.[53] While Horsley was certainly interested in the culture of ancient Rome, he was resistant to the kind of obsessive admiration that drove many of his contemporaries, not least Clerk and Stukeley:

> I KNOW the virtues of the antients have been largely applauded by many, and recommended as very worthy of our imitation. Tho' I cannot carry my compliment to the antients in this respect so far as some others have done; yet no doubt a great many things may be learned from those antique monuments, which are both instructive and useful.[54]

If anything, he saw the ruined remains of the distant past not as reminders of the noble beginnings of the nation, but instead as evidence of the transient nature of civilisation, a warning against the perils of pride and vanity.

Roman Scotland as portrayed in *Britannia Romana*

Although the *Britannia Romana* ably demonstrates John Horsley's expansive knowledge of both classical texts and more recent antiquarian publications (including Gordon, whom he cites throughout the work, sometimes favourably, sometimes critically), it was his extensive fieldwork that has won him the most respect. While Sir Robert Sibbald extolled the virtues of personally examining sites and William Stukeley also inspected and recorded many such places on his travels, neither came close to matching Horsley for coverage and accuracy. 'Several thousand miles were travelled on this account', he wrote in his preface, also labelling his research 'expensive and tedious'.[55] Aware of the problems that could arise from repeating the reports of others and critical of existing scholarship, Horsley claimed that he had viewed as many of the Roman sculptures and inscriptions in Britain as possible. This made a trip to Scotland obligatory, and he travelled widely in the country, visiting the collection of stones in Glasgow (Figure 4.2) as well as Sir John Clerk. The journey to Aberdeen proved too daunting, however, and instead he copied a sketch of an inscription held at Marischal College supplied by one of its professors.[56] Despite his undeniable commitment, the enormous scope of the project meant that Horsley did require assistance on occasion, so as well as co-opting George Mark, who was probably his assistant at the school in Morpeth, he also called on Newcastle businessman and antiquarian

Figure 4.2 Illustration of an Antonine Wall distance slab (RIB 2208) in John Horsley's *Britannia Romana*, 1732.

Robert Cay and solicited the opinions of Clerk, Stukeley, Gale and others on the readings of various inscriptions.[57]

The content of the completed book reveals the military focus of Horsley's research, since the only monuments that he describes in any detail are the two Roman walls. References are made to Roman towns and cities in England, but they are dealt with briefly. Regarding Scotland, he does hint at Roman civility when he mentions 'the ruins of a Roman town or outbuildings' next to the fort at Balmuildy and the faint vestiges of a possible 'Roman fort or town' at Cadder.[58] Like all of his predecessors, he also believed that he had seen the 'manifest remains of a considerable town' at Camelon, but in general his account of the history of Caledonia talks more of conflict than settlement.[59] Horsley proposes that the gains made by Agricola were probably eroded by the Caledonians in the years that followed, so that none of Scotland was in Roman hands by the time Hadrian became emperor; also that the Antonine Wall was breached by the Caledonians almost as soon as it was completed, although he refused to speculate on whether the region was reconquered under subsequent emperors.[60] Severus' endeavours in Scotland are described, although the author was unsure about how far north the Romans reached and debates at some length which wall was built or restored at the end of this expedition and what lands were given up by the Romans when a peace treaty was agreed.[61] He was more confident in stating that the south of Scotland was fully relinquished during the reign of Caracalla, with maybe only a few 'advanced stations' remaining beyond the boundary of Hadrian's Wall.[62]

As noted in the previous chapter, Horsley believed that the Romans had not failed to conquer the north, but rather had seen no benefit in doing so. He describes the area surrounding Hadrian's Wall as 'wild and desolate', and notes that it would have been even more so during the Roman period; although he identifies signs of Roman civility beyond the Antonine Wall, he was convinced that there were no such settlements north of the Tay.[63] In his eyes, the present inhabitants of the Highlands had changed little from the barbarians faced by Septimius Severus fifteen centuries before.[64] Furthermore, the Roman remains that he found in Scotland were judged to be of inferior quality to those further south: 'I think it also remarkable, that in the *Roman* stations and forts in *Scotland*, there does not appear such large remains of stone buildings, either without or within, as are frequent in England'.[65] Such evidence suggested to Horsley that Roman involvement in Scotland had been brief and had made little impact on either its people or its landscape. Indeed, his portrayal of Britain as a whole implies that the Roman occupation was more military than civil. In discussing the surviving Roman inscriptions in Britain, he notes that most relate to military matters, 'since there were few *Romans*, but soldiers, in this island'.[66] In the years that followed, such a focus on the militaristic aspects of the Roman past, encouraged by the military nature of many of the written sources and material remains, was to become common amongst many antiquarians both Scottish and English.[67]

The reputations and influence of Stukeley and Horsley

Stukeley and Horsley met in 1729 and hit it off, with the former writing to Roger Gale that they spent an evening inspecting Stukeley's collection and reporting that they 'had a world of discourse' on Horsley's work in progress.[68] Nevertheless, it is hard to think of two men whose approaches to uncovering the distant past were more different. While Stukeley created a history that fitted his preconceptions, Horsley stuck more closely to the sources and was reluctant to indulge in conjecture where no evidence existed. As a consequence, their descriptions of Roman Scotland were at odds with one another, one presenting Scotland as largely a settled Roman province, the other portraying it as an unstable warzone. Ultimately, the reputations of the two men were just as divergent, and while both are recognised as pioneers, one is often regarded as something of an eccentric, the other admired for his unusually (for the eighteenth century, at least) balanced approach.

Even during his lifetime, doubts were expressed about Stukeley's accuracy and objectivity. Thomas Hearne, who was no fan of the antiquarian, described him as a 'very fancifull Man, and the things he hath publish'd are built upon fancy'.[69] Stukeley's habit of conjuring up Roman settlements where none existed was not limited to Scotland: after a meeting with him in Oxford in 1724, Hearne recorded the following day that 'he told me he had been at Thame thinking it was a Roman City. Good God! this is nothing but idle dreaming'.[70] Later, fellow antiquarians John Whitaker, Thomas Pennant and Robert Masters were all to take issue with Stukeley's ambitious conjectures.[71] In 1782 John Nichols applauded his learning and inexhaustible commitment, but also acknowledged that he was 'a little too much transported by a lively fancy and invention'.[72] Today his work on Roman sites has faded into obscurity, a situation surely exacerbated by the prehistoric bias of his principle biographer, Stuart Piggott. While his plans and drawings of ancient sites that are now lost or altered are valuable to modern historians and archaeologists, his writings are less admired. Here was a man whose good intentions tended to be sabotaged by his regular diversions into romance and fantasy. As Piggott himself notes, 'though outstanding as a field archaeologist, he was no scholar'.[73]

John Horsley, meanwhile, is recognised as a ground-breaking antiquarian who was ahead of his time. *Britannia Romana* is certainly regarded as more accurate than Gordon's *Itinerarium Septentrionale*, and during his lifetime

Horsley was admired by Stukeley, Gale and Clerk (although their praise was not absolute, Clerk writing to Gale in February 1729 that Horsley 'affects now and then a singularity in his readings and opinions' and Gale informing Stukeley not much later that 'I find he has his fancys as well as others of our fraternity').[74] His book was slow to sell at first, but within a few decades it was considered rare and attracted high prices at auction.[75] In 1831 a new biography of Horsley by John Hodgson brought the antiquarian back into the public eye, while five years later the bibliographer Thomas Frognall Dibdin wrote during a visit to the north of England that 'they are all at Newcastle, necessarily, Horsley-mad'.[76] His investigations into Roman Britain were praised in the twentieth century by such greats as Francis Haverfield, R. G. Collingwood and George MacDonald, who ended his 1933 essay on Horsley with the warning that 'even to-day, the student of the subject who chooses to neglect the *Britannia Romana* will do so at his peril'.[77]

Of all the men discussed so far in this book, John Horsley remains the most opaque, not just because we know little about his life, but also because he reveals little of himself in his writing, aside, of course, from his impressive objectivity. Apparently devoid of any personal agenda, *Britannia Romana* stands out from the mass of contemporary antiquarian publications, which was so often mired in politics, religion, patriotism and prejudice. Comparing him to Stukeley, Boyd Haycock describes Horsley as 'more cautious – and in the long run more reliable'.[78] It is this careful, non-partisan approach that has ensured for his book an unrivalled reputation, which endures almost three centuries after its initial publication.

Other English views of Roman Scotland

John Strachey and John Horsley were not the only Englishmen to venture north of the border to investigate the Roman remains and other antiquities to be found there. Roger Gale too made the journey, although what he discovered would fail to live up to expectations. Sir John Clerk wrote to Gale in 1733 with effusive thanks for the hospitality shown him during a visit to England and invited Gale to Scotland: 'The old saying *turpi est peregrinari domi*, will, I hope, hold good as to Scottland, as well as England, since our interests, as well as territorys, are united and inseperable'.[79] Following an aborted attempt that same year, Gale finally arrived in Scotland in 1739. While the places of interest that he visited there were not all Roman, he did view the Roman coins in Edinburgh's Advocates Library and a supposed Roman camp near Penicuik, also taking a trip to the Roman fort at Middleby, no doubt at the bidding of Clerk, who had previously described it to him as 'the most remarkable station I ever saw'.[80] Overall, Gale was underwhelmed by what he found during his stay, and told Stukeley as much in no uncertain terms:

> We have no reason to complain of the country, but I think I shall hardly take a journey of pleasure to it again. We saw everything that was remarkable, found them much short of our expectations, & the eulogiums bestowed upon them by the natives.[81]

It is tempting to suggest that it was an ebullient Clerk himself that Gale had in mind when accusing the 'natives' of exaggerating the qualities of Scotland's antiquities.

Just as pertinent to English perceptions of ancient Caledonia as the antiquarians from the south who studied and recorded Scotland's Roman remains were those who ignored them altogether. Although Bedfordshire-born antiquarian Nathaniel Salmon travelled many miles in search of Roman monuments and was aware of such antiquities in Scotland, he paid little attention to those north of the border 'since it is out of my province'.[82] In 1724 John Pointer had produced an earlier *Britannia Romana*, with the subtitle *Roman Antiquities in Britain viz. Coins, Camps, and Publick Roads*. The content is largely based on the text and images found on coins, objects which Pointer himself described as 'not so much a Treasure of Money, as of Knowlege'.[83] Despite his belief in the importance of fieldwork, his book is in fact sketchy and error-ridden, described by Rosemary Sweet as 'almost entirely derivative'.[84] Although its title suggests that the book will include a survey of Roman sites across the British mainland, Pointer's map and written description of what he refers to as Roman Britain tell a different story. No Roman remains north of Hadrian's Wall are mentioned in either. For this antiquarian, Roman Britain meant Roman England. Whether this was due to apathy towards Scottish affairs or the misconception that Hadrian's Wall represented the endpoint of Roman power is not clear. Either way, it seems likely that Pointer would not have been the only Englishman to perceive Scotland as a country with little or no Roman past to speak of.

As this chapter has shown, the history and geography of Roman Scotland were as disputed amongst English antiquarians as they were by their Scottish counterparts, despite those south of the border being less patriotically invested in the subject, and interpretations changed dramatically in the space of a decade. For both the Scottish and the English, the story of Caledonia and its interactions with Rome presented something of a conundrum. A close study of written sources offered little clarification, and the discovery, identification and description of material remains only added to the confusion. Patriotic Scots such as Alexander Gordon remained adamant that the Romans had failed to conquer the north and thus had not been the masters of arms that Stukeley had so confidently proclaimed them. As the next chapter will demonstrate, the artefacts and monuments that the Romans left behind in Scotland also suggested, to some at least, that they were far from masterful when it came to the arts.

Notes

1. BL Harley MS 7055, f. 9. This incarnation of the Society of Antiquaries folded in 1708 when Wanley's patron Lord Harley was forced to resign from government.
2. NRS GD18/5027/3: Stukeley to Clerk, 7 June 1725. The 'vallum' in question is that of Hadrian's Wall.
3. Stukeley, *The Commentarys, Diary, & Common-Place Book & Selected Letters*, pp. 11–12; Lukis, *The Family Memoirs of the Rev. William Stukeley*, Vol. 1, p. 16.
4. Stukeley, *The Commentarys, Diary, & Common-Place Book & Selected Letters*, p. 14; ibid. p. 34.
5. Bodl.MS.Eng.misc.c.113, f. 295: Johnson to Stukeley, 6 April 1714.
6. Stukeley, *Itinerarium Curiosum*, Preface.
7. Stukeley, *Of the Roman Amphitheater at Dorchester*, p. 1; ibid. p. 2; ibid. p. 15.
8. Stukeley, *An Account of a Roman Temple*, p. 15.
9. A copy of the manuscript is held on microfilm at the British Library, reference RP 8279.
10. Boyd Haycock, *William Stukeley*, pp. 119–20.
11. Stukeley quoted in: Boyd Haycock, *William Stukeley*, p. 120 n. 50.
12. Stukeley, *Itinerarium Curiosum*, Centuria II, p. 77.
13. For Clerk's attitude towards posterity, see: Brown, *The Hobby-Horsical Antiquary*, p. 17.
14. Stukeley, *Itinerarium Curiosum*, Centuria II, p. 77.
15. Stukeley, *An Account of a Roman Temple*, p. 2. This statement partly inspired Alexander Gordon's own investigations into Roman Scotland.
16. Stukeley, *An Account of a Roman Temple*, p. 2.
17. Ibid p. 3.
18. Ibid. p. 24.
19. Ibid. p. 4.
20. Ibid. p. 8.
21. Ibid. pp. 5–6.
22. Ibid. p. 11.
23. Ibid. p. 6.
24. Ibid. p. 26.
25. Ibid. pp. 23–4.
26. Stukeley, *Itinerarium Curiosum*, Centuria II, p. 56.
27. Stukeley mentions plans to visit Scotland in letters to Alexander Gordon, for example: NRS GD18/5023/3/12: Stukeley to Gordon, 24 October 1724.
28. Keppie, *The Antiquarian Rediscovery of the Antonine Wall*, p. 63.
29. Piggott, *William Stukeley*, p. 39.
30. Lukis, *The Family Memoirs of the Rev. William Stukeley*, Vol. 1, p. 25; Keppie, *The Antiquarian Rediscovery of the Antonine Wall*, p. 62.
31. Stukeley, *An Account of Richard of Cirencester*, p. 3.
32. Lukis, *The Family Memoirs of the Rev. William Stukeley*, Vol. 1, p. 25.
33. This letter is now in the collection of Stukeley's papers purchased by the Bodleian Library between 1924 and 1955, reference Bodl.MS.Eng.misc.c.114, f. 20.

34. Stukeley, *An Account of a Roman Temple*, p. 10; Sibbald, *Scotia Illustrata*, p. 41. Sibbald features the Antonine inscription in a chapter dedicated to the eating habits of the Caledonians, using it to support his (incorrect) conjecture that the tribe known as the Brigantes had inhabited Scotland.
35. Baxter, *Glossarium Antiquitatum Britannicarum*, p. 249.
36. Stukeley, *An Account of a Roman Temple*, p. 7.
37. Bodl.533.7 G.42 fol.
38. Stukeley, *The Commentarys, Diary, & Common-Place Book & Selected Letters*, p. 60.
39. For a similar myth of a bronze 'speaking-tube' running along Hadrian's Wall, see: Hingley, *Hadrian's Wall*, pp. 82–3.
40. For more on Stukeley's notes in his own copy of *An Account of a Roman Temple* that relate to the *De Situ Britanniae*, see Chapter 8.
41. Bodl.533.7 G.42 fol., p. 7.
42. Bodl.533.7 G.42 fol., p. 2.
43. Chambers, *A Biographical Dictionary of Eminent Scotsmen*, p. 91.
44. MacDonald, 'John Horsley, Scholar and Gentleman', pp. 6–7.
45. Hodgson, *Memoirs*, p. 40.
46. MacDonald, 'John Horsley, Scholar and Gentleman', p. 16.
47. NRS GD18/5034: Hamilton to Clerk, 30 October 1728.
48. NRS GD18/5038/4: Horsley to Clerk, 1 November 1729.
49. NRS GD18/5033: Clerk to Crawford, 6 January 1729.
50. NRS GD18/5023/3/41: Gordon to Clerk, 7 September 1728. The Latin phrase is derived from Plutarch, *Apophthegmata Laconica* 69. It can be translated as 'words and nothing more'.
51. For example, see: NRS GD18/5033: Clerk to Crawford, 6 January 1729. Also: NRS GD18/5036/4: Blackwell to Clerk, 17 December 1728.
52. NRS GD18/5030/25: Gale to Clerk, 15 April 1732. For a fuller account of Gordon's attitude towards Horsley, see: Keppie, 'John Horsley and the Britannia Romana', pp. 16–18.
53. Lukis, *The Family Memoirs of the Rev. William Stukeley*, Vol. 2, p. 390.
54. Horsley, *Britannia Romana*, p. iv.
55. Ibid. p. i.
56. Keppie, 'John Horsley and the Britannia Romana', p. 15.
57. Ibid. pp. 11–13.
58. Horsley, *Britannia Romana*, pp. 167–8.
59. Ibid. p. 172.
60. Ibid. pp. 48–9; ibid. p. 53.
61. Ibid. pp. 61–3.
62. Ibid. pp. 66–7.
63. Ibid. p. 65.
64. Ibid. p. 60.
65. Ibid. p. 66.
66. Ibid. p. 181.
67. Sweet, *Antiquaries*, pp. 181–2.
68. Lukis, *The Family Memoirs of the Rev. William Stukeley*, Vol. 2, p. 71.
69. Lukis, *The Family Memoirs of the Rev. William Stukeley*, Vol. 1, p. 169.
70. Ibid. p. 170.
71. Sweet, *Antiquaries*, p. 21.
72. Nichols quoted in: Boyd Haycock, 'William Stukeley', p. 239.

73. Piggott, *Ancient Britons and the Antiquarian Imagination*, p. 127.
74. Lukis, *The Family Memoirs of the Rev.William Stukeley*, Vol. 3, p. 390; ibid. p. 256.
75. For the rising value of the book, see: Bosanquet, *John Horsley and His Times*, p. 78.
76. Ibid. p. 80.
77. MacDonald, 'John Horsley', p. 164.
78. Boyd Haycock, *William Stukeley*, p. 6.
79. Lukis, *The Family Memoirs of the Rev. William Stukeley*, Vol. 2, pp. 270–1. Clerk is paraphrasing a quote by Italian humanist Aldus Manutius, '*turpe est in patria peregrinari, et in eis rebus quae ad patriam pertinent hospitem esse*' (it is disgraceful to live as a stranger in one's own country, and to be uninformed of the things that belong to it).
80. Lukis, *The Family Memoirs of the Rev. William Stukeley*, Vol. 1, pp. 317–18; NRS GD18/5033: Clerk to Gale, 10 September 1729.
81. Lukis, *The Family Memoirs of the Rev. William Stukeley*, Vol. 1, p. 316.
82. Salmon, *A New Survey of England*, p. 603.
83. Pointer, *Britannia Romana*, Preface.
84. Sweet, *Antiquaries*, p. 170.

5

'Monuments and delights of the arts': rediscovering the material remains of Rome in Scotland

> The sacred Reliques of old Greece and Rome
> Inscriptions, Statues, Bass Relieves and Coyns
> With every monument that may explain
> The Laws and Customs of the wisest States
> All such deserve their Place and cannot fail
> In some degree our Learning to advance.
>
> Sir John Clerk, *The Country Seat*,
> 1727 (NRS GD18/4404/1, f. 13)

In their attempts to retrieve the history and geography of Roman Scotland, early modern antiquarians turned to various sources. As we shall see in Chapter 7, the *Agricola* of Tacitus was to become their preferred ancient text, while other surviving classical writings were similarly examined for references to northern Britain. Also crucial to the task of understanding Scotland's ancient past were the surviving traces of Rome in the form of earthworks or foundations, as well as the inscriptions, coins and other ancient objects found around them. Throughout the eighteenth century such sites and artefacts were actively sought out and, once identified, were repeatedly inspected and measured, described and drawn, each visitor intending to correct the mistakes of his predecessors and hoping perhaps to uncover something new that had escaped their notice. For lovers of Rome, these remains were proof that classical civilisation had arrived in Scotland. For those of a more traditionally patriotic mindset, they could be interpreted as evidence of aborted attempts to conquer the north. More than just the indicators of the heritage of a place, Roman antiquities also became symbols of status and learning to be purchased, swapped and displayed. While the white marble statues being discovered in Italy and imported in bulk by Grand Tourists were a common sight in aristocratic houses in England (Wilton House, Ince Blundell Hall, Newby Hall and Charles Townley's London home to name but a few), they rarely made it north of the border. Instead, the two greatest Scottish collections of ancient objects were best-known for their Roman artefacts discovered on home ground, while gentlemen landowners also tended to display Roman items found on their own properties. Such artefacts were also searched out by the antiquarians, who endlessly discussed and analysed them amongst themselves, with Sir Robert Sibbald and Alexander Gordon amongst the first Scots to refer to their study of ancient objects as 'archaeology'.[1]

It soon became clear that the inscribed stones being dug up along the line of the Antonine Wall (referred to today as 'distance slabs') were something quite unique, and such discoveries attracted public attention both in Scotland and further afield: the uncovering of a group of Roman carvings by Gordon at Shirva near Kilsyth was reported in *The Caledonian Mercury* on 3 October 1726 (p. 6150, described as 'Evidences of the Roman Grandeur') and the excavation of an altar at Bar Hill was apparently reported in the *Daily Gazetteer* of 7 September 1736.[2] Larger monuments too, such as the Antonine Wall or the extraordinary and much debated Arthur's O'on, were to be explored and studied in depth, each often presented either as proof of large-scale Roman conquest or evidence of its failure. The Roman material remains found in Scotland would fascinate generations of antiquarians and collectors, but would also prove unsatisfying and confusing, seen as lacking in quality and regarded as disappointingly un-Roman in some quarters. The varied reactions, both positive and negative, of these men (and one woman) towards the vestiges of Rome in Caledonia, as well as the interpretations and misinterpretations of these tangible reminders of Scotland's early history, are the focus of this chapter.

Discovery and excavation

The majority of ancient objects unearthed during the eighteenth century were discovered by chance, often dug up by builders or turned up by the plough. Their historical importance unrecognised or unvalued, many carved stones were reused as building materials, a practice that had apparently begun almost as soon as the Romans left the north.[3] A collection of drawings of Roman carved stones in the papers of Sir John Clerk notes locations across central Scotland, some in the walls of barns, while Gordon mentions several stones built into cottages near the fort of Middleby.[4] Indeed, the panel that finally proved beyond doubt that the Roman wall in Scotland was Antonine thanks to its inscription bearing the name of Lollius Urbicus, a fragment described by Robert Sibbald as 'the most remarkable inscription we have', was used as a sill for a barn window until its rescue in the 1690s.[5] Clerk complained to Thomas Blackwell that even educated members of the Edinburgh Faculty of Advocates failed to appreciate the value of such stones: 'I'll adventure to pick out at least 50 of their number who if they found a Roman Altar would thinke they had got a prize of a large stone to be a lintle or rebet to a stable or house of office'.[6]

Over previous generations, ancient sites had become associated with mythical buried treasure and locals had a tendency to pillage places where old, potentially valuable things might be found, no doubt causing damage to the sites in the process. Gordon records the legend that treasure lay under Ardoch Fort, and towards the end of the century author and bookseller John Knox recounts the tale of a 'Goth' who ravaged the fort at Duntocher while searching for artefacts.[7] But the first signs of organised excavations can also be detected in the early eighteenth century. Following that aforementioned discovery of carved stones in a 'hollow mausoleum' at Shirva in 1726, one of which was damaged as it was removed, Gordon and his associates planned to go with the proprietor to 'dig up the rest carefully' and record their findings in a drawing.[8] Excited by the discovery of a statue of a goddess and two inscribed sculpture bases at Middleby in 1731, Sir John Clerk ordered further excavations: 'I believe there may be more stones of value lying there & possibly may be dig'd for'.[9] A cautious Roger Gale, however, warned him that the chances of finding the complete statue of Mercury associated with one of the bases were slim: 'I hope you will not loose your labour in searching for his Godship: I hardly think he was made of Metal but the danger of disappointment to you will be from his being broke to pieces, and then you will find the fragments of him'.[10]

Private collections of Roman antiquities

It was not unusual for rediscovered Roman stones to end up in the possession of the local landowner, several subsequently being incorporated into the walls of castles and houses for public display. Such buildings became places of pilgrimage for antiquarians and other curious types: early seventeenth-century Prussian traveller Crispin Gericke, for example, reported to Jan Gruter and Joseph Scaliger that one of the distance slabs was to be found in the wall of Cawder Castle in Lanarkshire, while Silesian visitor Servaz Reichel also sent word of it to William Camden.[11] The stone was valued enough to be reset in the west end of the new Cawder House in 1624, where it would later be viewed by John Adair, John Urry, Edward Lhuyd and Alexander Gordon. By the time John Horsley visited in the late 1720s the stone had been moved inside the courtyard, placed so high that a ladder was needed to inspect it.[12] Other gentlemen who had found or inherited such antiquities routinely welcomed interested visitors, with Alexander Milne of Carriden House telling Robert Sibbald about the (since lost) carved eagle discovered on the site of a neighbouring Roman fort and later built into the wall of his home, and also showing him a gold coin of Vespasian.[13] Further east at Cramond, Sir John Inglis displayed an inscribed altar in his garden and owned a collection of Roman coins found around the fort on his estate.[14] Edward Lhuyd recorded a collection of stones at Cumbernauld House as well as an altar at Castle Cary, a medieval tower house constructed largely from Roman masonry plundered from the ruins of the nearby fort of the same name.[15] While some of these landowners would have enjoyed the idea that their properties had once formed part of the Roman Empire, even those who were not particularly interested in Scotland's Roman past were no doubt aware of the prestige and elite associations of such classical objects.[16]

Undoubtedly the greatest eighteenth-century private collection of Roman objects of Scottish provenance was that accumulated by Sir John Clerk of Penicuik. Although he started collecting antiquities during his Grand Tour, on returning to Scotland he began to concentrate on objects found more locally. Clerk was aware of the contemporary portrayal of antiquarians as pedantic collectors of worthless trifles, and his attitude towards his own collecting habit seems at times rather defensive. His handwritten catalogue for the collection, produced in 1739, justifies such 'Cabinets or Repositories of Curiosities' by arguing that their preservation of ancient knowledge and skill had inspired modern developments in the arts and sciences.[17] A similar sentiment can be detected in the lines of his poetry included as the epigraph to this chapter.

Despite Clerk's insistence that a lack of funds limited his purchasing power, at its height the collection contained 395 Roman coins, six 'Roman' spearheads and a 'Roman' shoe, as well as numerous carved stones and countless other artefacts of all sorts.[18] It gained an unrivalled reputation amongst antiquarians, with Gordon stating in 1726 that 'Among all the Collections of *Roman* Antiquities in *Scotland*, that of the Baron Clark justly claims the Preference, both as to Number and Curiosity'.[19] In 1753, William Maitland similarly proposed that the Baron's collection of Roman artefacts 'is so considerable, that probably it is not to be excelled in this Part of the Island'.[20] While Clerk sourced a few objects himself on his travels, he tended to employ others to search out and acquire items for him. Wheeler-dealer Richard Burn supplied a number of inscriptions, a job that grew more difficult as the locals became aware of their value.[21] Alexander Gordon also kept an eye out for potential purchases during his antiquarian peregrinations. His letters to Clerk relate his latest discoveries, also revealing the tense situation that arose when he realised that his travelling companion James Glen was also on the lookout for Roman antiquities.[22]

Much consideration would have been given to how the objects in Clerk's collection were displayed. Writing to the Baron from Aberdeen in 1731, Thomas Blackwell underlined the importance of exhibiting artefacts correctly: 'Their Order and Arrangmt. is capable of adding a very great beauty to them; as they are to any Place where they are properly disposed off, at least to those that can feel, and have the *docti Oculi* celebrated by Cicero'.[23] Blackwell's suggestion that Clerk should display his collection at Mavisbank by constructing an 'Aeystus adorned with the rougher Monuments of Antiquity at proper Distances, and a

Repository for the smaller ones at the end of it', however, went unheeded. Instead, the antiquities remained at Penicuik, where many were placed in the library, as described in Clerk's letter to fellow Leiden alumnus Herman Boerhaave:

> There you will find books in all departments of literature . . . But lest my library should be quite empty of the monuments and delights of the arts, you may see there certain ancient bronze and marble statues, altar-pieces, inscriptions, and that sort of thing . . . There is also in the museum a number of Greek and Roman coins, incised vases, traces of a picture of ancient workmanship . . . for so I would imitate Julius Caesar and Augustus (according to Suetonius), and even if I had not the example of such great men, I should regard it as a mean thing to build up a library of huge volumes on antiquities, and yet to disdain as useless the very objects which the most learned men, as Graevius, Gronovius and Montfaucon, have explained with such expenditure of time and toil. The things themselves speak and for the most part explain themselves; but descriptions, however accurate, present to the mind only confused or shadowy ideas . . . [24]

In addition, a 1728 letter from Professor Matthew Crawford of Edinburgh University locates antiquities in both the Baron's study and garden at Penicuik.[25] Of all of the Roman objects in his collection, the carved Roman stones found at Middleby in 1731 (purchased from a local widow for two guineas) were surely Clerk's most prized, representing, as he saw it, 'the chief of the kind now in Britain'.[26] He corresponded with other antiquarians including Gronovius on their significance and the content of their inscriptions. An entire chapter of Gordon's 1732 *Additions and Corrections* is dedicated to them, as is one of Clerk's rare forays into print, the *Dissertatio de Monumentis Quibusdam Romanis in Boreali Magnae Britanniae Parte, Detectis, Anno MDCCXXXI* of 1750, which includes more information on their form and provenance.

After Clerk's death the Penicuik Roman stones were displayed in prominent positions in the Palladian mansion built in the 1760s by his son James, who also demonstrated an interest in the antique. Clerk's copy of the *Itinerarium Septentrionale* contains later eighteenth or early nineteenth-century pencil notes next to illustrations of some of them that record their presence in the house, one being located in the hall.[27] As a result, this was probably the only opportunity to see such Roman sculptures of Scottish provenance alongside their esteemed Italian counterparts, since Sir James also ordered a series of reproductions of celebrated ancient works from Rome; although these new white marble sculptures were commissioned to decorate the dining room, by the 1820s the Apollo, Flora, 'Piping Faun' and various classical antiquities were to be found in the hall alongside the stones from Middleby.[28] As an interesting aside, the ancient stones almost caused the destruction of the house in 1779, when a mob protesting against the repeal of anti-Catholic laws threatened to burn it down, believing that the 'Roman altars' inside demonstrated links with the Church of Rome.[29]

Institutional collections

As well as private collecting on both a small and a grand scale, the long eighteenth century also witnessed the development of the first institutional collections of Scotland's Roman antiquities. The largest group of such artefacts not in private hands was that at Glasgow University, which Horsley rated as equal to that of Sir John Clerk: 'The two principal collections in *Scotland* are those of the university of *Glasgow*, and of Baron *Clerk*; for I do not know of three inscriptions together in any other place in *Scotland*'.[30] Thanks to its reputation, the collection was to be visited by almost every antiquarian who took an interest in Roman Scotland as well as many a tourist, although, as we shall see, not all were entirely complimentary.

Most of the stones in Glasgow were donated by generous aristocrats including the Marquess of Montrose, the Earl of Perth and the Honourable Charles Maitland, a number of the donors also being ex-pupils. The first inscriptions probably arrived in the mid-1690s and were housed in the library. In 1697 Robert Wodrow accepted the role of librarian and henceforth took an active role in expanding the collection. Lawrence Keppie highlights the high status given to the stones by the professors in the eighteenth century.[31] Space limitations and presumably security concerns meant that they were eventually moved into locked 'presses', these cupboards being replaced and enlarged in 1728, 1760 and 1771.[32] The final enlargement was due to the discovery of several altars during the construction of the Forth and Clyde Canal that were acquired by John Anderson, the university's Professor of Natural Philosophy who had a particular interest in the finds being made along the Roman wall. The carved stones themselves seem to have been affixed with labels recording both their donor and their place of origin.[33]

Meanwhile, the university in Edinburgh was building its own collection of Roman objects with a Scottish provenance. Robert Sibbald donated a number of such items in the late seventeenth century along with antiquities from the collection of Andrew Balfour. Housed in the upper Common Hall of the Old College, Daniel Defoe described it as a 'curious and noble museum', adding that it was 'greatly valued by the Virtuosos'.[34] Edinburgh's Advocates Library, which promoted itself as a resource for the use of the legal fraternity, the virtuosi and the general public, also owned a similar collection.[35] The first acquisition made for the library's museum seems to have been coins belonging to Edinburgh botany professor James Sutherland, purchased in 1705.[36] As well as containing specimens from various periods including ancient Greek and modern European, this collection was notable for its Roman coins, many of which, according to Sibbald, had been discovered in Scotland.[37] Over the years the library's collection grew thanks to purchases and donations, and another group of objects belonging to

Sibbald ended up here after his death in 1722, including the 'Roman' sword found at Carriden that was to inspire Gordon to begin work on his *Itinerarium*.[38] Thomas Ruddiman, the celebrated classicist who was Keeper of the library from 1730–52, encouraged further acquisitions; in 1779 a small hoard of Roman coins unearthed near Linlithgow was also donated by the town's Provost and magistrates and a sandstone altar discovered at Newstead was added to the collection after its discovery in 1783.[39]

Following the foundation of the Society of Antiquaries of Scotland in 1780, a house was purchased in Edinburgh as their meeting place, library and museum. The need for such a place was stressed by the society's founder, David Steuart Erskine, the 11th Earl of Buchan, in his inaugural speech, in which he blamed the failure of a previous incarnation of the society on it 'having no house in property, nor any private interests to care for their books, museum, and other necessary appurtenances'.[40] Despite three changes of location in the following years due to financial problems, the society's collection of antiquities remained largely intact. Like that of Glasgow University, it grew thanks to private donations, and it also contained numerous natural curiosities, William Smellie attributing this to both the relative lack of antiquities in Scotland and a desire to encourage more scientifically-inclined men to join the society.[41] The comprehensive list of donations compiled by Smellie does, nevertheless, include several supposedly Roman items; most are coins and metalwork, such as the 'quantity of Roman arms' (actually Bronze Age) gifted by Sir Alexander Dick of Prestonfield and the Roman 'camp kettle' (an Iron Age cauldron) found in a peat bog near Stirling.[42]

Scotland's Roman inscriptions

For early modern antiquarians, ancient objects were invaluable tools for learning. Sir John Clerk saw them as vital for an understanding of ancient language and civilisation: 'Inscriptions, Altars, Vases, Urns &c . . . may be necessary as a better way to form our knowledge upon than we can have from any Grammars or Dictionaries whatsomever or even from any of the Ancient Authors'.[43] Most interesting for Clerk and his ilk were Roman inscriptions. In studying and collecting inscribed stones, Scotland's antiquarians were following a long tradition dating back to the sixteenth century, and were no doubt further inspired by European scholars such as Scaliger, Gronovius and Johann Graevius, whose twelve-volume *Thesaurus Antiquitatum Romanarum* was published in Leiden around the same time that Clerk himself was a student there.

Inscriptions were viewed as important sources of Roman history, an uncorrupted contemporary record of Roman thoughts and deeds and a way of verifying the claims of classical authors. Gordon refers to them as 'authentik vouchers of antiquity' and proposed that they could 'prove demonstratively those Facts which are asserted in History'.[44] He also realised the importance of the Antonine Wall distance slabs, writing that, thanks to them, 'there is scarce any Transaction asserted in the whole *Roman* History, the Veracity of which is better confirmed and proved to Posterity, than that this Wall in *Scotland*, was begun and perfected in the Reign of *Antoninus Pius*'.[45] John Horsley took a similar approach in the second chapter of his *Britannia Romana*, which is dedicated to recording and illustrating all of the known Romano-British sculptures and inscriptions, the author comparing the latter favourably to written sources: 'I am persuaded that fragments of Roman inscriptions will in time be as much esteemed, and as carefully searched for, as fragments of ancient authors. I have found those few, which are here intermixed, serviceable to good purposes on many occasions'.[46]

The letters between Gordon and Clerk written during the former's antiquarian explorations also demonstrate the emphasis placed on inscriptions by collectors. Roman stones without carved letters were apparently of little interest to Clerk, a fact that could lead to disappointment for potential vendors, and abuse for Gordon, as he relates in a note sent from Linlithgow in 1723:

> At Wiltons at Kilpatrick the fellow himself told me of a stone in his house with an inscription which I purposed to have bought for you but when it was taken out of its place had not one letter on it & because I would not give him a crown for showing me it (as I promised if it had letters on it) his wife & he scolded me like Kellwives.[47]

Similarly, Richard Burn wrote to Clerk of one particular stone that he dismissed as 'not of much value being[?] no leters on it' and Gordon decided against making a sketch of an altar in the garden at Carriden House since it was not inscribed.[48]

Although some uninscribed altars did make their way into his collection, Clerk's preference for inscriptions was encouraged by his love of discussing them with his friends and associates as they struggled to reveal the elusive meanings of these abbreviated, often eroded and fragmentary Latin texts. Every new discovery was analysed at length and the proposals of others debated both in letters and in print. William Stukeley points out mistakes made by Camden and Baxter in their interpretations of one Scottish stone and gives his own version of the text, while Clerk often wrote to Stukeley, Gale, Gresham College professor John Ward and others about inscriptions, also discussing with such men the images and text found on Roman coins.[49]

The artistic merits of Scotland's Roman stones

Writing in the early seventeenth century, Englishman Henry Peacham ranked antique statues highly in terms of their importance for scholars and gentlemen of taste: 'I began with them, because I suppose them of greater standing & antiquitie than even Inscriptions or Coines'.[50] At a time when the achievements of the ancients were widely revered and large quantities of marble sculptures were being shipped to Britain from Italy, Roman statues were also increasingly viewed not just as historical sources, but also as works of art and status symbols. The artistic merits of the sculptures produced by the Romans in Scotland were also scrutinised; their reception, however, was decidedly mixed. While the number of objects discovered in northern Britain that could be classed as 'statues' was limited, many of the inscribed stones contained decorative elements that could be rated according to their aesthetic qualities. Those that looked more typically Roman were often admired, but others were seen as crude, lacking the skill and finesse generally associated with the classical world at this time.

Although William Stukeley never saw the Scottish stones that he described in his *Account of a Roman Temple*, relying instead on drawings made by Edward Lhuyd, he was most taken with the distance slab found near the west end of the Antonine Wall and kept at Mugdock Castle before being donated to Glasgow University by the Marquess of Montrose sometime before 1694.[51] Impressed by its unmistakeably classical architectural elements, Stukeley described the panel as 'a very fine Stone like the Front of a Temple, adorn'd with two Pillasters supporting a Pediment with handsome Mouldings'.[52] Horsley places an image of this same stone on the title page of the plates in his *Britannia Romana* (Figure 4.2, Chapter 4), and it was also chosen as the first plate when a collection of engravings of the university's stones was published in the late 1760s. Having been presented with a set of these engravings during a visit to Glasgow in 1772, Thomas Pennant described the illustration of this particular slab as 'beautiful', also designating the figure on another 'very elegant' and revealing his preference for the Scottish Roman stones that were 'well cut and ornamented'.[53]

Elsewhere these stones were viewed less favourably. To many observers, both foreign visitors and proud natives, the Roman art found in Scotland was just not up to the expected standards. Alexander Gordon noted the varying quality of the carvings discovered at Shirva, describing some as 'much inferior in beauty', and suggested that this was evidence of a later date of fabrication. In fact, he saw the differences in such objects as proof of two periods of occupation of the Antonine Wall:

> When *Lollius Urbicus* first built the Wall, it was unquestionably in the Time of the higher Empire, when Arts and Politeness were at no small Height among the *Romans*; but when that Wall was rebuilt in *Honorius*'s Time . . . not only Arts and Politeness were greatly sunk, but even the Glory and Power of the Empire; and to confirm it, the literal Characters of the Monuments of that Age, whether Inscriptions or on Medals, are all of a rude Taste.[54]

Such (in this case erroneous) ideas regarding the dating of ancient sculptures by their quality could be compared to the work being carried out by

Montesquieu, who was also aiming to demonstrate the decline of art in the later empire through the sculptures that he had encountered in Italy in the late 1720s.[55] Perhaps Gordon's opinions were influenced by Sir John Clerk, who was certainly underwhelmed by a supposedly Roman carved stone that he saw on a journey to Perth in 1717, concluding that 'in all probability no body knew any thing of these matters here except the legionary souldiers who no doubt were but clumsy artists'.[56] French cartographer Louis de la Rochette, who travelled to Scotland in 1763 and visited several Roman sites in Perthshire, was impressed by the region's military remains, but not by the sculptures associated with them. Commenting on the illustrations in Gordon's *Itinerarium*, he believed that such carvings suggested that 'les bons artistes restoient a Rome et ne se trouvoient gueres dans le camp de légions' (the good artists stayed in Rome and rarely found themselves in the camp of the legions).[57] Scottish minister and antiquarian Robert Henry proposed in his popular *History of Great Britain*, the first volume of which was published in 1771, that the surviving examples of Romano-British sculpture were generally of lower quality than would be expected, but blamed this state of affairs on the fact that the more important works would have been removed by the Romans when they departed Britain, or were perhaps destroyed by the marauding Caledonians in their subsequent attacks. He also argued that much of the surviving sculpture dated from the end of the empire when, he believed, 'the sculptor's art was on the decline'.[58] Writing in the 1770s, John Anderson felt that the carving on one of the distance slabs was 'well executed compared to that of the rest', but that on another 'the ornaments are not very elegant'.[59] He also remarked on the fine quality of one of the sepulchral reliefs found at Shirva that features a reclining figure next to a dog, and proposed that 'there is an exactness in the contour of both and an elegance in the drapery which could not have been expected if we judge the statury's skill by the sculpture on the other stones'.[60] A report made by Polish Princess Izabela Czartoryska, who visited Glasgow University in 1790, was more damning: while she was interested in the content of the inscriptions, the decorative elements that surrounded them are described dismissively as 'crude'.[61]

Misunderstanding and misrepresentation of material remains

In this proto-archaeological age, the identification and dating of ancient remains was still something of a shot in the dark. As Sir John Clerk pointed out to Roger Gale, 'the Sepulchral *Cairns*, or *Tumuli*, in this Country, are so alike, in the Shape and Materials, that it is not easy to distinguish those that are *Celtick* or *British*, *Danish* or *Roman*'.[62] Given the admiration for ancient Rome and the persistent idea that the ancient Caledonians were barbarians, it was inevitable that artefacts were misidentified and misattributed, with objects perceived as being of finer quality automatically labelled Roman. Sibbald and Gordon were not the only antiquarians to regularly identify bronze (and generally Bronze Age) artefacts as Roman and, as we have already seen, Clerk was wont to imagine a classical provenance for all sorts of non-Roman monuments and sculptures. Non-antiquarians made similar errors, and local landowners were drawn to attribute finds on their estates or in their locality to the most revered of ancient civilisations. Robert Lumsdaine of Innergelly, for example, was surprised when a group of burial urns that he believed Roman were found near St Andrews, since he knew of no other evidence that the Romans had settled in that part of the country.[63]

In addition, at a time when illustrations were becoming a common feature in antiquarian tracts, visual representations of items believed to be Roman sometimes demonstrate aspirations to render them more recognisably classical. One striking example of this is the carved panel set into the wall of a building in Edinburgh's Netherbow and featuring two heads in profile that was incorrectly identified by Clerk as Roman and by several others as portraits of the Emperor Severus and his wife Julia Domna. The relief features regularly in eighteenth- and nineteenth-century antiquarian and travel books; in many of the illustrations of it, however, a carved panel in between the two heads bearing a biblical quote, and therefore suggesting a post-Roman date, was simply omitted.[64]

Although the object itself was admired by antiquarians, the various illustrations of the relief sculpture representing the Romano-British goddess Brigantia in Sir John Clerk's collection certainly show evidence of what might have been considered 'improvement'. Clerk himself optimistically compared his sculpture, which features a rather rudimentary and sturdy robed female figure in an architectural niche with an inscription below (Figure 5.1), with the Diana of Ephesus, and Gordon apparently viewed it as both a historical source and a work of art, describing it as 'very remarkable, both as to the Figure and Inscription upon it'.[65] William Maitland later labelled this 'very beautiful stonern Figure' the 'most curious' sculpture in the Baron's collection.[66] The men who discovered the sculpture, no doubt hoping to increase its financial value, made the unconvincing claim that it had been entirely gilded when first dug up, the gold then being scrubbed off as it was cleaned, a claim that was later repeated by both Gordon and Clerk.[67] The Baron's own sketch of the sculpture (Figure 5.2) shows a figure that is markedly more detailed and elegant than the original.[68] Printed images appear in Gordon's *Additions and Corrections* and Horsley's *Britannia Romana*, the latter taken directly from Clerk's sketch, and both feature fine classical modelling, detailed facial features and delicately rendered curls certainly not visible in the sculpture itself. The most artistically satisfying but also the most fanciful representation appears in Sir John's own *Dissertatio de Monumentis Quibusdam Romanis* (Figure 5.3); its use of perspective and shading gives a better sense of the sculpture's form than any of the previous images, but also exaggerates the

Figure 5.1 Sculpture of the goddess Brigantia, c.120–180 CE. (© National Museums Scotland: X.FV 5)

Figure 5.2 Ink sketch of the Brigantia sculpture, Sir John Clerk, 1732. (NRS GD18/5044, reproduced courtesy of Sir Robert Clerk)

Rediscovering the material remains of Rome

Figure 5.3 Illustration of the Brigantia sculpture in Sir John Clerk's *Dissertatio de Monumentis Quibusdam Romanis*, 1750. (© The British Library Board: G.5216)

depth of the carved relief. With its graceful proportions, softly flowing drapery, carefully delineated attributes and neatly inscribed letters, this illustration certainly looks more like the ancient marble sculptures being imported from Italy than the heavy, flattened forms of the real Romano-British Brigantia. Despite his criticisms of the images in a catalogue of the Roman marbles owned by the Earl of Pembroke, in which he proposed that Pembroke had 'set down his notion of each piece, and has obliged the etcher or engraver to make it, as he wrote it, part of the copper-plate', the Baron himself was obviously not averse to such manipulations in a bid to render his own sculpture more conspicuously classical.[69]

Given the strong desire to locate and collect Roman objects in Scotland and the various misattributions that resulted from it, it is rather ironic that the most classically Roman sculpture to be found north of Hadrian's Wall was for over a century believed to be medieval. A carved marble head found near a ruined chapel in Tweeddale and donated to the Society of Antiquaries in 1783, known today as the 'Hawkshaw Head' and thought to be Trajanic, was still catalogued as the 'Stone Head of a Tonsured Priest' in the 1890s.[70] Although its find spot probably threw the antiquarians off the scent, it is likely that the sculpture was also just too classical, too different from the other Roman objects of Scottish provenance to be recognised for what it truly was.[71]

Antiquarian interpretations of Scotland's Roman monuments

In the eighteenth century, before intensive farming, industrial development, urbanisation and environmental erosion took their toll on their fragile earthworks, the remains of the Roman military interventions in Scotland would have been considerably more impressive than they are today. Not only did the enormous ditches, earthen ramparts and roads of such sites capture the imagination of our antiquarians, but two of them also turn up regularly on early modern maps of the nation. The Antonine Wall appears on several, including military engineer John Elphinstone's 1745 *New & Correct Map of North Britain* (as an unidentified hatched line), on James Dorret's 1750 *General Map of Scotland* (as 'Graham's Dyke') and on John Ainslie's *Scotland* of 1789 (as 'Vallum Antonini'). The wall is also featured from time to time on continental maps such as Blaeu's 1654 *Atlas of Scotland* (as the 'Valli Adriani Vestigia' on the map entitled *Scotia Antiqua* and as an unidentified shaded line on other maps of central Scotland), Bellin's 1757 *Carte Réduite des Isles Britannique* ('Ancienne Muraille d'Antonin'), Brion de la Tour's 1766 *L'Écosse* ('Ruin du Mur de Severe') and Barbié du Bocage's 1790 *L'Écosse avec ses Isles* (as 'Graham's Dike'), also as an unnamed castellated line on maps printed in Paris by de Vaugondy in 1762 and by Rigobert Bonne in 1787. The Roman fort at Ardoch is included in some maps, with Dorret identifying it as 'A Roman Camp' (and including a 'Roman Paved Way' nearby) and Emanuel Bowen similarly labelling it 'Roman Camp' on his *Map of North Britain* published in London in 1769. While partly indicative of the source material for these maps (which were often based on the works of Scottish antiquarians such as Timothy Pont and William Roy), the fact that these are generally the only antiquities, indeed often the only man-made structures of any kind to appear on them also reveals the enduring impact of these imposing Roman monuments on the landscape and the importance that they held for the cartographers who recorded it.

Just like the smaller Roman items discovered in Scotland, the larger monuments were often admired, but could also sometimes confuse and disappoint those who viewed them. While it was visited and examined by most of the antiquarians already discussed in this book, the Antonine Wall did not impress everyone. Patrick Abercromby dismissed it as a 'weak Fence' in 1711, and while John Anderson himself praised it as a feat of engineering, he reveals that other contemporary commentators were less complimentary: 'For it is fashionable at present not only for antiquarians and other literary men to ridicule this wall, but even for soldiers and for those who have made lines of posts their particular study'.[72] Both men proposed that its main flaw was its position between two firths, which would allow easy access across the frontier for those who could cross the water, while Anderson also records that it was criticised for its length, the troops along it being thinly spread out and thus slower to gather in the face of attack.

Perhaps the most curious but also the most perplexing Roman monument in Scotland was the strange domed structure found not far from the River Carron near Camelon. Standing twenty-two feet tall and constructed from dressed ashlar without the use of mortar, a single arched doorway surmounted by a window and an open oculus at the top of the dome, the building was commonly known as Arthur's O'on ('Arthur's Oven', the name inspired by its shape and associations with Arthurian legend), or sometimes Julius Hoss (thanks to legendary links with Julius Caesar). Already well-known in the medieval period, it became a veritable obsession amongst early modern Scottish (and a few English) antiquarians, each carefully examining it in order to devise their own theories regarding its date and purpose. Gordon notes that the various conjectures regarding the structure were 'so opposite, that not two of them have assigned the Work to the same Man, or Use', while de la Rochette later recorded that 'les opinions on été fort partageé sur cet edifice' (opinions were strongly divided on this building).[73] For patriotically-minded Scots the idea first recorded by George Buchanan that it was a temple of Terminus that marked the furthest extent of the Roman Empire was convincing, while for those with more Romanist inclinations it demonstrated that Roman architecture and religion had reached the north.[74] Sir John Clerk was surely not alone when he expressed a marked ambivalence, describing it as 'a beautiful and elegant building', but also pointing out that it was hardly a typical piece of refined classical architecture: 'nobody doubts of its being Roman, though a very plain piece of work'.[75]

While earlier generations had compared it to local constructions (Fordun thought it looked like a doocot, George Buchanan a broch), eighteenth-century antiquarians looked further afield in their attempts to confirm the classical credentials of Arthur's O'on.[76] Stukeley likened it to the circular temple in Rome now known as the Temple of Hercules Victor and observed similarities with the Temple of Romulus in the Forum, also adding a sketch of this building with additional notes to his own copy of *An Account of a Roman Temple*.[77] Horsley thought it remarkably similar to a description that he had read of the tomb of Caecilia Metella just outside Rome, noting that this was a typical form of mausoleum and also noticing that neither employed mortar.[78] But the most common comparison was with the mighty Pantheon, a building that Stukeley viewed as 'the finest as well as the most ancient and entire Structure now on the Globe', and which Andrew Lumisden, who spent time as a Jacobite exile in Italy, described as 'the pride of Rome, and the admiration of every person of taste'.[79] While some similarities can be seen between the two structures, most notably the circular plan, dome and oculus, such comparisons are certainly ambitious; but then most of the antiquarians who presented Arthur's O'on as Scotland's own Pantheon had never actually been to Rome. Sibbald was the first to highlight the similarities between the two, claiming that Arthur's O'on was built by Severus to commemorate his reconquest of the region, intending it 'as a Model, imitating the *Pantheon* at *Rome*'.[80] The comparisons presented by Stukeley in his *Account of a Roman Temple* are the most convoluted, the author detailing at some length the structure and proportions of each building and supposing that 'the Reader is prepossessed into my own Opinion that it [Arthur's O'on] may well pass for an imitation of the *Pantheon* or *Rotunda* at *Rome*'.[81] Gordon agreed, and went as far as to say that Arthur's O'on surpassed its Italian equivalent, 'the One being only built of Brick, whereas Arthur's Oven is made of regular Courses of hewn Freestone'.[82] Even Horsley, who paid less attention to it than his Scottish counterparts, suggested that it resembled the Pantheon.[83]

Not everyone was so enthused. Stukeley suspected that some might see the building as 'contemptible' and that they could also view his comparisons with the Pantheon as far-fetched.[84] His predictions were proved correct on publication of his essay in 1720 when, as he later admitted to Clerk, 'people laughed at me for adorning a dovecoat as they called it'.[85] Unfortunately, the structure was also of no interest to its owner, Sir Michael Bruce, who demolished it in 1743 and used its stones to build a dam, provoking unanimous outrage amongst the antiquarians. Clerk compared him to Herostratus, destroyer of the Temple of Artemis, Gale nicknamed him 'the BRUTES' and Stukeley drew him yoked to an iron collar with a stone from Arthur's O'on suspended at each end, his name written in burning phosphorous on his back.⁸⁶ Some took their lamentations further, with Edinburgh antiquarian George Paton relating an intriguing anecdote to Richard Gough in 1779:

> The late Engineer & Surveyor the master of Elphinston made it a rule if within a few miles of the Place to compell all the people he met to accompany him to the spot where the Building stood, then forming a Circle on their bare knees, he in the midst solemnly pronounced a heavy malediction on Sir Michael Bruce.⁸⁷

Thanks to the Clerk family, however, the spirit of Arthur's O'on was to live on. Sir John's son James ordered a reproduction of the lost building to be constructed as part of his improvements at Penicuik House. Sitting atop the stable block, this full-scale replica (Figure 5.4) functioned as a dovecote, the very thing to which the original structure had been disparagingly compared in earlier times.

Although much admired and collected throughout the eighteenth century, it is clear that the material remains of the Romans in Scotland also proved to be problematic. While antiquarians were absorbed in studying the historical information that Scotland's Roman artefacts held, others were undoubtedly

Figure 5.4 Doocot in the form of Arthur's O'on, on the stable block at Penicuik, 1763. (© Alan Montgomery, reproduced courtesy of Sir Robert Clerk)

underwhelmed by their artistic qualities. Atypical or even primitive to early modern eyes, certainly not a patch on the handsome marbles or grand buildings found in Rome itself, the Roman sculptures and architecture uncovered in Scotland often fell below expectations. That the antiquarians were also apt to concoct fanciful, almost comic conjectures regarding such objects was widely recognised, even at the time. In Sir Walter Scott's novel *The Antiquary*, first published in 1816 but set two decades earlier, the eccentric antiquarian of the title laments the destruction of his precious (and distinctly dubious sounding) lachrymatory from 'Clochnaben' by his niece's dog, resulting in the loss of important evidence, he believed, that the Romans had not only conquered the Highlands, but also left behind them 'traces of their arts and arms'.[88] By the end of the eighteenth century, as the fervour for ancient Rome began to cool, it appears that interest in the relics of Roman Scotland was already on the decline. The once celebrated coin cabinet in the Advocates Library became difficult to access, neglected and disordered, with much of the museum's contents, including Sibbald's donations, no longer on view, apparently lost.[89] Looking back more objectively a century after its destruction, antiquarian Robert Stuart felt that the excitement surrounding Arthur's O'on (which he thought resembled a humble beehive) had been somewhat overblown: 'It was examined, measured and remeasured, again and again, even to its minutest details, with a care and devotion carried, many would say, somewhat to excess'.[90] In 1851, Sir Daniel Wilson was even harsher, describing it as 'the supposed *Templum Termini*, of which so much has been written to so little purpose', even expressing doubts that it was Roman.[91] That this lack of interest in Scotland's classical antiquities was indicative of a wider sea-change in attitudes towards the nation's ancient history will become clear in the closing chapters of this book.

Notes

1. Sibbald, *Historical Inquiries*, Preface ('Archeologie'); Gordon, *Itinerarium Septentrionale*, Preface ('Archiology').
2. NRS GD18/5030/52: Gale to Clerk, 2 June 1737.
3. See, for example, the Iron Age souterrain at Crichton, which has Roman masonry and a decorated stone built into its walls.
4. NRS GD18/5068/2: Clerk(?), undated portfolio of sketches; Gordon, *Itinerarium Septentrionale*, p. 18.
5. Keppie, *Roman Inscribed and Sculptured Stones in the Hunterian Museum*, p. 94. This stone is catalogued in the *Roman Inscriptions of Britain* as RIB 2191.
6. NRS GD18/5031/6: Clerk to Blackwell, 23 September 1734.
7. Gordon, *Itinerarium Septentrionale*, p. 41; Knox, *A View of the British Empire*, p. 611.
8. NRS GD18/5023/3/36: Gordon to Clerk, 24 September 1726.
9. NRS GD18/2109, f. 8: Clerk, 'A Journie to Carlyle & Penrith', 1732.
10. NRS GD18/5030/22: Gale to Clerk, 20 November 1731.

11. Keppie, *Roman Inscribed and Sculptured Stones in the Hunterian Museum*, p. 76.
12. Horsley, *Britannia Romana*, p. 198. This stone (RIB 2186) is now in the Hunterian Museum, Glasgow.
13. Sibbald, *Historical Inquiries*, p. 31.
14. Horsley, *Britannia Romana*, p. 205. The altar is RIB 2135.
15. Stukeley, *An Account of a Roman Temple*, p. 12.
16. For a brief summary of early modern attitudes towards the collecting of classical antiquities, see: Swann, *Curiosities and Texts*, pp. 21–2.
17. NRS GD18/1810: Clerk, catalogue of the collections at Penicuik and Mavisbank, 1739.
18. Clerk, *Memoirs of the Life of Sir John Clerk of Penicuik*, p. 237; Brown, The *Hobby-Horsical Antiquary*, p. 31.
19. Gordon, *Itinerarium Septentrionale*, p. 117.
20. Maitland, *The History of Edinburgh*, p. 506.
21. Brown, *The Hobby-Horsical Antiquary*, p. 20.
22. NRS GD18/5023/3/1: Gordon to Clerk, 19 September 1723.
23. NRS GD18/5036/12: Blackwell to Clerk, 24 September 1731.Cicero makes several references to the acquisition and display of art in his letters to Atticus, for example 1.4 and 1.8.
24. Clerk, *Memoirs of the Life of Sir John Clerk of Penicuik*, pp. 237–8.
25. NRS GD18/5035: Crawford to Clerk, 30 December 1728.
26. Clerk, *Memoirs of the Life of Sir John Clerk of Penicuik*, p. 139.
27. Brown, 'The Penicuik Copy of Alexander Gordon's Itinerarium Septentrionale', p. 67.
28. Neale, *Views of the Seats of Noblemen and Gentlemen*, Penicuik.
29. Keppie, *The Antiquarian Rediscovery of the Antonine Wall*, p. 90.
30. Horsley, *Britannia Romana*, p. 181.
31. Keppie, *Roman Inscribed and Sculptured Stones in the Hunterian Museum*, p. 20.
32. Ibid. p. 21.
33. MacDonald, *Tituli Hunteriani*, p. 3.
34. Murray, *Museums*, p. 153.
35. Ouston, 'York in Edinburgh', p. 148.
36. Brown, '"This Old Magazine of Antiquities"', p. 158.
37. Sibbald, *Historical Inquiries*, p. 51.
38. Brown, '"This Old Magazine of Antiquities"', pp. 164–5.
39. Ibid p. 161; ibid. p. 167. The altar is RIB 2121.
40. Smellie, *Account of the Institution and Progress of the Society of the Antiquaries of Scotland*, p. 13.
41. Ibid. p. 20.
42. Ibid. p. 39; ibid. p. 94; Stevenson, 'The Museum, Its Beginnings and Its Development', p. 37.
43. NRS GD18/4404/2, ff. 61-2: Clerk, 'The Country Seat', 1727.
44. Gordon, *Itinerarium Septentrionale*, Preface.
45. Ibid. p. 64.
46. Horsley, *Britannia Romana*, p. 177.
47. NRS GD18/5023/3/1: Gordon to Clerk, 19 September 1723. A kalewife is a female vegetable seller.
48. NRS GD18/5024/3: Burn to Clerk, 18 November 1723; Gordon, *Itinerarium Septentrionale*, p. 61.
49. Stukeley, *An Account of a Roman Temple*, p. 10.
50. Peacham, *The Compleat Gentleman*, p. 106.

51. The stone is RIB 2208.
52. Stukeley, *An Account of a Roman Temple*, p. 10.
53. Pennant, *A Tour in Scotland . . . Part I*, pp. 157–8.
54. Gordon, *Additions and Corrections*, p. 6.
55. For more on Montesquieu's ideas on the decline of Roman art, see: Haskell, *History and Its Images*, pp. 164–6.
56. NRS GD18/2099, f. 6: Clerk, 'A Trip to Perth', 1717.
57. NLS MS 3803 f. 27: de la Rochette, untitled notes. On de la Rochette's study of Scotland's Roman antiquities, see Keppie, 'The French Cartographer and the Clan Chief'.
58. Henry, *History of Great Britain*, p. 349.
59. SUL OA/5/5, f. 51: Anderson, 'Of the Roman Wall Between the Forth and Clyde', c.1770, referring to RIB 2204; ibid. f. 64, referring to RIB 2173.
60. Ibid. f. 67. This stone is now in the collection of the Hunterian Museum, Glasgow.
61. Keppie, *Roman Inscribed and Sculptured Stones in the Hunterian Museum*, p. 31.
62. Gordon, *Itinerarium Septentrionale*, p. 177.
63. NRS GD18/5056: Lumsdaine to Clerk, 26 February 1741.
64. For a discussion of the misrepresentation of the so-called 'Netherbow Heads', see: Brown and Montgomery, 'The 'Roman Heads' at the Netherbow in Edinburgh', pp. 258–64.
65. Clerk, *Memoirs of the Life of Sir John Clerk of Penicuik*, p. 140; Gordon, *Additions and Corrections*, p. 27.
66. Maitland, *The History of Edinburgh*, p. 506.
67. Gordon, *Additions and Correction*, p. 27; NRS GD18/2109, f. 4: Clerk, 'A Journie to Carlyle & Penrith', 1732.
68. NRS GD18/5044: Clerk, 'Roman Stones in Pennicuik House', 1732.
69. Nichols, *Bibliotheca Topographica Britannica*, Vol. 3, pp. 300–1.
70. *Catalogue of the National Museum*, p. 289.
71. For a discussion of the subject and provenance of the head, see Russell and Manley, 'Trajan Places'.
72. Abercromby, *The Martial Atchievements of the Scots Nation*, p. 23; SUL MS. OA/5/5, f. 108: Anderson, 'Of the Roman Wall Between the Forth and Clyde', c.1770.
73. Gordon, *Itinerarium Septentrionale*, p. 28; NLS MS 3803, f. 5: de la Rochette, untitled notes.
74. Buchanan, *The History of Scotland*, p. 15.
75. Nichols, *Bibliotheca Topographica Britannica*, Vol. 3, p. 321.
76. Fordun, *Chronicle of the Scottish Nation*, p. 46; Buchanan, *The History of Scotland*, p. 15.
77. Stukeley, *An Account of a Roman Temple*, p. 23; ibid. p. 27; Bodl.553.7 G.42 fol.
78. Horsley, *Britannia Romana*, p. 174.
79. Stukeley, *An Account of a Roman Temple*, p. 20; Lumisden, *Remarks on the Antiquities of Rome*, p. 277.
80. Sibbald, *Historical Inquiries*, p. 46.
81. Stukeley, *An Account of a Roman Temple*, p. 15.
82. Gordon, *Itinerarium Septentrionale*, p. 25.
83. Horsley, *Britannia Romana*, p. 174.
84. Stukeley, *An Account of a Roman Temple*, p. 12; ibid. p. 19.
85. NRS GD18/5027/1: Stukeley to Clerk, 21 March 1725.
86. Nichols, *Bibliotheca Topographica Britannica*, Vol. 3, p. 385; NRS GD18/5030/94: Gale to Clerk, 20 August 1743. Stukeley's cartoon was published posthumously in 1780 in Volume 3 of *The Antiquarian Repertory*.

87. NLS.Adv.MS.29.5.7(iii), f. 59: Paton to Gough, 5 October 1779.
88. Scott, *The Antiquary*, p. 288.
89. Brown, '"This Old Magazine of Antiquities"', pp. 171–2; Pennant, *A Tour in Scotland . . . Part II*, p. 246.
90. Stuart, *Caledonia Romana*, p. 184.
91. Wilson, *The Archaeology and Prehistoric Annals of Scotland*, pp. 370–1.

6

Reconquering the Highlands: Hanoverian interpretations of Roman Scotland

> Hence it is that military men, especially those who have been much accustomed to observe and consider countries in the way of their profession . . . are naturally led to compare present things with the past; and being thus insensibly carried back to former ages, they place themselves among the ancients, and do, as it were, converse with the people of those remote times.
>
> William Roy, *The Military Antiquities of the Romans in Britain*, 1793, p. i

The first half of the eighteenth century was a time of social and political disruption in Scotland and across Britain as a whole. Perhaps the most dramatic crises of the period were the Jacobite rebellions of 1715, 1719 and 1745, the last of which came close to bringing down the Hanoverian regime, Bonnie Prince Charlie marching his troops as far south as Derbyshire before losing his nerve and retreating back to Scotland. Having raised their standards in the far north and ultimately been defeated there at the Battle of Culloden, the Stuart uprisings were (and still are) often presented as a Highland phenomenon, although support for the Jacobite cause was certainly not restricted to that region. The idea of a harmonious Britain resulting from the Union of 1707 was shattered, anxieties about the internal divisions within Scotland itself re-emerged and the traditional vision of Caledonia as a place of conflict was revived, with memories of ancient battles between savage northerners and civilised southerners rekindled in eighteenth-century minds. In the wake of these unsuccessful rebellions, the ways in which the north of Scotland was to be viewed and governed were to radically change.

These events also had a notable impact on Scottish historiography and antiquarianism. A new breed of Romanist soldier antiquarian emerged, men who were less concerned with the civility that might result from Roman conquest and more focused on the military expertise required to conquer. As Hanoverian forces were deployed to the Highlands to suppress any potential Jacobite resurgence, some soldiers turned their attention to the study of the area's Roman remains, particularly those believed to be Agricolan. Eighteenth-century generals followed in the footsteps of their Roman equivalents and some early modern Scots developed new interpretations of their nation's ancient heritage, identifying aspects of it that resonated with their own experiences and harnessing their military expertise while conjecturing Roman tactics. Although these were not the first Scots to try to track the Roman expeditions into the north, their approach to the distant past and the techniques that they used to uncover and record it can be related to emerging Enlightenment attitudes towards documenting the landscape and society of the early modern nation.

Hanoverian 'Romans' versus Highland 'Caledonians'

For centuries the Highlands of Scotland had resisted the control of centralised government and as a consequence were commonly viewed by southerners as a separate, troublesome region that at times even threatened national stability.[1] Antiquarians often expressed such prejudices. William Camden made reference to the savagery of the Highlanders who 'are rude & unruly, speake Irish, & go apparailed Irishlike' in the earliest editions of his *Britannia*, while Sir Robert Sibbald noted in the late seventeenth century that Lowlanders were more civilised (by which he meant anglicised) than the barbarous, Gaelic-speaking Highlanders.[2] The idea that the inhabitants of the north were more Irish than Scottish was commonplace: writing at the time of the Union, Daniel Defoe stated that the Highlanders retained the names, manners and language of the Irish or ancient *Scoti* and that the Lowlanders were a mongrel race partly descended from the Romans.[3] Furthermore, the early modern inhabitants of the Highlands were at times conflated with the ancient barbarians described by the Romans centuries before. The wording chosen by English scholar and Royal Society member John Chamberlayne to describe the purpose of Agricola's fortifications across the Forth/Clyde isthmus in his *Magnae Britanniae Notitia*, published just after the first Jacobite uprising, is telling: 'to exclude the *Scotch-Highlanders*'.[4] And while Alexander Gordon may have seen the supposed similarities between ancient Caledonians and modern Highlanders as admirable, referring in particular to their abstemiousness, his patron Sir John Clerk was less flattering, also believing the current inhabitants of northern Scotland to be little different from the tribes met there by Agricola, but describing them disdainfully as lazy, untrustworthy and lawless.[5]

The Jacobite rebellion of 1745–6 proved the most significant of the various attempts by the house of Stuart to regain the British throne, and the chaos and fear that it spread throughout Britain only confirmed such ideas of barbaric Highlanders for many southerners. Having allowed the Jacobite army to get within 100 miles of London, the Hanoverian regime was well aware of how close it came to defeat. It became clear that the Highlands of Scotland, where this and previous uprisings had germinated, needed to be brought under tighter control. The now notorious Duke of Cumberland was sent north to violently supress any signs of remaining insurrection and a road-building policy initiated by General Wade after the 1715 rising was continued. Fort George was constructed near Inverness, the estates of Jacobite supporters were seized and Highlanders were forbidden from carrying arms. Less bellicose (although no less controversial) techniques including the ban on traditional Highland dress, improved education, plans for 'model villages', attempts to eradicate Gaelic and the promotion of Protestantism all aimed to integrate the Highlands with the rest of Britain, reduce the power of the clan chiefs and encourage loyalty to the Crown.[6]

The similarities between these Hanoverian strategies and those used by the Romans to subdue conquered nations have been noted in modern scholarship, with Hingley calling it the imposition of a 'neo-Roman concept of order across the Scottish Highlands'.[7] Those involved in the pacifying project were obviously aware of these similarities, and at times made explicit links to Roman precedents, particularly when constructing roads and bridges. The elegant bridge over the Tay built by General Wade, for example, features a Latin inscription highlighting its position 250 miles beyond the limits of the Roman Empire (which presumably means Hadrian's Wall), while the edition of *Britannia* edited and extended by Richard Gough in 1789 notes that 'the troops employed in making these roads left engraved on the rocks the names of the regiment each party belonged to after the manner of the Romans'.[8] Visiting Englishman Thomas Pennant made several references to the Roman methods employed by the Hanoverian army, and the parallels were also not lost on the locals, with Elgin church minister and local historian Lachlan Shaw relating Wade's road building in the north of Scotland to the 'Military ways' constructed by Septimius Severus as described in Xiphilinus' epitome of Dio.[9]

Since the Hanoverians were effectively imagining themselves, and indeed publicly presenting themselves as inheritors of the classical world, it also suited their purpose to carry on the tradition of portraying the indigenous Highlanders as savages similar to those faced by the invading Romans. Descriptions of the Highlands suggested that they were a virtual time capsule, a place where little had changed for centuries, even millennia. Many commentators would, like Shaw, have known the *Roman History* of Cassius Dio, which includes descriptions of the native tribes, named by the ancient author as the Caledonians and the Maeatae, and depicts them as hardy, tent-dwelling naked herders who were also terrifying warriors fond of plunder.[10] Thomas Ashe Lee, a captain-lieutenant in the government forces who spent time in the Highlands following Culloden, kept a copy of Caesar's *De Bello Gallico* with him on his travels and studied it for parallels with modern tactics. His description of the Highlanders he encountered suggested that they were even more barbarous than ancient tribesmen: 'The most savage of the Gauls shall be outdone by the gentlest rebels of these Highlanders, & it surprised me to find the confusion at Falkirk [the 1746 battle at Falkirk Muir] printed there in very elegant Latin, for I imagined it was unparalleled in History'.[11] Hingley suggests that Scottish Hanoverian statesman Duncan Forbes held similar opinions on the inhabitants of the north, describing his writings from the mid-1740s as 'reminiscent of the observations of Tacitus, Posidonius and Caesar about the Celtic and Germanic tribes of Iron Age Europe'.[12] Such attitudes persisted into the 1770s, when John Anderson proposed in his paper on the Antonine Wall that the tribesmen met by Severus were similar to those that Agricola had encountered over a century before, and that the manners of the present Highlanders were comparable in several respects to those of their ancient forebears.[13] In a description of one of the Antonine Wall distance slabs in the same essay, Anderson describes the weapons carried by Caledonian captives shown in the carving and considers a comparison with Highland dirks, also noting that 'the Highlanders had the same kind of broadsword in the time of Agricola which they have at present'.[14] Southern audiences could well have taken such accounts at face value: Edmund Burt, who seems to have been an English engineer working on the new Highland road system in the 1720s, records in his extensive correspondence (which was published in London in 1754) that Lowland Scots knew little about the Highlands, and the English virtually nothing.[15]

General Robert Melville and the rediscovery of Agricola's campaigns

Robert Melville (sometimes Melvill), the first of our Hanoverian antiquarians to display a notable interest in Scotland's Roman military history, was born in Monimail in 1723 as the son of the local minister. Orphaned in his teens, his education was overseen by his uncle Robert Whytt, a physician and later a professor of medicine at Edinburgh University. Melville himself studied medicine, first at Glasgow University and then in Edinburgh, but dropped his studies in favour of a military career. He spent time fighting in Flanders during the War of the Austrian Succession, but his involvement there was interrupted when he was called back to Scotland to help combat the 1745 Jacobite rising. Although posted to Ireland between 1749 and 1755, he made more return visits to his native land in 1751 and 1754 to recruit for the 25th Regiment of Foot.

It was during this 1751 sojourn in Scotland that Melville's interest in his homeland's Roman history was first ignited during a visit to Penicuik House. Although Sir John Clerk himself was not at home, his son James showed (by now Captain) Melville a sword believed to be a Roman *gladius* from Clerk's extensive collection of antiquities. The description of this encounter, written later in an adulatory biographical essay by Melville's secretary, captures the Captain's pragmatic, hands-on approach to the past:

> He at once discarded his systematic knowledge and, wielding the weapon, asked himself in what manner men armed with such a sword in the right hand, and with a legionary shield on the left, ought to be arranged in order to make the best use of their arms offensive and defensive.[16]

The impact of this experience was such that Melville began to research Roman warfare more extensively. He spent several months scrutinising the writings of sixteenth-century humanist philosopher Francesco Patrizi and read Justus Lipsius' *De Militia Romana* along with other antiquarian tracts in a bid to read 'all the writers who had either briefly touched on, or more largely treated of the military branch of Roman antiquities', and also spoke to other soldiers who had read up on the subject.[17] His secretary, no doubt echoing the thoughts of Melville himself, argued that previous work on the matter had been inferior due to the fact that its authors had rarely been military men. Melville's studies, however, offered new insights and gave 'further proofs of the versatility as well as of the extent of his genius'.[18]

As his fascination with the Roman army and its Caledonian campaigns grew, Melville became particularly interested in Agricola's expeditions into the north. His second return to Scotland in 1754 allowed him the opportunity to scour the Scottish landscape in search of Roman military remains. An essay detailing two journeys designed to trace Agricola's progress made during the summer of that year was included in the 1789 *Britannia*, while a manuscript essay on the same subject entitled 'Agricola's Camps in Scotland' can be found amongst Melville's papers in the National Records of Scotland. The exact date of the manuscript essay remains unclear (the author's suggestion that it was composed nearly ninety years after the publication of Gordon's *Itinerarium Septentrionale* of 1726 cannot be correct, since Melville died in 1809), but it must have been written towards the end of his life.[19] Melville was accompanied on his travels by John Clerk of Eldin and Matthew Clerk, sons of the celebrated Sir John. In the unpublished essay 'Captain M', who refers to himself throughout in the third person in a style reminiscent of Caesar, proposes that the subject of war and its history should be approached methodically: 'War says a French writer is a trade for the ignorant, but a science for the skillful'.[20]

His first antiquarian tour, which followed the Antonine Wall before heading up towards Strathearn and was carried out on foot to avoid missing any evidence on the ground, was largely unsuccessful, so Melville retreated to Edinburgh to reread his Tacitus and reconsider the landscape he had just explored whilst also taking into account 'the rational principles of the art of war'.[21] As many have discovered both before and since, the *Agricola* is frustratingly limited when it comes to geographical information. Melville was certainly aware of its shortcomings, noting that 'the text of Tacitus is summary and not sufficiently circumstantial in detailing the operations of Agricola's army'.[22] He also found the more recent publications of Sibbald, Gordon and Horsley largely unsatisfactory, dismissing such scholars as 'unmilitary antiquaries'.[23] Instead Melville turned to his own military expertise and experience to put together a conjectural route for the first-century Roman invasion, plotting an itinerary past Stirling, across Fife and over the Tay into Perthshire. Determined to prove the veracity of his conjectures by locating physical evidence of Agricola's advance, Melville set off northwards once again. With the help of local inhabitants, he finally located four previously unknown camps at Lintrose, Battledykes, Kirkbuddo and Keithock in the region north of Dundee, all of which he confidently attributed to the Agricolan invasion. While many observers were initially sceptical of his research, his discoveries inspired much excitement, the sites becoming 'a topic of curiosity and conversation every where near them'.[24] He also developed a new theory regarding the much debated site of the battle of Mons Graupius, a subject that will be discussed further in the next chapter. The antiquarian's delight that the evidence on the ground appeared to confirm the effectiveness of his methods is demonstrated by his proud claim that he 'sketched out for Agricola a plan of operations which incontrovertible facts afterwards most completely supported and confirmed'.[25] Melville's attempt to put himself in the sandals of a Roman general had proved an unmitigated success.

It was probably around the time that he was searching out Agricolan remains that Melville also wrote his most extensive published work on the subject of Roman history, his *Critical Enquiry into the Constitution of the Roman Legion*, which was printed in 1773 after apparently lying 'neglected and almost forgotten upwards of twenty years'.[26] Depicting the organisation of the Roman army and also describing the 'Military Art of the Ancients', Melville's book often challenges the work of his predecessors and contemporaries who, he reiterated, lacked an understanding of the martial world.[27] Although he realised the different challenges they faced compared to their ancient counterparts, Melville clearly intended his work as an instruction manual for fellow military commanders. He believed that the structure of the Roman army and the layout of their camps allowed its generals to work more closely with their troops, and thought that the Roman army was more efficient due to the fact that the average legionary 'was attended with a considerable degree of dignity', while the modern army tended to recruit 'the dregs of the people'.[28]

Melville was to spend much of his later life far from Scotland, but his admiration for the Romans never dimmed. He was posted to the Caribbean and became involved in British attempts to establish colonies there. Following various successes against the French during the Seven Years' War, he was appointed lieutenant-governor of Guadeloupe in 1759 and became governor of the Ceded

Islands in 1763. In 1774–6 the now General Melville took himself on a Grand Tour of Europe, during which he explored the sites of ancient battles and tracked the route of Hannibal over the Alps armed with copies of Caesar and Polybius. During the French Revolution he even lobbied for the introduction of swords modelled on the Roman *gladius*, although his letters to several influential figures, including the Duke of York and distinguished Scottish officer Sir John Moore, met with polite refusals.[29]

The genesis of William Roy's *Military Antiquities of the Romans in Britain*

While the inclusion of his essay in Gough's 1789 *Britannia* suggests that Robert Melville's antiquarian work was highly regarded during his lifetime, it is less widely recognised today. His entry in the 2004 *Oxford Dictionary of National Biography*, for example, makes only passing note of an interest in Roman history, focusing instead on his military and imperial achievements.[30] That his researches on Roman Scotland are remembered at all is largely due to his influence on another military antiquarian whose reputation has since greatly surpassed Melville's own, namely Major-General William Roy. Melville himself was proud that his inquiries had inspired the work of a man he termed 'my first proselyte': 'General Melvill concludes upon the whole, that it is to him a most pleasing reflection, that his small but fortunate discovery should have proved to have been the original cause of those ingenious productions, from so meritorious an officer and so esteemed a friend'.[31]

Roy originally hailed from Lanarkshire, born there in 1726. His father was a gardener for the Hamiltons of Hallcraig and his uncle was Land Steward to the Lockharts of Lee. We also know that he attended the local parish school in Carluke and the grammar school in Lanark, where George MacDonald proposes he would have received a thorough training in Latin and mathematics.[32] How he was occupied in the years following his education remains a mystery; suggestions have been made that he helped his father to map the estate that he oversaw, or that he was employed as a road surveyor for the Post Office, also that he worked as a draughtsman for the Edinburgh Ordnance Office.[33] In 1747 he became clerk to Lieutenant-Colonel David Watson, deputy quartermaster-general in Scotland in charge of improving communications in the Highlands following the '45 uprising. In Roy's own words:

> The rise and progress of the rebellion which broke out in the Highlands of Scotland in 1745, and which was finally supressed by his Royal Highness the late Duke of Cumberland . . . convinced Government of what infinite importance it would be to the State, that a country, so very inaccessible by nature, should be thoroughly explored and laid open, by establishing military posts in its inmost recesses . . .[34]

Watson began work on a military survey of Scotland, creating accurate maps of the Highlands to replace the old and insufficiently detailed ones used during the Jacobite revolt. By this point Roy seems to have already been a competent surveyor.[35] Although it can be assumed that mapping was not his only task, with responsibility for the quartering of the troops, improvement in communication and the movement of supplies also falling under his remit, it is his cartographical skills that he himself chose to emphasise: '[Watson] first conceived the idea of making a map of the Highlands. As assistant Quarter-Master, it fell to my lot to begin, and afterwards to have a considerable share in, the execution of that map'.[36] Roy was employed on this project to map the Highlands from 1747–52, after which it was extended for another three years to include southern Scotland. He began the survey of the north at Fort Augustus and was probably the lone surveyor for almost two years. Later, three assistants from the engineer cadets were employed alongside him; according to Watson's nephew David Dundas, Roy worked with an iron chain, a 'Magnetic Needle' and a 'good plain Theodolite with a needle box made by Cole'.[37] Although never completed and restricted to the Scottish mainland, the map that resulted from his endeavours is generally referred to as the 'Great Map'. Roy himself felt that it ably served its purpose, but was aware of its shortcomings, blaming poor quality instruments and a lack of funding for the fact that it should be 'considered as a magnificent military sketch, [rather] than a very accurate map of a country'.[38]

It seems to have been during his three years surveying southern Scotland that Roy became interested in Roman antiquities. As he later recorded in the Prefatory Introduction to his *Military Antiquities*, such a hobby was unusual but not unique among his colleagues: 'though at that early period, the study of Antiquity was but little the object of the young people employed in that service, yet it was not wholly neglected; many sketches of Roman works having been made in the ordinary course of the other observations'.[39] The only surviving letter from Roy to Watson, dated 20 September 1752 and written at Berwick-upon-Tweed, provides some evidence of his growing preoccupation with Roman remains. Composed following a journey along the Scottish border, it contains topographical information and details of how the Jacobite army had traversed the region while marching into and later retreating out of England, but also includes descriptions of ancient sites encountered along the way:

> Netherby an old Roman Station, is situated on a rising Ground, on the English side exactly over against Kirk Andrews. Here I had the pleasure of seeing the Remains of a very Curious Roman Temple or Bath, it is not yet entirely discovered, but what is I have made a plan and section of. Mr Beatty the parson of Kirk Andrews, gave me Baron Clarks exposition of the inscription on an Altar found in the Sacrifice Room of this Bath which was discovered in the year 1732.[40]

Later in the same letter Roy also makes note of another supposed Roman camp further along the border as well as the well-preserved remains of Watling Street. His study of Roman sites progressed from there, with several of the plans that would later appear in his book probably dating from the early 1750s.[41]

The year 1754 was to prove pivotal for Roy, as it was then that his fateful meeting with Robert Melville took place. While Roy was already aware of the general attributes and layout of permanent Roman forts, Melville apparently introduced him not only to his methods for searching out and identifying marching camps, but also to the idea that the progress of Agricola's troops across Scotland could theoretically be tracked by mapping such fortifications.[42] Melville's aforementioned respect for Roy was reciprocated, with Roy later modestly suggesting that his own research would have been unnecessary if Melville's antiquarian work had not been brought to an end by his foreign postings, since Melville was 'much better qualified to treat the subject as it deserves'.[43] Roy's new focus on camps led to a series of plans, including several sites in Perthshire, and in 1755 he completed the most detailed survey to date of the Antonine Wall. He probably formally joined the army around the same time after several years of working on these military projects as a civilian.[44] By now the military survey was at almost an end and it was in this final stage that Roy seems to have added several Roman forts and camps to his map in the form of reduced versions of his own plans and sketches.[45]

In the later 1750s Roy too was called away to the Seven Years' War, during which he saw active service on the continent. He was promoted to the position of deputy quartermaster general to the forces in South Britain in 1761 and settled in London. During a visit to his mother's house in Lanarkshire in 1764, however, he stumbled across a Roman camp at Cleghorn and his passion for antiquity was revived. Roy was unable to investigate further himself due to his duties in England, so asked George Clerk, the second son of Sir John, to explore Annandale in search of more Roman sites, with some success. It was another five years before Roy himself was back in Scotland and he conducted another extensive tour in 1771. What had begun as a relaxing sideline had grown into a plan for two essays on the subject of the Roman military remains in Scotland. Largely inspired by the discovery of a new source on the geography and history of Roman Britain, a supposed medieval manuscript now known as the *De Situ Britanniae*, Roy finally decided that his work could be expanded into a book. The text for what would become his *Military Antiquities of the Romans in Britain* was largely complete by the summer of 1772.

Over the next few years Roy put his antiquarian research to one side in favour of his military career, and this time there would be no return to such pursuits. During the 1780s, now a major-general, he was largely occupied by a project to accurately triangulate the south east of England, but plans to create a map of England to accompany his survey of Scotland ultimately remained unrealised largely due to the costs of the American War of Independence. He died on 1 July 1790, his obituary in *The Gentleman's Magazine* recording his antiquarian reputation, highlighting the inclusion of Roman monuments on his Great Map and also mentioning the production of a smaller version (called here the 'King's Map'), which included 'many camps, a good number of Roman names'.[46] His antiquarian research was contained in two manuscripts, one in the King's Library and another in the collection of the Society of Antiquaries of London. Two years were spent collating the two versions before the Society published the work with great fanfare in 1793, a copy being sent to each of its members and others presented to the King and Queen, the British Museum, the Royal Society, the Vatican Library and the Universities of Oxford and Cambridge. An unspecified number were also released for sale, with Robert Melville strongly encouraging Danish scholar Grímur Thorkelin to acquire a copy for his own use and for inclusion in the Royal Library of Denmark.[47]

Roy's interpretation of Scotland's Roman heritage

Given its reference to the '*Romans in Britain*', the title that appears on the first title page of Roy's posthumous publication is rather misleading as regards the geographical coverage of its content. More accurate is that printed on the following page, *The Military Antiquities of the Romans in North Britain*, which make its focus on Scotland more apparent. Given its author's skills as a draughtsman and cartographer, it is fitting that this book is now most highly regarded for its maps and plans (Figure 6.1). In terms of accuracy and detail they far surpass any previous efforts to record Scotland's Roman monuments and several remain valuable today as evidence of lost or damaged sites. The text, however, is often overlooked. Roy himself described his writing in modest terms: 'Though the Essays which compose this collection, considered in a military light, bear some relation to the profession in general, and particularly to those employments the author hath the honour to hold; yet he wishes them to be regarded rather as the lucubrations of his leisure hours, than as tending to any great utility'.[48] His reliance on the completely unreliable *De Situ Britanniae* (the creation and content of which will be explored in Chapter 8) unfortunately renders much of his conjecture worthless to historians of Roman Britain. Nevertheless, Roy's proposals regarding the first-century invasion of Scotland still deserve attention, particularly for the attitudes that they demonstrate towards Scotland's history and its role in the formation of national identity.

The second title page of the *Military Antiquities* states that the book intends to study the structures of the surviving vestiges of Roman camps across Scotland and employ them to track the progress of Agricola's expedition, also highlighting

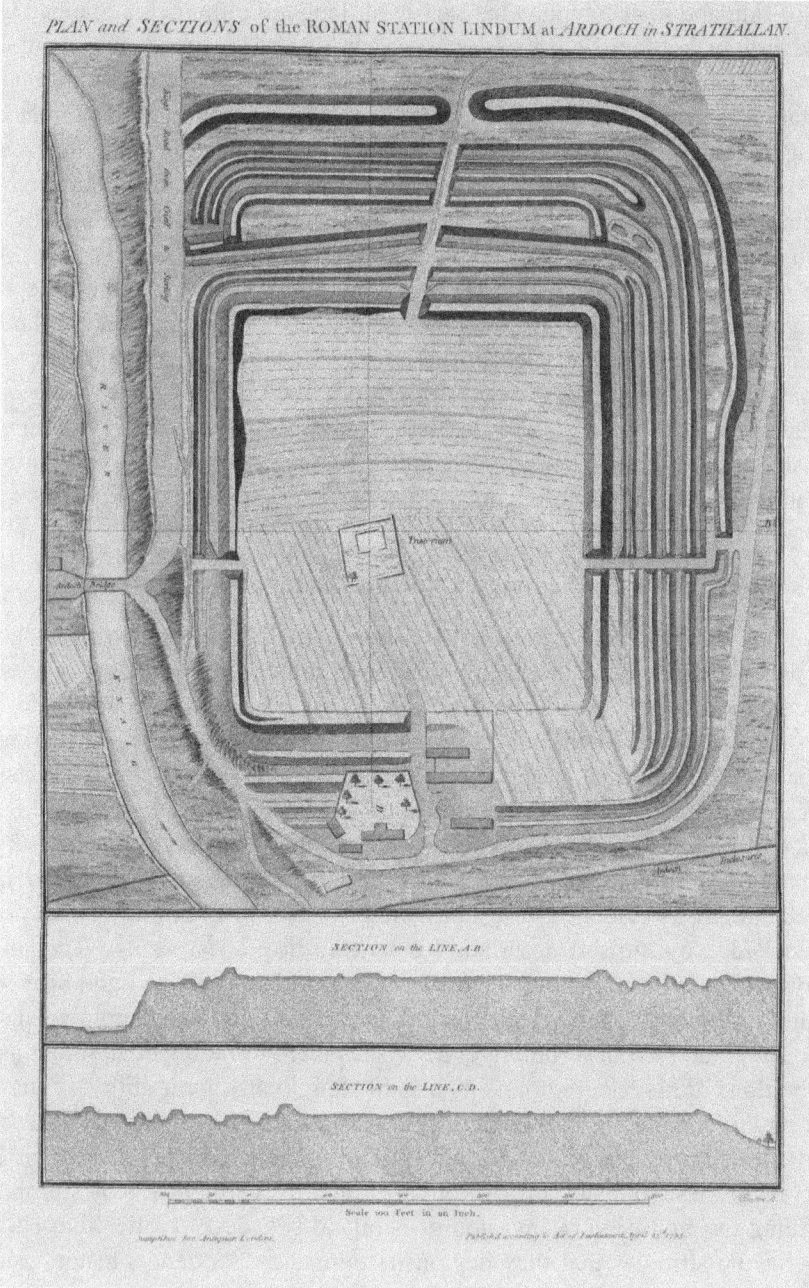

Figure 6.1 Plan and section of Ardoch Fort, Plate 30 in William Roy's *Military Antiquities of the Romans in Britain*, 1793. (Reproduced by permission of National Library of Scotland)

the inclusion of a treatise that employs the apparent revelations in the *De Situ Britanniae* to correct previous conjectures on ancient geography. The book consists of four main sections: a brief history of the Romans in Britain, a description of the Roman army under the monarchy and early Republic, details of the Agricolan camps found in Scotland and a new description of ancient Scotland based on the content of the *De Situ Britanniae* (which also includes a survey of the Antonine Wall). These are followed by five short appendices, four by Roy and another contributed by John Anderson on the subject of recently discovered stones and inscriptions from the wall.

While his fieldwork was vital to Roy's understanding of both the layout of Roman camps and their locations across Scotland, the author also mined the classical sources for information. Greek historian Polybius provides useful detail on both the hierarchy of the Roman army and the techniques used to set up, run and then take down their temporary camps.[49] Where Polybius falls short Roy turned to Vegetius, whose *Epitoma Rei Militaris*, although written around 400 CE, was largely a compilation of works by earlier Roman writers and contains a chapter entitled *Quemadmodum castra debeant ordinari* (How the camp should be arranged).[50] Roy also analysed the history of Livy, which contains accounts of military conflicts during the third and second centuries BCE, for its references to the layout of a typical *castra*.[51] As well as listing the scientific and mathematical instruments used in his work, the catalogue printed by Christie's to accompany the 1790 sale of Roy's possessions also gives insight into his literary researches. The contrast with the previous antiquarians discussed in this book is notable, for while Sir Robert Sibbald had studied Stoic philosophy and Sir John Clerk pored over the poetry of his beloved Horace, Roy preferred books dealing with the art of war. At his death, his library included many such classical texts including Hampton's *General History of Polybius* of 1761, three editions of Caesar's works including William Duncan's *Commentaries of Caesar, Translated into English* (which also features his 'Discourse Concerning the Roman Art of War') and *Mémoires Militaires sur les Grecs et les Romains* by Guischardt, as well as various other antiquarian books such as Horsley's *Britannia Romana* and Warburton's *Vallum Romanum*.[52] Numerous publications on modern warfare were also present, such as Dulacq's 1741 *Théorie Nouvelle sur le Mécanisme de l'Artillerie* and de Puységur's 1748 *Art de la Guerre*.[53] On a similar note, the only antiquity listed in Roy's collection is distinctly brutal, described by Christie's as '1 of the cowie stakes driven into the bed of the Thames by the Britons, to hinder the passage of Julius Caesar'.[54]

Roy noticed that antiquarians tended to focus on aspects of history that mirrored their own occupations, with 'each, according to his particular taste, inquiring into that favourite branch that pleases him most; and in this choice he seems generally to be directed by the relation which it bears to his ordinary employments in life'.⁵⁵ He also shared Melville's view that military experience was crucial to a proper understanding of the Roman incursions into Caledonia. Although Roy's knowledge of modern warfare undoubtedly informed his interpretations of the past, he also implies that modern soldiers could learn from historical precedents since, as the epigraph to this chapter demonstrates, this was a two-way exchange. He believed that the techniques of warfare had changed little over the centuries, allowing him to establish links between himself and the Romans in a way that men like Sibbald and Clerk had also attempted, arguably less successfully, to do:

> That the principles of war are fixed and general, varying only with the local circumstances and situation of the country, we doubt not will be admitted: whence it follows, that some knowledge of modern military operations seems necessary, to enable us to trace with success the motions of a Roman army; and whoever hath been accustomed to observe the one with most attention, will, in all likelihood, not only find it easiest to trace the other, but, at the same time, will perceive a very great resemblance in the leading principles upon which they respectively acted.⁵⁶

Roy also proposed that the military remains of the Romans in Britain were more important and impressive than those of civil monuments such as temples, amphitheatres and baths. He suggested that, although the surviving camps, which consisted largely of earthworks, were more susceptible to the destructive forces of agriculture and weather, there was little evidence of more sturdy public buildings in Britain, and Roy thought it unlikely that the Romans had ever built many such 'costly edifices in this island'.⁵⁷ He believed that these military sites were the only antiquities in Britain that could outshine those found in other parts of the Roman Empire, echoing a claim made by Alexander Gordon several decades before.⁵⁸ His research may have concentrated on military antiquities at the expense of civil remains, but he did recognise a certain degree of Roman civilisation in Scotland, no doubt influenced by the *De Situ Britanniae*, which seemed to reveal the locations of several previously unknown Roman settlements in the north. But while Roy accepted the existence of two Roman provinces in the region, he believed that even the southern reaches of Scotland were held only briefly and were racked by insurrection throughout these short occupations. Although, like most of his predecessors, he identifies Camelon as a city, he makes no other mention of a Roman civil settlement in Scotland.⁵⁹ Rather than the era of civility portrayed by Sibbald and Stukeley, Roy depicts the Roman occupation of Scotland as a period of 'rapine, devastation and blood-shed'.⁶⁰

In including Roman sites in his map of Scotland, William Roy may have followed a tradition that dated back to Timothy Pont's late sixteenth/early seventeenth-century cartographic practice, but his work should also be viewed in the context of Enlightenment attitudes towards recording and mapping. Sponberg Pedley identifies a two-wave revolution in the way that the world was recorded and described in the early modern period: the first wave, which began around 1650 and lasted for around a century, witnessed technological improvements as scholars began to comprehend the shape and size of the Earth; the second, which would carry on until the early nineteenth century, saw state agencies commission large-scale national surveys and support schools to fulfil the growing demand for surveyors and engineers.[61] This latter trend for more precise and extensive mapping of nations and their overseas colonies, which emphasised the importance of original surveys and the use of state-of-the-art instruments, was evident throughout Europe at this time, as scholars increasingly employed reason and research to answer their questions regarding the nature of the world that they inhabited. MacDonald describes Roy's work as being imbued with a 'scientific spirit', and the antiquarian certainly made use of the latest technology available to him.[62] He was accompanied during many of his travels by the artist Paul Sandby, who painted views of the landscapes they found as well as working on the maps themselves, and their methods can be associated with a desire in Enlightenment Scotland to, as Charles Withers describes it, 'understand its present constitution and to provide a vision of the nation in the future'.[63] Forward-thinking Scots of the later eighteenth century were intent on understanding even the remotest corners of their nation with a view to improving it throughout. Visual records of the landscape, both cartographic and artistic, allowed this understanding to be disseminated to a wider audience in polite society.[64]

A sense of how much things had changed over the previous decades can be found in a comparison of the reception of Roy's research with the fate of Sir Robert Sibbald's work around a century before. Both men were appointed by the State to map Scotland and both developed a fascination with the geography of ancient Caledonia in the process. Withers locates in the writings of Sibbald and his circle the beginnings of a belief that geographical knowledge represented a vital element in the formulation of national identity.[65] Sibbald's research into the landscape of the ancient nation also inspired the generations of antiquarians who were to follow, a trend that reaches its apogee in Roy. But while Sibbald, partly restricted by challenging travelling conditions but also following the scholarly tradition of the day, often depended on the reports of others for his information on antiquities across Scotland, Roy travelled widely and viewed sites himself, using a new generation of mathematical instruments to record them in unprecedented detail. Neither lived to see their magnum opus published. A man ahead of his time, Sibbald struggled unsuccessfully for years to get his *Scotish Atlas* to the press. Roy's *Military Antiquities of the Roman in Britain*, on the other hand, was posthumously published to great acclaim in a sumptuous folio format, copies of it ending up in many of the great libraries of Europe.

Alexander Shand and his 'esteemed discoveries of the greatest importance'

Although Roy and, to a lesser extent, Melville have received the most attention from modern scholars of eighteenth-century antiquarianism, they were not the only soldiers studying Scotland's Roman patrimony in the years following the '45. Alexander Shand, born in 1731 in Forgue, Aberdeenshire, proved to be a bright and enthusiastic pupil in his youth, and by 1760 this ambitious young man had joined the army. Thanks to an impressive military record in Germany, America and Gibraltar he was eventually promoted to the rank of colonel. In later years he retired to an estate in Templeland, not far from his birthplace. As well as dedicating himself to agricultural improvement, Shand filled his leisure hours with investigations into the Roman antiquities that lay north of the Antonine Wall. In 1785 he located the vestiges of a camp at Glenmailen; three years later he presented a paper to the Antiquarian Society of Perth that included a description of both that site and another camp at nearby Old Meldrum, a manuscript copy of which survives in the archive at Perth Museum.

Shand had a high opinion of the significance of his finds, stating that 'as they furnish positive evidence that the Romans passed the Grampians . . . and had possessed the country, in their usual manner, by a strong permanent praesidium, [they] are esteemed discoveries of the greatest importance, not only as mere evidence of an historical point, but as tending to shew the true impact of the itinerary, and pointing out methods of further investigation'.[66] He was particularly optimistic regarding both the success of the Severan invasion of Caledonia and the potential to identify surviving remains of it, proposing that evidence might be found as far north as Inverness or even Tain on the Dornoch Firth if searches were made.[67] The essay received praise from Robert Melville, who described it as 'vigorous' and was suitably impressed by the author's adoption of a 'military view' during his investigations.[68] Shand's work even attracted international attention, leading to a correspondence with Grímur Thorkelin, who wrote to the Scot seeking details of Roman remains in his locality. A reply from Shand to Thorkelin sent in 1790 contains information on Aberdeenshire antiquities and folklore.[69]

Duplicates of the drawing that Shand made of the camp at Glenmailen were widely distributed, one version ending up as Plate 51 in the *Military Antiquities*. Shand, however, was unhappy with the quality of the plan reproduced in Roy's book, noting errors in spelling that he believed were a result of his original being corrupted as it was copied and recopied.[70] Despite Shand's own confidence in the significance of his antiquarian work and the admiration that it inspired in his contemporaries, some aspects of it do not stand up to modern scrutiny. The camp near Old Meldrum that he designated Roman, often referred to today as Barra Hill, is now considered Iron Age. While Shand claimed that it had been 'executed exactly in the same manner as the praetorium at Ardoch', its circular plan and position atop a hill clearly suggest otherwise.[71]

Roman Scotland as British history

The second half of the eighteenth century witnessed new attitudes towards Scotland's ancient past as military-minded antiquarians steered their national historiography in a different direction. Finally, in this age when southern civility was again perceived to be under threat from rampaging northern hoards, the endeavours of the Romans in northern Britain seemed more relevant to many early modern Scots. While previous generations had employed the battle of Caledonia against Rome as a metaphor for Scotland's struggle for independence from England, now specific aspects of it were interpreted as analogous to the conflict between Hanoverian and Highlander as the British regime strove to impose a veritable *Pax Romana* on the north. In this way Scots who supported the government could more convincingly associate themselves with the Romans rather than their Caledonian enemies, while the portrayals of the Highlands as a savage wasteland to be tamed by the forces of empire found in classical texts gained new pertinence. Meanwhile, similar comparisons between Roman troops and the Hanoverian redcoats were made by English antiquarians George Smith and John Warburton in their writings on Hadrian's Wall.[72]

Although obviously proud of their homeland and intent on uncovering its earliest history, both Melville and Roy were also active members of the Society of Antiquaries of London. Along with Alexander Shand, these men were not the opponents of empire, rather they were its builders and consolidators, and in many ways their work reflects their own sense of being British as much as Scottish. Their reinterpretation of Scotland's distant past effectively rebranded it as an element of British history, making it more suitable for the construction of a new historical narrative for the recently unified nation. As a tale of a martial but benevolent force bringing stability to the north, the invasions of Agricola and Severus fitted more easily into a Whiggish historiography in which a thread of political and social progress could be charted from the ancient to the modern state. Indeed, William Roy's *Military Antiquities* could be seen, just like the Latin inscriptions placed in the Highlands, as a piece of Hanoverian propaganda; it is certainly appropriate that it was published in London, rather than Edinburgh or Glasgow. Like Robert Sibbald before him, Roy saw the accurate surveying of a country as an act of 'great public utility'.[73] In looking forward to the pacification and prosperity of a new Britain, both men also looked back to the past. While his work finally revealed the topography of the wild and mysterious Highlands to enlightened southern audiences, Roy's inclusion of Roman sites in his maps also presented a satisfyingly progressive interpretation of the previously frustrating and muddled story of Roman Scotland. For those in power, his work helped to establish their hold on troublesome regions, and his interest in the similar endeavours of the Romans centuries before was perfectly apt. The notion of Roman Scotland as a military landscape, its history waiting to be uncovered using a combination of scholarship, fieldwork and military expertise, appealed not just to Melville, Roy and Shand, but also to an international audience. Signs of classical civility in Scotland might still be proving elusive, but evidence of Roman military prowess and power was now there for all to see.

This did not mean, however, that the debate over the true nature of Roman Scotland was over. In fact, the years following the last Jacobite rebellion saw a further polarisation in political interpretations of Scotland's ancient history as two new, apparently revelatory sources were uncovered, each offering completely different visions of the past. And while Tacitus' *Agricola* had played a key role in the research of the military antiquarians, it was also mined for more patriotically Scottish material by other antiquarians with distinctly different viewpoints. As the following chapters will reveal, the idea of a modern, stable British nation may have begun to settle into the national consciousness in the later decades of the eighteenth century, but the extent of ancient Britannia and the influence of Rome in Caledonia would remain as contentious as ever.

Notes

1. For a concise history of 'Highland separatism' pre-1707, see: Turnock, *The Historical Geography of Scotland Since 1707*, pp. 19–22.
2. Camden, *Britain*, Scotland, p. 5; NLS Adv.MS.33.5.16, f. 81: Sibbald, 'Discourses Anent the Improvements May Be Made in Scotland', 1698.
3. Defoe, *The History of the Union of Great Britain*, p. 2.
4. Chamberlayne, *Magnae Britanniae Notitia*, p. 356.
5. Gordon, *Itinerarium Septentrionale*, p. 67; Nichols, *Bibliotheca Topographica Britannica*, Vol. 3, p. 358; Brown, 'Modern Rome and Ancient Caledonia', p. 46.
6. On the pacification of the Highlands post-1745, see: Plank, *Rebellion and Savagery*, pp. 103–29.
7. Hingley, *The Recovery of Roman Britain*, p. 102.
8. Gough, *Britannia*, pp. 384–5.
9. Pennant's comparisons of the Roman and Hanoverian military campaigns in the north are discussed in: Constantine, 'Heart of Darkness: Thomas Pennant and Roman Britain'; Shaw, *The History of the Province of Moray*, p. 228.
10. Dio, *Roman History* 77.12.2–3.
11. Ashe Lee quoted in: Hingley, *The Recovery of Roman Britain*, p. 150.
12. Hingley, *Roman Officers and English Gentlemen*, p. 40.
13. SUL OA/5/5, ff. 23–4: Anderson, 'Of the Roman Wall Between the Forth and Clyde', c.1770.
14. Ibid. f. 53, referring to RIB 2193.

15. Burt, *Burt's Letters from the North of Scotland*, p. 3.
16. Balfour-Melville, 'A Biographical Sketch of General Robert Melville', pp. 122–3.
17. Gough, *Britannia*, p. 414*.
18. Balfour-Melville, 'A Biographical Sketch of General Robert Melville', p. 122.
19. NRS GD126/box 28: 'Agricola's Camps', f. 43.
20. Ibid. f. 9.
21. Ibid. ff. 8–9.
22. Ibid. f. 16.
23. Gough, *Britannia*, p. 416*; Stuart, 'Notice of Letters Addressed to Captain Shand', p. 30.
24. Gough, *Britannia*, p. 416* n. k.
25. NRS GD126/box 28: 'Agricola's Camps', f. 9.
26. Melville, *A Critical Enquiry into the Constitution of the Roman Legion*, p. vii.
27. Ibid. p. 28.
28. Ibid. p. 42; ibid. pp. 31–2.
29. Balfour-Melville, 'A Biographical Sketch of General Robert Melville', p. 122.
30. Cornish, 'Robert Melville', p. 788.
31. Stuart, 'Notice of Letters Addressed to Captain Shand', p. 30; Gough, *Britannia*, p. 417*.
32. MacDonald, 'General William Roy and his "Military Antiquities of the Romans in North Britain"', p. 163.
33. Baigent, 'William Roy', p. 50.
34. Roy, 'An Account of the Measurement of a Base on Hounslow Heath', pp. 385–6.
35. Hodson, 'William Roy and the Military Survey of Scotland', p. 7.
36. O'Donoghue, *William Roy, 1726–1790*, p. 3; Roy, 'An Account of the Measurement of a Base on Hounslow Heath', p. 386.
37. Hodson, 'William Roy and the Military Survey of Scotland', p. 10.
38. Roy, 'An Account of the Measurement of a Base on Hounslow Heath', pp. 386–7.
39. Roy, *Military Antiquities*, pp. iv–v.
40. RA Cumberland Papers Box 44/268. This plan of Netherby bath house was included as Plate 46 in Roy's *Military Antiquities*.
41. MacDonald, 'General William Roy and his "Military Antiquities of the Romans in North Britain"', p. 168.
42. Ibid. p. 171.
43. Roy, *Military Antiquities*, p. vi.
44. For the various possible dates that Roy joined up, see: MacDonald, 'General William Roy and his "Military Antiquities of the Romans in North Britain"', pp. 174–6.
45. Hodson, 'William Roy and the Military Survey of Scotland', p. 14.
46. *The Gentleman's Magazine*, p. 670. For more on this so-called King's Map, see: Gardiner, 'William Roy, Surveyor and Antiquary', pp. 442–3.
47. EUL MA Laing III.379, f. 1092: Melville to Thorkelin, 16 May 1792.
48. Roy, *Military Antiquities*, p. ii.
49. For Polybius' description of the structure of the Roman army and its camps, see: Polybius, *Histories* 6.19–42.
50. Stelten, 'Introduction', p. xiii.
51. For mentions of camps in Livy's writings, see: Livy, *Rome's Italian Wars* 10.32–33; also: Livy, *The Dawn of the Roman Empire* 34.46–7 and 40.27–28.
52. Christie's, *A Catalogue of a Select, Well-Chosen, Valuable Library of Books, Maps &c.*, p. 5; ibid. p. 7; ibid. p. 17; ibid. pp. 6–7.
53. Ibid. p. 7; ibid. p. 8.

54. Ibid. p. 18.
55. Roy, *Military Antiquities*, p. i.
56. Ibid. p. v.
57. Ibid. pp. ii–iii.
58. Ibid. p. iii; Gordon, *Itinerarium Septentrionale*, Preface.
59. Roy, *Military Antiquities*, p. 126. Also: ibid. p. 162.
60. Ibid. p. 92.
61. Sponberg Pedley, *The Commerce of Cartography*, p. 2.
62. MacDonald, 'General William Roy and his "Military Antiquities of the Romans in North Britain"', p. 179.
63. Withers, *Geography, Science and National Identity*, p. 142.
64. For more on Roy's place within a global trend for Enlightenment mapping, see: Withers, 'William Roy's World'.
65. Withers, *Geography, Science and National Identity*, p. 69.
66. Stuart, 'Notice of Letters Addressed to Captain Shand', p. 28.
67. PM 266, f. 14: Shand, 'Some Observations on the Great Roman Road and Adjacent Camps, and Stations to the North of Graemes Dyke', 1788.
68. Stuart, 'Notice of Letters Addressed to Captain Shand', p. 29.
69. EUL MS Laing III.379, ff. 1380–1: Shand to Thorkelin, 29 September 1790.
70. Stuart, 'Notice of Letters Addressed to Captain Shand', p. 28.
71. PM 266, f. 8: Shand, 'Some Observations on the Great Roman Road and Adjacent Camps, and Stations to the North of Graemes Dyke', 1788.
72. Hingley, *Hadrian's Wall*, p. 121; ibid. p. 124.
73. Roy, 'An Account of the Measurement of a Base on Hounslow Heath', p. 385.

7

The age of 'Agricolamania': early modern uses and abuses of Tacitus' *Agricola*

> ... that most valiant *Chieftain* of Great fame,
> Brave *Julius Agricola* by name.
> Henry Adamson, *The Muses Threnodie*, 1774, p. 86

Throughout the long-running and often acrimonious early modern debates regarding the historiography of Roman Scotland, one source dominated the discussion, namely the *Agricola* of Publius Cornelius Tacitus. This relatively short work, written around 98 CE and purporting to describe the life of the author's father-in-law Gnaeus Julius Agricola, was recognised by antiquarians as the most extensive primary source for events in first-century Britain, containing an account of the subjugation and civilisation of much of the island by its titular general. A large proportion of the text relates specifically to Roman exploits in what is now Scotland, and a comprehensive knowledge of it was vital for any eighteenth-century Scot who professed an interest in the nation's earliest history. As a result, it was translated, read and re-read, analysed, interpreted, misinterpreted and quoted endlessly by antiquarians seeking to substantiate their conjectures regarding the extent of Roman power in the north. Its protagonists became heroic figures to many, while the potential geographical locations of the incidents that it describes were scrutinised and deliberated ad nauseam.

Although some doubts about its accuracy and reliability were to emerge during this period, the *Agricola* was generally viewed as a factual record of historical figures and events. Tacitus himself was typically held in high regard, nominated an 'irrefragable Voucher of the *Scots* Antiquities' by Patrick Abercromby in his 1711 *Martial Atchievements of the Scots Nation* and referred to as the 'father' of Scottish history by John Pinkerton almost eight decades later.[1] The content of his first published work, with its often ambiguous language and its apparently contradictory impressions of Rome and its imperial ambitions, was examined for information relating to Scotland and often used as evidence for opposing (and patriotically and politically partisan) visions of ancient Caledonia. James Boswell and Dr Johnson were not alone in bemoaning the challenging nature of Tacitus' Latin, both agreeing that it was 'too compact, too much broken into hints, as it were, and therefore too difficult to be understood'; but for some commentators the very ambiguity of the text presented the potential for fanciful hypotheses, effectively rendering it more malleable to biased interpretations that were, thanks to the relative lack of other source material, difficult to refute.[2] That it told of a successful invasion culminating in a glorious Roman defeat of the Caledonians was problematic for many Scots, but, as we shall see, such men were not averse to cherry-picking its content for material more suitable to their patriotic visions of national heroism. Towards the end of the eighteenth century the conjectures relating to Agricola and his impact on Scotland were to sometimes verge on the ludicrous thanks to a combination of admiration for the man himself and a prevailing desire to locate evidence of Roman or Caledonian greatness. By the early nineteenth century this phenomenon, already identified as 'Agricolamania', was to become the subject of comic fiction, those suffering from it recognised as credulous, their proposals often based more on a desire for personal aggrandisement than any convincing historical evidence. This chapter will explore the early modern Scottish obsession with both *Agricola* the text and Agricola the man, demonstrating how the source's form and content allowed it to be manipulated and misrepresented by Scots determined to prove either that their native soil had been a settled part of the Roman Empire, or on the other hand that it had never been Roman at all.

The rediscovery and early reception of Tacitus' *Agricola*

For Scotland's early modern antiquarians, the survival of the *Agricola*, this shining light in the otherwise shadowy early history of their nation, was a stroke of incredible luck. While the construction of the Antonine Wall is mentioned in a single sentence of the *Historia Augusta* and the histories of Herodian and Dio both relate some limited detail on the third-century Severan invasion, Tacitus dedicated sixteen chapters of his text to the late first-century Roman military expeditions into Scotland. Perhaps most inspiring for Scots was his description of the great battle between Rome and Caledonia known in the eighteenth century as 'Mons Grampius' (now referred to as 'Mons Graupius' in accordance with a more recently discovered manuscript of the *Agricola*), as well as the two orations proceeding it given by the (otherwise unattested) Caledonian chief Calgacus and Agricola himself, each written in direct speech as if recorded verbatim.

That the *Agricola* survived into the eighteenth century at all is something of a miracle, all thanks to a single manuscript known as the Codex Hersfeldensis. Written around the middle of the ninth century and possibly held in the library of Hersfeld Abbey in Hesse, the book was rediscovered by Italian scholars on the hunt for classical texts in the fifteenth century. In late 1425 Gian Francesco Poggio Bracciolini received a report in Rome of this codex containing previously unknown works by Tacitus, news that generated great excitement in humanist circles. For reasons that remain unclear, it was seemingly thirty years before the codex, which contained the *Agricola*, the *Germania* and the *Dialogus de Oratoribus* by Tacitus as well as the *De Grammaticis et Rhetoribus* of Suetonius, made its way to Italy. After its arrival its fate becomes even more mysterious. The *Agricola* somehow became separated from the rest, perhaps sold when its owner failed to find a buyer for the complete book.[3] The whole codex was later lost, but the texts that it contained were transcribed before its disappearance and thus preserved for posterity.[4]

In the German-speaking states, scholars quickly recognised the potential of Tacitus' *Germania* for their own patriotic histories. Although the text's descriptions of the region's indigenous tribes contain both positive and negative attributes, the positives were promoted and the less admirable characteristics largely ignored in the works that cited it. Particularly welcomed by Germans was the notion of an uncorrupted racial heritage, its popularity inspiring early sixteenth-century humanist and Lutheran reformer Andreas Althamer to refer to the author fondly as 'our Tacitus'.[5] Between 1500 and 1650 more than twenty editions of the *Germania* were produced in central Europe and the patriotic myths that emerged from it were to endure (with sinister results) into the twentieth century, as Christopher Krebs demonstrates in his 2011 volume *A Most Dangerous Book*.[6]

The *Agricola* took longer to reach the attention of Scottish scholars, however, and its initial reception was more limited, perhaps lending some weight to persistent early modern claims that historical study in Scotland had been hindered by religious and political upheaval during this period (John Pinkerton for one blamed 'fanaticism', poverty and geographical remoteness).[7] As mentioned in the Introduction, Hector Boece certainly knew of the *Agricola* when he composed his 1527 *Historia Gentis Scotorum*. He was also rather free with his interpretation of Tacitus' text, giving the events it describes spurious geographical locations in Scotland and significantly increasing the number of deaths (claiming 12,000 Romans and 20,000 Caledonians lost compared to 360 Romans and 10,000 Caledonians in Tacitus) during the battle at Mons Graupius.[8] While the famous pre-battle speeches by Agricola and Calgacus are included in full, as previously noted, Boece also added a new sequel in which Calgacus wins back the lands lost to the Romans. George Buchanan also includes information from the *Agricola* in his *Rerum Scoticarum Historia*, completed just before his death and published in 1582, but treats it more briefly, running through it in less than two pages and sticking faithfully to the original before including Boece's fictional claims of a Caledonian resurgence following the departure of Agricola from Scotland.⁹ Published in Paris in 1599, Justus Lipsius' two volume collection of the works of Tacitus with associated essays included a commentary on the *Agricola* by his pupil William Barclay (c.1570–c.1627), a Banffshire-born writer and Latin poet whose Catholic faith forced him to spend much of his life on mainland Europe. While he was highly regarded by Lipsius, Barclay's analysis of Tacitus was not so appreciated by Scottish readers. Sibbald was shocked that he made no reference to Scotland other than noting his own place of birth, while English bishop and antiquarian William Nicolson records similar criticism of the commentary by Scottish historian Thomas Dempster, blaming Barclay's lack of accuracy on his long absence from his homeland.¹⁰

Even by the end of the seventeenth century Scottish scholarship on the *Agricola* was almost non-existent, an issue raised by Alexander Gordon in his 1726 *Itinerarium Septentrionale*, where he cited William Nicolson's claim 'That some have admir'd why so few of the learned Men of the Scotish nation have not given their Commentaries on the Life of Agricola, which is so full of what relates to the Antiquities of their Country'.¹¹ Although Gordon seems to suggest that it was his own book that would finally fill this lacuna, in fact he had already been beaten to it by his predecessor Sir Robert Sibbald, who discusses the Roman general in several of his manuscript and published works. Sibbald viewed Agricola as a heroic figure, the man who introduced civilisation and stability to Scotland, and he was not alone in this. In fact, the idea that Agricola laid the very foundations of the Scottish nation was one shared by antiquarians both north and south of the border.

Agricola the hero

The extensive writings of Sir Robert Sibbald reveal him to be a great admirer not only of Rome, but also of the Roman general Agricola. Several of his works endeavour to relate the events described in Tacitus' text with the early modern Scottish landscape; indeed, the *Agricola* takes first place in the list of sources that Sibbald used while researching his *Historical Inquiries, Concerning the Roman Monuments and Antiquities in the North Part of Britain Called Scotland*, in which he describes it, alongside the works of Herodian, Dio and Ammianus Marcellinus, as the 'best Help we have for discovering the *Roman* Monuments in this Country'.¹²

Sibbald's opinion of the *Agricola* and its main protagonist altered over time as his familiarity with both the text and the topography of Scotland increased. An early manuscript, which appears to relate to the unpublished *Scotish Atlas*, contains a brief account of the Romans in Scotland and includes details of Agricola's endeavours in the region. Although Sibbald cites Tacitus in the margins, the content of the body text is largely conjectural, aiming to plot the Roman advance in the Scottish landscape using evidence of surviving sites and artefact findspots.[13] He proposes here that the Roman 'town' at Camelon was founded by Agricola and also attributes the nearby Arthur's O'on to him, suggesting that the Romans habitually 'planted new Colonies in ye New Conquest Lands'.[14] At this point he remained unsure about how far north Agricola had actually reached, and does not commit to a definite location for the battle of Mons Graupius, although he did believe that it must have taken place somewhere near Ardoch, stating (erroneously) that Tacitus describes a post-victory march to the nearby river *Taus*, which Sibbald identifies as the Tay.[15] In this essay Sibbald mentions no retreat from the north following Agricola's departure, but instead jumps from the general's exploration of the northern extremities of Britain to the reign of Septimius Severus, when the Romans 'lost ground more and more', also proposing (surely inspired by George Buchanan, who makes a similar error) that it was this emperor who then built the wall in Scotland now attributed to Antoninus Pius. In doing so, he appears to suggest that most of Scotland was under Roman control for over a century, with only 'the Highlanders Country being untouched by ym'.[16]

Sibbald's growing interest in Agricola would lead to further research over the following years. A letter sent by him to Hans Sloane in late 1698 reveals that he had already prepared for printing some dissertations on the *Agricola* illustrated with 'Mapps and Tables', which placed the incursions securely within a Scottish geographical context by cross-referencing the text with surviving material remains such as coins, inscriptions and monuments.[17] William Nicolson's *Scottish Historical Library* of 1702 records that Sibbald had composed a manuscript essay compiling all of the information on ancient Britain contained in the writings of Tacitus, and yet another manuscript notebook, which appears to date to the last two decades of the seventeenth century, contains a tract dedicated to Agricola's fourth campaign.[18] At the opening of this (probably incomplete) essay the author states that his intention is to 'comment upon that [fourth expedition] and to illustrate it from the Roman inscriptions and other monuments that are found yn it [Scotland] and from theme to gather as much as may be for demonstrating the Antiquity of the Scotish nation: and our ancient possession of yt part of the country'.[19] While he may not achieve such grand ambitions here, this rather rambling and conjectural text does suggest that Sibbald viewed the *Agricola* as a valuable source not just for Roman exploits in the north, but also for the condition and territories of the indigenous tribes and thus the provenance of the early modern inhabitants of Scotland.

In his later publications it becomes clear that Sibbald's notion of a strong and enduring Roman presence in Scotland is based largely upon the content of the twenty-first chapter of Tacitus' *Agricola*, which he quotes in full in both Latin and English at the beginning of his 1707 *Historical Inquiries*. This famous, much quoted chapter describes how Agricola subdued the inhabitants of Britain by introducing Roman manners, dress and architecture to the island:

> *adiuvare publice ut templa fora domos extruerent . . . iam vero principum filios liberalibus artibus erudire . . . ut qui modo linguam Romanam abnuebant, eloquentiam concupiscerent. Inde etiam habitus nostri honor et frequens toga; paulatimque discessum ad delenimenta vitiorum, porticus et balineas et conviviorum elegantiam.*

This was (liberally) translated by Sibbald as:

> he openly assisted them to build temples, Courts of Justice, and Places for Assemblies, Houses and Cities, where they might live in Societies . . . then he took Pains to instruct the Sons of the Nobles and chiefest Men in the Liberal Sciences and Arts . . . So that they, who a little before that refused to learn the *Roman* Language, became now desirous to speak it Elegantly, and came to love their Habit, and used much the Gown, and so by degrees they yielded to the soft Pleasures of Vice, building Sumptuous Galleries and Baths, and making costly Feasts and fine Intertainments.[20]

While this section of the *Agricola* had already been employed by English seventeenth-century antiquarians such as John Clapham and William Burton to demonstrate the Roman roots of their nation, the idea that it also referred to Scotland was new.[21] Rather inconveniently for Sibbald, it appears in the text well before Tacitus recounts Agricola's invasion of Scotland. This, however, was to prove no impediment to a man determined to demonstrate the existence of a truly classical Caledonia. Sibbald convinced himself that the general's civilising project must have extended into the north, stating that 'through these cunning ways, and the good Order he had settled amongst the Officers under him, many of the South *Picts*, who lived upon this side of the Firth of *Forth* and *Clyd*, came to be under the *Roman* Province'.[22]

The heroic exploits of Agricola also earn mentions in Sibbald's *History, Ancient and Modern, of the Sherrifdoms of Fife and Kinross* and his *History, Ancient and Modern, of the Sherrifdoms of Linlithgow and Stirling*, both published in 1710. Despite it today being recognised as a region with little evidence of Roman activity, it is in his history of Fife that Sibbald emphasises how the surviving material remains demonstrated Agricola's intentions:

> Without doubt, After-times may discover in this Shire, and in other Parts of North *Britain*, many *Roman* Antiquities, when Curious Persons will search for them: for *Tacitus* telleth us, that it was one of the Means that *Agricola* used to Tame the *Britains*, that he privately exhorted and publickly joined with them to Build Temples, Houses, Seats of Justice; and by degrees brought them to erect *Portico*'s and *Baths*.[23]

In his 1711 tract on the supposedly Roman sites around the south-eastern coast of Scotland Sibbald takes inspiration from *Agricola* 20.2, which states that the general explored the estuaries and shrewdly chose his own sites for camps, and the antiquarian refers on two occasions to Agricola's ability to locate the best harbours.[24] He also stresses the importance of these supposedly Agricolan sites for later Scottish history, proposing that royal seats such as St Andrews, Dunfermline and Kinghorn were built on the location of Roman fortifications and similarly highlighting the importance of Inverkeithing, 'which in *Agricola's* time, 'tis like was a very convenient Harbour, and had such Vestiges of *Roman* Forts upon the Brink of it, as made our Kings choose it for one of their principal Seats, and build a town of large extent there'.[25] Also in 1711 Sibbald finally published a Latin essay on Agricola's Scottish expeditions entitled *Commentarius in Julii Agricolae Expeditiones 3.4.5.6.7*, which, although it lacked the maps and plans he had earlier promised Sloane, certainly consolidated many of his previous conjectures.

Although he seems to have had a limited knowledge of Sibbald's published works, William Stukeley's favourable impression of Agricola is not dissimilar to that of his Scottish predecessor. He makes similar reference to the 'wise' general's skill in locating the best places for forts and garrisons and proposes that he fortified the Forth/Clyde isthmus in order to separate the barbarous northerners from those to the south who had adopted the Roman way of life. The Agricolan invasion was, he believed, a monumental moment in Scotland's history, describing it as 'this warlike and glorious Peoples conquests over the Caledonian Britons'.[26] Stukeley also concluded that the foundation of many of Scotland's major towns could be attributed to Agricola:

> He laid the Foundation, in all Probability, of those Cities or defensible places hereabouts, mention'd in the *Annotations to Camden's Britannia*, publish'd by the present Bishop of *Lincoln*, 1695, p.957 [such as Camelon, Stirling, Kirkintilloch, Paisley and Dumbarton], continuing nevertheless to advance his victorious Arms still further into the Country Northward, as Occasion offer'd, where many Cities, Camps and Military Ways occur.[27]

As will be revealed in the next chapter, Stukeley's admiration for Agricola also lead him to claim that he had identified the Roman general's lost memoirs, although this apparently sensational new source would later turn out to be not what it had at first appeared.

Back in Scotland, Agricola was to become something of a Whig icon. He was admired by Sir John Clerk, an establishment figure and commissioner for the Union who took the pseudonym 'Agricola' in Stukeley's society of *Equites Romani*, as commemorated in a charming coin-style portrait sketched by Stukeley himself that is now in the collection of the Bodleian Library (Figure 7.1). As the previous chapter demonstrated, Hanoverian soldiers such as Melville, Roy and Shand spent much of their leisure time tracing Agricola's footsteps, studying

Figure 7.1 Portrait of Sir John Clerk as 'Agricola', ink on paper by William Stukeley, 1727. (© The Bodleian Library, University of Oxford: Bodl.MS.Eng.misc.e.136, f. 89 recto)

Tacitus and comparing his text with material remains as they went. This ancient narrative of an invading empire subduing native peoples with civility fitted well with the early modern Whiggish interest in the progress of man from savagery to civilisation.

One of the most popular translations of the *Agricola* during the eighteenth century was that produced by Scottish scholar Thomas Gordon in 1731. Born in Kirkcudbright and possibly educated at Aberdeen University, Gordon became famous for his Whiggish political writings, which would have a profound impact across Europe and America. His two-volume *Works of Tacitus* (the volume containing the *Agricola* dedicated to the Prince of Wales) also included a political discourse on the Roman author's oeuvre. While the *Agricola* offered less potential for political analysis than the *Histories* or the *Annals* with their tales of cruel dictators and unstable regimes, or even the *Germania* with its portrayal of political and social liberty amongst ancient tribes, it did offer some scope for interpretation. Herbert Benario, for example, suggests that the choice to translate the word *imperium* in the speech of Calgacus as 'government' was an unusual one made to support Gordon's own theories on the potential powers of the state.[28] Sir John Clerk was apparently impressed with Gordon's approach, noting after a meeting with him at the London home of John Campbell, 2nd Duke of Argyll, that he was a 'jolly man full of vivacity & vanity as appears in all his writtings but particularly his political observations on Tacitus'.[29] The 1763 Glasgow printing in octavo of Gordon's translation was the first publication of the *Agricola* as a stand-alone text in Scotland. This posthumous production (Gordon had died in 1750) was perfectly timed to take advantage of a surge in interest in the work. Its dedication to the (by now also deceased) Duke of Argyll, a committed supporter of both the Union and the Hanoverian regime who had taken an active role in supressing the 1715 Jacobite uprising, compares him to the Roman general, describing Agricola (and by implication Argyll) as 'that polite and most accomplished Patrician, that Great Commander, great Statesman and, which is above all, that Great Honest Man'.[30]

Agricola the enemy

While arch-Romanists Sibbald and Stukeley were confirmed devotees of the Roman general, both confident that his civilising spirit had left its mark on Scotland's landscape and society, others were not so favourable, particularly those of an anti-unionist persuasion. In his *Martial Atchievements of the Scots Nation* of 1711 Patrick Abercromby paraphrases that twenty-first chapter of Tacitus' *Agricola*, which relates his efforts to subdue the natives with Roman ways, before stating defiantly that 'the *Northern-Britains*, I mean the *Scots* and the *Picts*, were not to be Tam'd by those Methods'.[31] Like many of the Scots who were to follow, Abercromby was much more interested in Agricola's opponent, the courageous Calgacus. Taking his cue from Boece and Buchanan he portrayed the Caledonian chieftain as a fearless resister of Roman rule, part of an extended family of indefatigable freedom-fighters. Calgacus' heroic reputation is emphasised here by the inclusion of an excerpt from a poem by eminent Scottish Latinist Arthur Johnston (c.1579–1641), which ends with the claim that '*Nemo armis major, consiliisque prior*' (Noone was greater in arms, or superior in judgements).[32]

Fierce patriot Alexander Gordon was predictably ambivalent towards Agricola; this was, after all, the man who took the pseudonym 'Galgacus' on joining Stukeley's *Equites Romani*. Throughout his *Itinerarium Septentrionale* Gordon downplays the Roman victory at Mons Graupius and focuses instead on the evidence of Caledonian bravery that the *Agricola* contains. Like Sibbald,

Gordon was determined to pinpoint the geographical locations of the *Agricola*'s key events. Indeed, in the proposal for the *Itinerarium* he promised a whole essay dedicated to locating Mons Graupius, although in the completed book the subject is accorded just part of a longer chapter on the Roman general's invasion.[33] But unlike Sibbald, Gordon had actually put in the necessary legwork required to locate Roman sites all over Scotland, embarking on an extensive tour in 1723 for that very purpose. Perhaps against his better judgment, he did admit to some signs of Agricola's bid to bring Roman civility to the north, attributing Arthur's O'on to him: 'it seems most natural to conclude, that this Building of *Arthur's Oven* is the very temple, or one of them, mention'd by *Tacitus* to have been made by *Agricola* in that part of *Britain*'.[34] The ruins of Camelon, he surmised, 'confirm the truth of Tacitus', and although he could not be sure where the 'Galleries and Bagnios' mentioned in the *Agricola* were, the arches and lead pipes apparently found at Camelon appeared to show that it once contained sumptuous baths. Gordon also suggested that the extensive ruins and terraces he found at 'Coudon' (Cowden Hill at Bonnybridge) might have been a settlement established by Agricola, citing the 'visible Marks of *Roman* Grandeur' to be found there.[35]

Gordon found much to admire in the exhilarating speech given by Calgacus in the moments before he faced the Roman army in battle, with its valiant call to defy foreign oppression and protect Caledonian liberty, even to the death. As already noted in Chapter 2, Gordon's assumption that it was a true record of a real speech was scorned by his patron Sir John Clerk, who correctly viewed it as a piece of writing more literary than historical. Even Patrick Abercromby had been forced to admit that, although Calgacus was undoubtedly a hero, his speech had probably been tidied up by Tacitus to render it more elegant.[36] Gordon, however, was not to be dissuaded from citing such a rousing call to arms, one which reflected so many of his own attitudes towards Scotland's present situation. It was, he proclaimed, 'such a Strain of Patriotism and Love of Liberty, that *Tacitus* has not neglected to give his Speech Word for Word', adding that Justus Lipsius had declared it the greatest example of Latin eloquence.[37] Gordon was wont to quote it here and there, inserting a key phrase into a letter to Sir John Clerk in which he praised his patron's scholarship: 'blessed be God by this been able to shew the English what kind of men of Learning Caledonia has yet reserved for her self as Galgacus said *quos tibi Caledonia viros seposuerit*'.[38] In 1732 he quotes the speech again, this time in the Dedication at the beginning of his *Additions and Corrections*, when he identifies the Romans as '*Raptores Orbis*, The *Plunderers of the World*'.[39]

Even foreigners recognised the patriotic potential of this speech, or at least hoped to curry Scottish favour with it. In November 1732 the Irish poet Samuel Boyse, then resident in Edinburgh and actively seeking patronage, wrote to Sir

John Clerk to praise his poem *The Country Seat* and offer his own translation of Calgacus' address in (rather laboured) heroic couplets, which opens as follows:

> When round this Camp I cast my ravishd Eyes,
> And view the glorious cause for which we rise;
> Methinks, my Freinds, the happy day is come,
> To stop the Progress of usurping Rome![40]

If this work was supposed to convince the Baron that he should provide a regular stipend to the struggling poet then it seems to have proved unsuccessful, as Boyse's increasingly desperate letters (including one that unsubtly expresses his desire to be employed in the service of 'some man of quality who lov'd letters') were to continue until early 1734.[41] He was later forced by his debts to leave Scotland altogether. A slightly different version of his translation of Calgacus' speech would be published in London (alongside two poems dedicated to Clerk) in his 1738 *Translations and Poems, Written on Several Occasions*, but Boyse, like Calgacus, was doomed to failure, dying in abject poverty in 1749.

Later in the century the speech was used to demonstrate the Latin skills (and no doubt also stir up the patriotic spirits) of Edinburgh's schoolboys: a report in *The Edinburgh Evening Courant* of 16 August 1780 records the performance during a school inspection of the 'elegant speech of Galgacus, the Caledonian Chief, to his soldiers, before they engaged the Romans at the Grampian Hills' by the Dux of Canongate High School, which was 'received with universal applause'.

Agricolamania

The intense focus of Scottish antiquarians on a single ancient source, a text that promised much but often delivered only hints and clues, together with the lionisation of two of its (opposing) protagonists, inevitably led to some conjectures and conclusions that pushed beyond the bounds of reason and into the realms of fantasy. Throughout the eighteenth century we see the desire of Scots to locate Agricolan history in their own locality or even to own mementoes of it. Robert Sibbald placed the major events of the invasion in Fife, where he had many family connections, and also incorrectly attributed inscribed stones in his collection to the period of the campaigns, while Robert Barclay wrote to the Earl of Buchan to inform him that the battle actually occurred on his estate at Urie in a letter published in the 1792 *Archaeologia Scotica*.[42] Folklore and spurious etymology also played their part. Gordon's favoured site for Mons Graupius was based upon his understanding that a Perthshire moor was known locally as 'Galgachan Ross', its name supposedly recalling that of the Caledonian chieftain who once fought there, a notion that Horsley properly dismissed as a mishearing of 'Dalgin

Ross'; James Playfair, minister at Bendochy in Perthshire, claimed it for nearby Stormont, since 'stour' was Scots for a struggle or battle.[43] Numerous other theories regarding the field of Agricola's final battle were presented stretching from Ardoch in Perthshire to the top of north-eastern Aberdeenshire, suggestions including Comrie, Stonehaven, Blairgowrie and Fortingall (a place also identified as the birthplace of Pontius Pilate, with medieval earthworks there assumed by many antiquarians to be Roman). Anywhere with evidence of old ditches, a standing stone or some burial mounds, or even better all three, could be nominated a potential Mons Graupius. The popularity of such speculations did not go unnoticed: French cartographer Louis de la Rochette was aware of 'une idolatrie qui lui fait attribuer la plupart des travaux militaires dans les parties reculeés' (an idolatry that results in the attribution to him [Agricola] of most of the military works in the further regions), while in 1789 John Pinkerton indignantly recorded the tendency of 'infantine Scotish antiquists' to claim everything Roman as Agricolan.[44] The term 'Agricolamania' was in use by 1796, when it was employed by David Macpherson to characterise the Scottish fascination with Agricola and its negative impact on objective historical research.[45] For some Scottish antiquarians there was a compulsion not just to make sense of Tacitus' text, but also to bring it back to life by finding the visible remains of the notable events that it describes, events that many believed had shaped the very beginnings of the nation.

The widely read (and also heavily criticised) *History and Antiquities of Scotland* published by William Maitland in 1757 contains much material on the history and geography of Roman Scotland. Although largely reliant on previous scholarship such as that of Gordon and Horsley, Maitland himself had spent some time studying Roman remains, writing to Sir John Clerk in 1742 of his successful search for ancient sites north of the Tay.[46] Perhaps the most striking example of the author's admiration for the classical world is his claim that the existence of a rocky outcrop in the ditch of the Antonine Wall at Croy Hill was proof that stone could 'vegetate'; that the Roman engineers and builders had been unable or unwilling to remove it was simply unthinkable.[47] The author's veneration of Agricola is also frequently apparent. The Agricolan conquest is referred to as 'the most memorable expedition that had ever been known in Britain' and, like Sibbald, Maitland repeatedly presents the twenty-first chapter of Tacitus as evidence of Roman civilisation in Scotland.[48] Camelon is identified as a large Roman *oppidum*, Middleby is described as a Roman 'town of great note' and Cramond is labelled 'one of the most considerable Roman towns in Scotland'.[49] Maitland also speculated that a Roman bath house discovered (and, he believed, subsequently destroyed) at Inchtuthil in Perthshire was one of those *balinea* mentioned by Tacitus, proposing that this was the site of another Roman town.[50] He was confident that the civilising effect of Agricola had been felt even in the Highlands, claiming that the Gaelic spoken in the region included a number of

Latin words and phrases and that Highland dress was a direct descendant of the Roman toga.[51] Later in the book he also asserted that a comparison of traditional Highland attire with the drapery of Roman sculptures proved his point, adding that the bonnet of a modern Highlander had evolved from the Roman *pileus*.[52] He had obviously been considering this idea for some time, having asked Sir John Clerk in that 1742 letter for his opinion 'concerning some parts of the Highland dress and arms . . . which of them you take to be Roman'.[53] Clerk's response is now unfortunately lost, although he clearly discussed the correspondence with Roger Gale, who declared himself disappointed with Maitland's 1739 *History of London* but remained hopeful (mistakenly, as it turned out) that he might yet prove to be 'a second Camden'.[54]

A tradition existed at this time amongst the inhabitants of Perth that Agricola and his troops had reacted to their first sight of the location of the town, which sits on a plain by the river Tay, by exclaiming '*Ecce Tiber, ecce Campus Martius*' (behold the Tiber, behold the Field of Mars). Readers of Tacitus will fail to find any such exclamation in his text, and it does not appear in any medieval or Renaissance histories, but in 1899 James MacDonald traced it back to a mid-seventeenth-century poem by Perth native Henry Adamson entitled *The Muses Threnodie*.[55] By the eighteenth century Adamson was remembered chiefly as a classical scholar who wrote decent Latin verse; this poem (in English) relates the history and antiquities of his home town. Its fabulous account of Roman activity in the area includes claims that, when the Romans arrived on the plain, 'Incontinent they *campus Martius cry*', and that Agricola constructed a fortified wooden bridge across the Tay before rebuilding and rededicating a Caledonian temple and planning a new settlement inspired by Rome itself:

> Thus fortified, lest that they should neglect,
> Due honour to their gods they did erect,
> To *Mars* a temple, rather did restore
> The temple built by Cunidad before.
> For time on all things worketh demolition,
> And heathen men maintaine like superstition.
> Then did this valiant chieftaine name the river
> In *Italies* remembrance *New Tiber*,
> Which afterwards it kept for many a day,
> How long I know not. Now 'tis called *Tay*,
> Likewise an house of mighty stone he framed,
> From when our *Castle-gavil* as yet is named,
> And if *Domitian* had not call'd him home,
> I think he should have built another *Rome*.[56]

That the Romans proclaimed '*Ecce Tiberim*' on encountering the Tay is mentioned in Thomas Pennant's first *Tour in Scotland*, which relates his travels in

1769, but MacDonald attributes the transfer of such ideas from recognised fiction to supposed historical fact to a new edition of *The Muses Threnodie* that appeared in 1774.[57] Although its editor, Dunkeld bookseller James Cant, who also prefaced the poem with his own history of Perth, dismissed its account of the town's Roman heritage as 'poetical fable', it is after this publication that the romantic notion becomes more concrete.[58] Local minister James Scott's contribution to the *Statistical Account of Scotland* on the history of the town contains the assertion that the Romans 'cried out with one consent, Ecce Tiber! Ecce Campus Martius!' on their arrival, with the *Guide to the City and County of Perth* of 1805 noting how the spot 'excited the admiration of the Romans, who in this scenery saw the Tiber, the field of Mars, and the Apennine mountains again stretched out before them'.[59] The story would be repeated (often as factual) in publications of all sorts throughout the nineteenth century. Elsewhere, de la Rochette records another local legend that the troops who fought with Agricola at Mons Graupius were the same ones who sacked Jerusalem in 70 CE, only to point out that the records of the legions stationed in Britain ('Angleterre') prove that this could not in fact have been the case.[60]

While James Cant may have highlighted the improbability of Henry Adamson's claims regarding the Roman heritage of Perth, he was not immune to bouts of Agricolamania himself. In one of the many footnotes that he added to his edition of *The Muses Threnodie* he relates the discovery of two ash-filled urns on the banks of the River Almond in Perthshire. After giving a brief summary of the incidents described in the *Agricola*, including the deaths of Agricola's own son and his captain Aulus Atticus during the Caledonian campaigns, and speculating (correctly) that a Roman fort probably stood at nearby Bertha, Cant conjectures on the contents of these urns:

> It is not improbable that the large *plated urn* found at *Bertha* might be the repository of the ashes of *Agricola*'s *son*, and that the *urn* in which we saw the *lachrymatory* might contain the ashes of *Atticus*, who would be interr'd with military honours.[61]

Cant's ambitious claim even makes its way into Richard Gough's 1789 edition of Camden's *Britannia*, although a note of scepticism can perhaps be detected here:

> He supposes Bertha was a Roman castellum, and this the burying-ground, that Agricola lost his infant in the seventh summer of his command here-abouts, and that the large plated urn contained his ashes, and the other those of Aulus Atticus praefect of a cohort slain in the battle with Galgacus.[62]

The fanciful nature of such Agricolamaniac conjecture was even mined for its comic potential. Jonathan Oldbuck, the lead character in Walter Scott's *The Antiquary*, is evidently a man who displays all the symptoms of Agricolamania. The earthworks on his estate that he proudly shows off to a young visitor named

Lovel, for example, are identified by him not just as an Agricolan camp, but also as proof that Mons Graupius must have taken place nearby. Laughable etymology and a dubious inscription are presented as evidence and Oldbuck confirms his intention to publish an essay on his discovery, pointing out that it had escaped the notice of Sibbald, Gordon, Stukeley and Roy. That these ditches are then exposed by the local mendicant as having been dug within living memory leaves Oldbuck embarrassed but reluctant to abandon his conjectures.[63] In a later episode the eccentric antiquarian tries to convince his protégé to compose an epic patriotic poem describing the battle between Agricola and the Caledonians. 'The Caldedoniad; or Invasion Repelled – Let that be the title', announces Oldbuck, to which the young man points out that the Agricolan invasion was not in fact repelled. 'No; but you are a poet – free of the corporation, and as little bound down to truth or probability as Virgil himself', replies the antiquary. 'You may defeat the Romans in spite of Tacitus'.[64]

Even today, the *Agricola* of Tacitus divides scholars of ancient Scottish history and is viewed differently by historians, classicists and archaeologists.[65] Archaeological discoveries have called into question the idea that Agricola was the first Roman to lead an army into the north, and hints have also been found in other literary sources of earlier Caledonian expeditions.[66] By its very nature it is a text that lends itself to various interpretations, filled as it is with contradictions, paradoxes and ambiguities: Tacitus himself appears to criticise Roman imperial ambitions and, while the text is intended to eulogise Agricola, it also includes a heroic adversary in the form of Calgacus, who has recently been described as 'almost more Roman than the Romans themselves'.[67] Its description of Roman events in Scotland is cut short when Agricola leaves the region, giving no hints as to what followed there. Dylan Sailor sums up its problematic nature, explaining that '*Agricola* gives us important historical information, but its value has to be assessed in light of the work's literary and political functions . . . *Agricola* is not a history; it is a work whose purpose is precisely to fulfil a personal obligation to Agricola'.[68] Even more shocking to the Scottish antiquarians would be modern claims that Calgacus was nothing more than a fictional character created by Tacitus for dramatic effect.[69]

All of these problems and the questions that they raise, however, only enhanced the popularity of the *Agricola* amongst eighteenth-century Scots, allowing them to manipulate and misinterpret it to fit their own desires and expectations. Those who saw the Roman conquest of Scotland as a victory of civilisation over barbarism could isolate the parts that suited their agenda and ignore the more troublesome implication that such conquest actually constituted virtual slavery. Those who preferred to highlight the brave Caledonian resistance could also selectively cite the text, overlooking the resounding defeat of Calgacus to focus instead on his inspiring call to arms. For both, the perceived

Scottishness of the text was key: Patrick Abercromby roundly criticised two (unnamed) English writers who had dared suggest that the events it described had not actually taken place in Scotland at all.[70] A few more perceptive commentators expressed doubts as to its reliability. As we shall see in the following chapters, some, discomfited by his portrayal of Caledonian defeat, would even denounce Tacitus as biased and completely untrustworthy. But no matter what the author's stance might be, any study of Roman Scotland had to include an analysis of the *Agricola* and, despite its relative lack of geographical detail, antiquarians were fixated on relating it to the early modern landscape that they themselves inhabited. The more preposterous interpretations of the text exposed these antiquarians to ridicule, and mockery of their bizarre and unsubstantiated claims would only grow as the century neared its close. If, as will be proposed in the Conclusion of this book, Roman Scotland was to become increasingly sidelined in nineteenth-century conceptualisations of a noble Scottish past, then the Agricolamaniacs certainly must share some of the blame for its demise.

Notes

1. Abercromby, *The Martial Atchievements of the Scots Nation*, p. 8; Pinkerton, *An Enquiry into the History of Scotland*, p. 9.
2. Boswell, *The Life of Samuel Johnson*, p. 378.
3. Krebs, *A Most Dangerous Book*, p. 80.
4. For a detailed discussion of the rediscovery of the manuscript and dissemination of its content, see: Schaps, 'The Found and Lost Manuscripts of Tacitus' Agricola'.
5. Mellor, 'Introduction', p. xxiii.
6. Ibid. p. xxiv.
7. Pinkerton, *An Enquiry into the History of Scotland*, pp. xlv–xlvi.
8. Bellenden, *The Works of John Bellenden*, p. 154.
9. Buchanan, *The History of Scotland*, pp. 109–11.
10. Sibbald, *Commentarius in Julii Agricolae Expeditiones*, Praefatio; Nicolson, *The Scottish Historical Library*, p. 2.
11. Gordon, *Itinerarium Septentrionale*, Preface, quoting Nicolson, *The Scottish Historical Library*, p. 1.
12. Sibbald, *Historical Inquiries*, p. ii.
13. NLS Adv.MS.15.1.1, f. 5: Sibbald, 'Atlas Scoticus', c.1682.
14. Sibbald later attributed the construction of both Camelon and Arthur's O'on to Septimius Severus.
15. Agricola's arrival at the *Taus*, still generally accepted to be the Tay, is mentioned much earlier (*Agricola* 22.1) in the narrative.
16. NLS Adv.MS.15.1.1, f. 5: Sibbald, 'Atlas Scoticus', c.1682.
17. BL Sloane MS 4037, f. 175: Sibbald to Sloane, 29 December 1698.
18. Nicolson, *The Scottish Historical Library*, p. 2.
19. NLS Adv.MS.33.3.26, f. 63: Sibbald, 'Ane Essay Upon Julius Agricola His Expeditions in Scotland Beginning at the Fourth He Made', undated.
20. Sibbald, *Historical Inquiries*, p. 2.

21. On Burton's portrayal of Roman civility in England, see: Hingley, *The Recovery of Roman Britain*, pp. 67–71.
22. Sibbald, *Historical Inquiries*, p. 2.
23. Sibbald, *The History, Ancient and Modern, of the Sheriffdoms of Fife and Kinross*, pp. 31–2.
24. Sibbald, *Conjectures Concerning the Roman Ports, Colonies, and Forts*, p. 2; ibid. p. 4.
25. Ibid. p. 7.
26. Stukeley, *An Account of a Roman Temple*, p. 3.
27. Ibid.
28. Benario, 'Gordon's Tacitus', p. 110.
29. NRS GD18/2110, f. 47: Clerk, 'Travels at Home'.
30. Gordon, *The Life of Agricola*, pp. 4–5.
31. Abercromby, *The Martial Atchievements of the Scots Nation*, p. 21.
32. Ibid. p. 55.
33. Gordon, *Proposals for . . . a Book, Intitled, Itinerarium Septentrionale*, p. 2.
34. Gordon, *Itinerarium Septentrionale*, p. 29.
35. Ibid. p. 23.
36. Abercromby, *The Martial Atchievements of the Scots Nation*, p. 51.
37. Gordon, *Itinerarium Septentrionale*, p. 37.
38. NRS GD18/5023/3/28: Gordon to Clerk, 29 January 1726. The Latin is from *Agricola* 31.4. The Loeb version reads '*quos sibi Caledonia viros seposuerit*' (those men that Caledonia has kept in reserve for her cause).
39. Gordon, *Additions and Corrections*, p. ii, quoting *Agricola* 30.4.
40. NRS GD18/4518(iv): Boyse to Clerk, 10 November 1732.
41. NRS GD18/4520: Boyse to Clerk, 24 May 1733.
42. Gibson, *Britannia*, p. 904; Barclay, 'On Agricola's Engagement with the Caledonians', p. 568. Sibbald's stones, now in the National Museum of Scotland (ref. X.FV 30, RIB 2313.), are actually part of a milestone dating to the Antonine period.
43. Gordon, *Itinerarium Septentrionale*, p. 40; Horsley, *Britannia Romana*, p. 44; Sinclair, *Statistical Account*, Vol. 19, p. 369.
44. NLS MS 3803, f. 17: de la Rochette, untitled notes; Pinkerton, *An Enquiry into the History of Scotland*, p. 222.
45. Macpherson, *Geographical Illustrations of Scottish History*, Mounth.
46. NRS GD18/5058: Maitland to Clerk, 1 October 1742.
47. Maitland, *The History and Antiquities of Scotland*, p. 176.
48. Ibid. p. 58.
49. Ibid. p. 173; ibid. p. 192; ibid. p. 203.
50. Ibid. p. 149; ibid. p. 199. For a discussion on how Maitland's supposed bath house may relate to modern discoveries on the site, see Pitts and St Joseph, *Inchtuthil*, p. 38.
51. Maitland, *The History and Antiquities of Scotland*, p. 80.
52. Ibid. pp. 149–50.
53. NRS GD18/5058: Maitland to Clerk, 1 October 1742.
54. NRS GD18/5030/88: Gale to Clerk, 26 December 1742.
55. MacDonald, 'The Origin and Growth of the Tradition, "Ecce Tiber! Ecce Campus Martius!"', p. 118.
56. Adamson, *The Muses Threnodie*, p. 87; ibid. p.89.
57. MacDonald, 'The Origin and Growth of the Tradition, "Ecce Tiber! Ecce Campus Martius!"', pp. 121–2.

58. Adamson, *The Muses Threnodie*, p. 89.
59. Sinclair, *Statistical Account*, Vol. 18, p. 493; *Guide to the City and County of Perth*, p. 3.
60. NLS MS 3803, f. 4: de la Rochette, untitled notes.
61. Adamson, *The Muses Threnodie*, p. 27.
62. Gough, *Britannia*, p. 399.
63. Scott, *The Antiquary*, pp. 40–7.
64. Ibid. pp. 134–5.
65. For a discussion of the differing modern attitudes towards the text, see Hoffman, 'Tacitus, Agricola and the Role of Literature in the Archaeology of the First Century AD', pp. 151–7.
66. Woolliscroft and Hoffmann, *Rome's First Frontier*, pp. 187–90.
67. Clarke, 'An Island Nation', p. 106.
68. Sailor, 'The Agricola', pp. 39–40.
69. Woolliscroft and Hoffmann, *Rome's First Frontier*, p. 217.
70. Abercromby, *The Martial Atchievements of the Scots Nation*, p. 51.

8

Forging a nation: the spurious histories of Charles Bertram and James Macpherson

> *Mundus vult decipi, ergo decipiatur.*
> (The world wants to be fooled, therefore
> let it be fooled.)
>
> J. B. Mencke, *De Charlataneria Eruditorum Declamationes Duae*, 1715, p. 119

As we have seen, early eighteenth-century antiquarian research into the Roman history of Scotland was dogged by contradictions and disagreements. Sir Robert Sibbald broke with tradition when he described the south of Scotland as a veritable Roman province, and not much later William Stukeley concocted a similar vision of the Scottish Lowlands dotted with the remains of classical culture. In 1726, however, Alexander Gordon denounced such ideas in favour of an indomitable Caledonia that the Romans had tried but ultimately failed to conquer, and while English antiquarian John Horsley agreed with the proposal that Scotland had largely remained outside of Roman control, the reasons he gave were far less flattering to the Scots. Despite such assertions, some commentators, no doubt swayed by the 'high idea which is commonly entertained of Roman greatness' later described by John Anderson, continued to search for the remains of Rome in the north, intent on discovering evidence of a truly classical Caledonia.

Then, between 1747 and 1763, two new sources emerged that both appeared to shed dramatic new light on the history and geography of Roman Scotland. But rather than bring a conclusion to the ongoing disputes surrounding the nation's distant past, these sources, each of which presented a radically different impression of ancient Caledonia, only served to confuse matters further. It was William Stukeley who brought the first of these sources, an apparently medieval manuscript discovered in Denmark, to the attention of Britain's antiquarians; no doubt he would have been pleased to find that it not only proved many of his earlier conjectures correct, but also demonstrated that almost all of Scotland had once been part of the mighty Roman Empire. Just over a decade later a cycle of ancient Gaelic poems was unearthed that would lead many of its readers to reassess their previous ideas of the indigenous Caledonian tribes who had faced the invading Romans, and once again the reception of Roman Scotland was turned upon its head. The impact of these two texts on Scotland's historiography was to be both far reaching and enduring, the latter in particular altering the way in which Scots viewed themselves and their historic nation for ever. That both texts were also largely bogus, consisting of elements from other sources stapled together with elements of pure fantasy, makes their composition, dissemination and influence all the more intriguing.

Charles Bertram and the *De Situ Britanniae*

The continuing early modern arguments regarding the true nature of Roman Scotland can be blamed partly on the relative paucity of ancient literary evidence available to the antiquarians. As the previous chapter demonstrated, the *Agricola* of Tacitus was the most comprehensive documentary source to hand, and as a result it was examined, analysed, and discussed exhaustively; but it was also a text notable for its ambiguities and lacunae that offered the potential for various contradictory interpretations. The *Roman History* of Cassius Dio was useful for the material that it included on the Severan invasion, but it contained little in the way of geographical information. Scottish scholars also spent much time poring over the Antonine Itinerary, the Ptolemy map, the *Notitia Dignitatum*, the Ravenna Cosmography and the *Tabula Peutingeriana*, but these also had their drawbacks. As Sibbald pointed out, the Antonine Itinerary was created after the Romans had abandoned Scotland, while William Roy held similar reservations about the *Notitia Dignitatum*, also viewing the *Tabula Peutingeriana* as 'incomplete' and the Ravenna Cosmography as 'confused'.[1] Given the limited and imprecise information contained in all of these sources, the conclusions that the antiquarians reached from studying them were often starkly different.

A plausible solution to this problem appeared in 1747, when William Stukeley received a letter (dated the previous year) from a stranger named Charles Julius Bertram, a young expatriate in Copenhagen employed as an English tutor at the Royal Marine Academy who was also a budding antiquarian. Bertram hoped to strike up a correspondence with Stukeley and introduced himself in suitably florid and sycophantic style: '*Nemo sine crimine vivit*, says the great Horace; and mine is to love Antiquities, a fault which in itself would easily have been pardoned, by You Great Sir who has made yourself so beloved, by the cultivating them'.[2] He declared himself a great admirer of Stukeley's *Itinerarium Curiosum* and wondered if his own knowledge of 'Northern tongues' might be useful for the preparation of the antiquarian's planned (but never published) history of the Celts. This letter was clearly received favourably in Stamford, and a reply was sent by Stukeley on 12 June that same year.

Bertram wrote again full of thanks and expressed his sadness at the loss of Arthur's O'on, nominating its destroyer Sir Michael Bruce an 'ignorant mean Wretch'.³ Towards the end of this letter he casually mentioned that he had recently acquired a copy of an 'old manuscript fragment' entitled *Richardi Monachi Westmonasteriensis Comentariolum Geographicum de Situ Britanniae & Stationum quas Romani ipsi in ea Insula Aedificaverunt* (A geographical description of the places of Britain and the stations that the Romans themselves built in that island by Richard, Monk of Westminster). Bertram wondered whether Stukeley was aware of copies of it in England and seemed keen to find out what the renowned antiquarian's opinions on it might be.

Stukeley replied enthusiastically, already declaring the said manuscript to be 'a Cimelium & Great curiosity' and advising that it should be printed.⁴ Bertram's next letter included a report on Scandinavian antiquities with descriptions and sketches of burial mounds and associated artefacts, but again towards the end of the missive he returned to the subject of his mysterious manuscript, quoting a short section to give Stukeley a taste of the author's writing style. Finally, in his postscript, Bertram included some tantalising hints regarding its content, focusing exclusively on what it said about Roman Scotland and placing it in the context of recent scholarship on the subject:

> I have perused Mr Gordon's Iter Septentrionale with great delight: it is well wrote, &, tho I cannot agree with his opinion at all times, believe good use may be made of him in illustrating the Monk of Westminster. I could wish I were acquainted with him, that I might enquire some things concerning Scotland, beyond the Tay, the Monk placing several stations there & makes the Roman roads to run as far as the Varar Aestuary [Moray Firth], tho hitherto none, that I have heard of, have discovered any vestigia in those parts.⁵

At this point the letters from Stukeley stopped (perhaps, as Piggott suggests, due to his move from Stamford to London in early 1748); two short notes from Denmark that followed seem to have met with no response, but a longer letter sent by Bertram in August 1748 rekindled the relationship.⁶ Apparently assuming that his previous letter had been lost in transit, Bertram summarised its content, again concentrating on new information regarding ancient Scotland but this time revealing even more specific detail:

> at the end I observed, that he not only places many Stations north of Bodotria [the Firth of Forth] but also makes the military rout stretch to the very Mouth of the River Varar [the Moray Firth], where he places the Metropolis of Vespasiana Πτερωτον the same as is commonly called Castra Alata, and generally, tho' falsely, ascribed to Edenburg; this is so much the more curious, seeing all I have hitherto read give no Account of the Roman Roads stretching farther North than Perth; nay Mr. Gordon (at the end of his Iter Sept.) seem's positively to affirm, tho' I hope too hastily, they

extended no farther. If I might be indulged my conjecture, I should think the present Road leading from Perth, by Dunkeld, Blair and Fort Augustus, either to be the Roman Road reedify'd, or that upon strict scrutiny One would be found not far off; Reason seeming to indicate the Romans had a station not far from that said Fort. The like I should think of that running from Nairn by Forres, Elgin, Banf, Turref, Five, Aberdeen, Montross, Dundee, to Perth. In like manner, that that which goes from Blair North by Ruthven upon Spey, turning to the left Hand leads to Inverness, I imagine to be a Roman Military Way, & that its course was formerly directly to Nairn. All this very probably your Honor'd self can inform me of, seeing you have Acquaintance with Scotch Persons of Erudition, some without doubt dwelling in those Parts. In my humble Opinion the Search would not be fruitless seeing we have no less than XXXVIII stations to fix N. of Antoninus's Praetentura.[7]

Bertram added that he had recently acquired a copy of Horsley's *Britannia Romana* and, while he was impressed with its collection of inscriptions and its descriptions of the two Roman walls, he declared himself unconvinced by many of Horsley's speculations on the geography of Roman Britain.

If Bertram was banking on the fact that such ground-breaking new information on the extent of Roman activity in Scotland would pique Stukeley's interest, then he was not to be disappointed. Following another eager reply from England, Bertram sent over a transcript of the first three chapters in October 1748. In February of the following year he finally sent a copy of the rest. By now he was no longer holding back on the importance of his discovery:

> The Chronology contains many choice pieces of Antiquity; and provided the Authoritys made use of be genuine, the whole Book, for the completeness of its System, has no peer in any tongue, or of any Nation. I must beg your candid Opinion on this behalf, and upon your Vindication shall esteem Britain, tho' once thought to be out of the ancient world, to be the only Region in it: this Libel comparing with Pausanias of Greece, and far exceeding Tacitus of Germany; then what other Nation can produce the Life of an Agricola![8]

Back in London an increasingly excited Stukeley showed a copy of the script to David Casley, the deputy keeper of the Cottonian Library, who pronounced it 400 years old. Discussions with the librarian at Westminster Abbey allowed Stukeley to confidently attribute the work to Richard of Cirencester, a fourteenth-century monk already known as the author of a history of England entitled *Speculum Historiale de Gestis Regum Angliae* along with other manuscripts, mostly of a religious nature. Encouraged by the fact that the author of this rediscovered medieval text claimed that it was based on an older work '*a quondam Duce Romano consignatis, et posteritati relictis*' (written down by a certain Roman general and left to posterity), Stukeley made what was perhaps his boldest claim yet, that the itineraries recorded in the manuscript were the only remains of a lost memoir written by none other than Agricola himself.[9]

Frustratingly for Stukeley, he was never to see the original manuscript himself, despite requests that it be sent to London: Bertram explained, rather improbably, that the current owner had stolen it as a youth from a public library (possibly in England) and as a result now preferred to keep both his own name and his precious manuscript out of the public eye.[10]

Stukeley's faith remained undimmed, but his dissemination of the text was nevertheless a slow process, and it was only in the later 1750s that it would become widely available in antiquarian circles. Stukeley presented two papers to the Society of Antiquaries of London in 1756 in which he discussed the life and work of the monk Richard and outlined some of the exciting information contained in his *De Situ Britanniae*, then in 1757 he published them in his *Account of Richard of Cirencester, Monk of Westminster, and of His Works*. That same year Bertram published the original Latin text alongside well-known works by Nennius and Gildas in a volume entitled *Britannicarum Gentium Historiae Antiquae Scriptores Tres* (An Ancient History of the British Peoples by Three Authors).

The *De Situ Britanniae* and Roman Scotland

Bertram's emphasis on the content of his manuscript that relates particularly to Scotland in his letters to Stukeley is striking. Although the *De Situ Britanniae* contained new information on many aspects of the geography and society of ancient Britain, Bertram obviously considered these Scottish revelations to be its most compelling, and apparently believed that they would also be the most interesting to Stukeley. Containing accounts of the 'Ancient State of Britain', the routes of eighteen itineraries across its landscape and also including a handy map, the manuscript revealed that Scotland had been almost completely conquered by Rome. The region had been divided into two provinces: to the south, the province of Valentia (named in honour of the family of Theodosius) lay between the two walls; in the north could be found a province named Vespasiana (after the father of Domitian, during whose reign it was first conquered).[11] Although it was a region much coveted by the Romans, Richard explained that Vespasiana did not remain under their control for long.[12] Despite this, it still contained thirty-eight Roman 'stations' and three important Roman cities named Victoria (Perth), Pteroton or Alata Castra (Inverness) and Theodosia (Dumbarton). All three were included in Richard's list of the thirty-three cities of 'greatest eminence' in Britain, and they were also among the ten described as *Civitates Latio jure donatae*, translated by Stukeley as 'Citys honor'd with the Italian Freedom'.[13] Victoria in particular is depicted as a place of some importance, 'a city in reality as well as name more splendid than the rest', founded by Agricola and named in honour of his success at Mons Graupius.[14] Two altars were constructed near modern-day Cromarty to mark the boundary of Roman power, beyond which lay the unconquered region of Caledonia, an impenetrable place of 'woods & forests, & continual ridges of rocky mountains'.[15]

The *De Situ Britanniae* was welcomed with open arms by the antiquarian community, largely thanks to Stukeley's enthusiastic support. He declared Richard of Cirencester's tenth itinerary, which charted a route from Inverness to Exeter, 'the only remaining monument of Roman power in Scotland' and lamented the fact that the manuscript had not been found sooner, when it could have been of use to scholars such as Camden and Gale.[16] It forced antiquarians to reconsider the extent of Roman influence in the northern regions of Scotland in particular: 'Our writers scarce knew, that the *Romans* had conquered this country, till *Richard of Cirencester*'s manuscript was brought to light'.[17] Stukeley's hand-written list of the many 'hitherto unknown' Roman cities in Scotland now identified thanks to the manuscript ran to almost four pages of a notebook.[18] As mentioned in Chapter 4, Stukeley also felt compelled to update his personal copy of his 1720 *Account of a Roman Temple* with various hand-written additions.[19] On page three he amended his description of the fortifications built across the Forth/Clyde isthmus by Agricola in which he had stated that they 'bounded the imperial conquests in these parts' by scoring through the word 'bounded' and replacing it with 'secured'; on an interleaf next to this he added 'even till he intirely subdued the whole country as far as Inverness, building a great & strong fortress there, called Alata Castra, where was his summer station for his fleet'. On a blank sheet next to page twenty-six, where he had debunked the notion that Arthur's O'on was a temple of Terminus that marked the end point of the Roman world, he wrote, 'Rich'd of Cirencester lets us know that this was far from being the terminus of the Ro. Conquests when all the country hence to Inverness was subdued & called Vespasiana: roads and stations all the way and many roads'. In smaller handwriting below this he also invoked the spirit of Virgil: '*His ego nec metas rerum nec tempora pono Imperium sine fine dedi* – Virg. & of this k.do there shall be no end'.[20]

The content of the *De Situ Britanniae* contradicted the findings of Alexander Gordon and John Horsley, who had both spent much time and effort searching Scotland for Roman remains. Fortunately for Bertram, neither man was around to defend their work, since Gordon was by now in America and Horsley long dead. Despite some doubts amongst English antiquarians regarding its authenticity, the next generation to investigate Roman Scotland generally accepted the manuscript without question.[21] While General Robert Melville's hunts for Agricolan sites were carried out before it was published, a note in his later manuscript essay entitled 'Agricola's Camps' describes the *De Situ Britanniae* as a 'valuable work'.[22] William Roy believed that, thanks to the discovery of Richard of Cirencester's text, 'the curious have thereby been furnished with many new lights concerning the Roman history and geography of Britain in general, but more particularly the north part of it; which, from the deficiency of materials, was hitherto not near so well ascertained as that of South Britain'.[23] Although he warned that it should be used with caution due to its late date, John Pinkerton (himself no stranger to literary forgery) confidently stated in 1789 that 'it's authenticity has not been questioned, and appears unquestionable'.[24]

In the nineteenth century things began to change. In 1846 the German scholar Karl Wex highlighted transcription errors in the text that must have arisen from a fifteenth-century edition of Tacitus' *Agricola*. We can assume that most of the antiquarians who had consulted it had relied on Stukeley's translations, with few referring to the Latin text. But when the original Latin was studied more closely in the late 1860s by B. B. Woodward and J. E. B. Mayor, who compared it to the language used in Richard of Cirencester's other works, countless anachronisms and inconsistencies were exposed. Both published scathing articles revealing their findings in *The Gentleman's Magazine*. Finally, over a century after it was first 'rediscovered', the *De Situ Britanniae* was completely discredited and exposed as an elaborate fraud.

James Macpherson and Ossian

The life of James Macpherson (Figure 8.1) and the origins of the poems of Ossian have been much discussed over the last two and a half centuries, and as such require only a brief summary here. Born in 1736 in Inverness-shire, Macpherson studied at Aberdeen and Edinburgh Universities before returning to his hometown of Ruthven to take up teaching. He also dabbled in poetry around this time, producing a (largely ignored) epic entitled *The Highlander*. In 1759 he was introduced to successful playwright John Home, with whom he discussed his researches into traditional Highland poetry. Home encouraged Macpherson to produce English translations of these Gaelic verses and was so impressed with the results that he rushed them to Edinburgh, where they met with great acclaim from the literati. By 1760 a book of these *Fragments of Ancient Poetry* was published, to be followed in late 1761 by *Fingal, An Epic Poem in Six Books, Together with Several Other Poems Composed by Ossian, the Son of Fingal*, with *Temora* completing the cycle in 1763. A compilation of all three volumes was published in 1765, followed by numerous other editions and translations into several languages. Readers not just in Britain but across Europe and America were mesmerised. Macpherson claimed to have collated these works from various manuscript and oral sources discovered during his tours of the Highlands and attributed them to a third-century blind bard named Ossian. Largely comprising accounts of how the early inhabitants of Scotland battled alongside their Irish allies to repel marauding Scandinavians, these poems depicted the Caledonians

Figure 8.1 James Macpherson, oil on canvas by George Romney, 1779–80. (© National Portrait Gallery, London)

not as Sir John Clerk's 'barbarians with no claim to civilisation whatever', but rather as an eloquent, courtly and cultured race possessed of outstanding bravery and soft sensibilities.

The verses of Ossian, with their themes of love, honour and loss amongst an ancient race of noble warriors and winsome maidens, all set in a nebulous landscape of windswept heaths and rolling seas, satisfied an emerging taste for Primitivism and the sublime. They were often compared with the works of Homer, which had enjoyed something of a renaissance since the publication of Pope's translations and the 1735 *Enquiry into the Life and Writings of Homer* of Thomas Blackwell (who also later taught Macpherson at Marischal College). Hugh Blair, professor of Rhetoric and Belles Lettres at Edinburgh University and one of Macpherson's greatest supporters, proposed that many aspects of the poems outshone even Virgil's *Aeneid*, arguing that Fingal was a more relatable and 'real' hero than the 'unanimated, insipid' Aeneas, and that the 'abrupt boldness, and enthusiastick warmth' of Ossian's verse offered a stark contrast to Virgil's 'correct elegance' and 'Roman stateliness'.[25] Now, as a new age of Romanticism dawned, the sophistication and civility of the Romans so admired by men like Sibbald, Stukeley and Clerk seemed restrained, cold and distinctly old-fashioned.

The argument over the authenticity of these poems has raged almost since the day that they were first published. Claims regarding their antiquity were loudly ridiculed, particularly south of the border where Samuel Johnson made several scathing attacks on Macpherson's credibility, while a number of Scottish scholars including Hugh Blair and Adam Ferguson remained steadfast in their support of Ossian. To some extent the war of words developed along patriotic lines, and a belief in the poems in defiance of English mockery became something of an imperative for many proud Scots.[26] The debate, however, was more complicated than a simple conflict between Scottish and English, or Classicist versus Primitivist: the ever-credulous William Stukeley wrote to Macpherson to declare himself 'charm'd with Ossian's poem' and confirmed Romanist William Roy owned an early edition of *Fingal*.[27] Several Scots also turned against Macpherson. While Arran-born William Shaw, a native Gaelic speaker, was initially convinced, he later published an *Enquiry into the Authenticity of the Poems Ascribed to Ossian* in which he recorded his frustrated attempts to view any of the original manuscript sources or locate any Highlander with a convincing knowledge of the poems. He was surprised that the Roman authors had made no mention of Ossian, since 'a man so thirsty after fame, would surely court an opportunity of meeting the cotemporary Romans, who certainly would not fail to make mention of so great a hero'.[28] Shaw also lambasted his fellow Scots for their credulity and complained that 'Caledonians, naturally partial to their country and its antiquities, were not "sturdy enough moralists" to disown an honour politically done them by a politically cunning *translator*'.[29] An indignant response from fellow Gael John Clark declared Shaw to be anti-Scottish, a traitor to his own island roots who spoke a 'corrupt' dialect hardly intelligible to true Highlanders.[30]

Much ink has been spilt since the 1760s on the 'Ossian Fraud', but recent scholarship has tended to be more sympathetic towards Macpherson, portraying him as a man striving to rescue a disappearing Highland culture and highlighting his role in the development of literary historicism, romantic literature and nostalgic nationalism. It has long been recognised that elements of his texts are loosely based on Irish myth and that they also contain some fragments of medieval and later Irish and Scottish literature, while investigation into his source material has uncovered links between the Ossianic poems and popular Gaelic ballads.[31] As we shall see, however, at least one key aspect of the poems, namely the references that they contain to the battles between the Caledonians and the invading

Romans, is entirely bogus, inserted by Macpherson for his own ends: that is, to deceive.

Rome versus Caledonia in the poems of Ossian

Since modern research into the themes and impact of the poems of Ossian has largely focused on their content relating to the provenance and fate of Gaelic culture, almost nothing has been said about the role played by the Romans in either the narrative or the reception of the texts. Despite the aforementioned air of anti-classicism that pervades contemporary critiques, as well as suggestions that Macpherson presented Ossian as 'totally ignorant of *Roman* and *Greek learning*', Macpherson's own extensive knowledge of Roman literature can be detected throughout the Ossianic poems.[32] Fiona Stafford, for example, identifies echoes of and allusions to the works of Lucan, Horace and Virgil.[33] References to Roman writers also regularly appear in the marginal notes included by Macpherson in his early printed editions.

Many readers no doubt enjoyed the poems as works of expressive and emotive literature. Even sceptics such as William Shaw recognised their potential as 'entertainment'.[34] Macpherson, however, was keen to present them as a major historical source, writing in the preface to *Fingal* that 'the compositions of Ossian are not less valuable for the light they throw on the ancient state of Scotland and Ireland than they are for their poetical merit'.[35] Other scholars of some note agreed: William Robertson, Lord Kames and Adam Ferguson saw the texts as evidence of the manners and society of the ancients, while Robert Henry echoed Macpherson in his popular *History of Great Britain* of 1771 when he wrote that 'the poems of that venerable bard are not only valuable for their poetical beauties, but also for the light which they throw on the history and antiquities of our country'.[36]

The verses included in the first volume, *Fragments of Ancient Poetry* of 1760, include no recognisable historical events, and Macpherson admits in the preface that, while their style suggests great age, 'their date of composition cannot be exactly ascertained'.[37] Several of those included in *Fingal*, however, contain oblique references to the Romans and their invasions of Scotland that are glossed by Macpherson in his accompanying notes. The Caracul mentioned in the poem entitled *Comala* is explained as early third-century emperor Caracalla, while the Caros who appears in *The War of Caros* is identified as the late third-century usurper Carausius who, Macpherson's notes inform us, rebuilt the Roman wall in Scotland to keep out the Caledonians.[38] The Romans remain enigmatic and distant, their actions relayed to us by the Caledonian protagonists who make vague references to eagles and name the Roman emperor 'the king of the world', a moniker that Macpherson explains was common 'in old composition'; Carausius' position in the Roman navy, meanwhile, was recognised in his title 'the king of ships'.[39]

While these could be described as only brief 'cameo appearances' with little importance for the (often hazy and confusing) narratives of the poems, the fact that these battles with Rome are so prominently flagged by Macpherson reveals that he viewed them as significant. The interactions between Ossian's Caledonian heroes and the Romans are the first evidence of a discernible chronology in the poetic cycle, anchoring the texts in the third century, a disrupted time loitering on the border between history and prehistory of the kind that Thomas Blackwell had previously identified as conducive to the creation of great epic poetry.[40] The importance of the Romans in establishing the antiquity, and thus the authenticity of Ossian is repeatedly stressed throughout Macpherson's essay and notes in *Fingal*. Colin Kidd observes that, while Hugh Blair's analyses of the poems tended to focus on their aesthetic and sociological aspects, Macpherson's glosses relate largely to their historiographical significance.[41] The note that highlights the first appearance of the Romans in the narrative declares that 'this poem is valuable on account of the light it throws on the antiquity of Ossian's compositions. The Caracul mentioned here is the same with Caracalla the son of Severus, who in the year 211 commanded an expedition against the Caledonians'.[42] In the essay included in the first edition of *Fingal*, entitled *A Dissertation Concerning the Antiquity &c. of Ossian's Poems*, Macpherson writes: 'Several other passages in the poems allude to the wars of the Romans; but the two just mentioned [*Colama* and *The War of Caros*] clearly fix the epoch of Fingal to the third century; and this account agrees exactly with the Irish histories, which place the death of Fingal . . . in the year 283, and that of Oscar . . . in the year 296'.[43] He also rather self-consciously attempts to pre-empt any scepticism regarding the sudden appearance of the Romans:

> Some people might imagine, that the allusions to the Roman history might have been industriously inserted into the poems, to give them the appearance of antiquity. This fraud must then have been committed at least three ages ago, as the passages in which the allusions are made, are alluded to often in the compositions of those times.[44]

In doing so he surely reveals his very modus operandi: as a result of the wave of incredulity that greeted his first collection, Macpherson 'industriously inserted' the Romans into the narrative in order to provide the Ossianic myths with a temporal framework. The fact that they appear for the first time in the second volume suggests that he was responding to specific criticisms of the earlier *Fragments*. As Ian Haywood has pointed out, the creation of the Ossianic poems was a 'process', with each instalment adapted to meet the apparent shortcomings of what had come before.[45]

While much of the depiction of the Caledonians in Ossianic poetry would have appeared new, even surprising to an early modern audience, not least the idea that these ancient people could compose such hauntingly beautiful verse, many elements were also reassuringly familiar. A blind author, for example, would no doubt evoke memories of Homer, perhaps even Milton, while *Fingal* and *Temora* shared their epic form with many of the greatest masterpieces of ancient literature. Although the texts themselves contain only vague allusions to landscape and a few archaic place names, Macpherson's notes often relate these to real locations in Scotland, Ireland and Scandinavia that readers themselves might have known of or visited.[46] The subplot of the Caledonian resistance to Rome would also be recognisable to many both in Scotland and further afield, since, as has already been demonstrated, this theme had been a staple of Scottish history since medieval times.

The poems of Ossian paint a rousingly patriotic picture of the Caledonians as noble freedom fighters that sharply contrasts their depiction of the Romans, who are shown in both *Comala* and *The War of Caros* to be a feeble enemy forced into retreat. Despite early reports that Fingal has been lost in a battle against Caracul/Caracalla near the River Carron in Stirlingshire, it later transpires that he has in fact been victorious, leading him to declare that 'Caracul has fled from my arms along the fields of his pride. He sets far distant like a meteor that incloses a spirit of night, when the winds drive it over the heath, and the dark woods are gleaming around'.[47] It is Ossian's own son Oscar who faces Carausius in battle, again near the Carron, which also happens to run close to the Antonine Wall. Macpherson's notes inform us that the 'gathered heap' mentioned in the texts is indeed this Roman frontier, although he calls it 'Agricola's Wall', this mistake surely arising from a misreading of the twenty-third chapter of Tacitus' *Agricola*, which describes the Roman general's fortification of the Forth/Clyde isthmus. This time the defeat of Rome is even more decisive:

> WHAT does Caros king of ships, said the son of the now mournful Ossian? Spreads he the wings of his pride, bard of the times of old?
>
> HE spreads them, Oscar, replied the bard, but it is behind his gathered heap. He looks over his stones with fear, and beholds thee terrible, as the ghost of the night that rolls the wave to his ships.[48]

And later:

> The warriors of Caros fled, and Oscar remained like a rock left by the ebbing sea . . . Happy art thou, O Oscar, in the midst of thy rushing blast. Thou often goest to the fields of thy fame, where Caros fled from thy lifted sword.[49]

Thus these Ossianic texts represent another example of that well-worn trope of valiant Scots standing up to and successfully resisting a foreign threat, an idea originally propagated by early historians and chroniclers such as John of Fordun, Hector Boece and George Buchanan, which had become only more popular during the eighteenth century. As if to make this link even more apparent, Macpherson directly cites Buchanan in a note accompanying *Comala*, quoting that famous section of his poem dedicated to Mary Stuart that celebrates Scotland's claim to have set the limits of Roman power along the line of the very same river Carron.

Macpherson's decision to set this Caledonian conflict with Rome in Stirlingshire close to the 'gathered heap' of the Antonine Wall is notable. While his glosses reveal a knowledge of the works of Tacitus and Buchanan, his proposal that the Roman advance was halted along the frontier that he erroneously believed to be 'Agricola's Wall' suggests that he had a rather muddled and outdated understanding of the history of Roman Scotland and was unfamiliar with more recent scholarship on the subject. Perhaps he simply preferred to ignore the evidence, both literary and material, which had already forced even the most patriotic eighteenth-century Scottish antiquarians to admit that the Roman army had, for a short time at least, marched into the Highlands. That this Ossianic conflict zone lay not too far from the notional early modern boundary between Lowland and Highland is surely no coincidence. Macpherson was certainly intent on demonstrating that his fellow Gaelic-speaking inhabitants of the north were the direct ancestors of those courageous tribes who had faced and defeated the Romans several centuries before, describing them as 'the genuine descendants of the ancient Caledonians'.[50] That many of the poems composed by Ossian had supposedly been passed down orally across the generations and centuries to Macpherson only seemed to confirm this idea. So, while many previous commentators had used comparisons with ancient Caledonians to denigrate the Highlanders, to frame them as barbaric and uncouth, now such comparisons were something of which the downtrodden Gael could be proud. In one fell swoop the troubling notion of a post-Roman Gaelic immigration from Ireland was scotched and the harsh image of the Highlander as unruly, untrustworthy and probably Jacobite was softened for southern audiences.

Determined to bolster the shaky historical foundations of his great 'discovery' in the face of an ever-growing swell of criticism, whilst also hoping to establish his reputation as a historian, Macpherson published his *Introduction to the History of Great Britain and Ireland* in 1771. This largely fanciful work not only reiterated the Scottish (as opposed to Irish) origins of Gaelic culture, but also tied the Ossianic tales more securely into a historical period and confirmed their picture of the brave Caledonian standing up to and defeating the weak and degenerate Roman. Macpherson expands his coverage of the Roman period by dealing here with the events of the Agricolan invasion, but claims that the Roman general was so highly regarded by posterity more thanks to the efforts of his (biased and untrustworthy) son-in-law biographer than his skills on the battlefield.[51] He even proposes that the Caledonian losses at the battle of Mons Graupius were greatly exaggerated by Tacitus, confidently declaring that 'the Caledonians suffered little from Agricola'.[52] Such was the threat posed by the inhabitants of Caledonia, Macpherson reminds the reader, that both Hadrian and Severus were forced to come to Britain in failed attempts to subdue them.[53] Their constant rebellions led to the construction of the two Roman walls and even resulted in the shameful bribery of the Caledonians by Roman general Virius Lupus following repeated raids on the Roman province to the south.[54] The fact that this Caledonian resistance is not recorded in Roman literature was, Macpherson declared, the result of a desire to erase it from history: 'The Roman writers with one consent seem to have entered into a conspiracy against the military fame of the Royal line of [mythical king] Heremon . . . foreign writers, with a scandalous partiality, not only concealed the exploits, but even the very names of those heroes'.[55] Ignored by history until now, the noble deeds of the Caledonians were overshadowed by Roman debauchery and 'Fingal passed away unnoticed in Caledonia, at the time that Heliogabalus employed the page of the historian at Rome'.[56] With this book, James Macpherson presented himself as the man who would finally right that wrong.

Any hopes that this publication might quell the rising tide of doubt were to be disappointed. William Shaw stated in 1781 that 'this book was published on purpose to support the imposture of Fingal', and eight years later John Pinkerton (who, as we have already seen, was completely taken in by the *De Situ Britanniae*) was even more damning, writing that 'the empty vanity, shallow reading, vague assertion, and etymological nonsense of this production, are truly risible'.[57] Macpherson's risky attempts to pull the tales of Ossian out of (Irish) myth and into (Scottish) history by introducing the Romans could be seen as something of a failure, as cracks soon began to show in their historical framework. While he was inclined to believe in the authenticity and historical value of the poetry, Edward Gibbon was confused by the use of the name 'Caracul', noting that the nickname Caracalla for the emperor more properly called Antoninus was not coined until four years after the Romans had left Scotland and only came into general use after his death.[58] A sceptical Malcolm Laing saw through the ruse, stating in his *History of Scotland* that (the by now deceased) Macpherson had 'found a convenient chasm in the history of Britain under the Romans, and connected Fingal with Caracalla in 208, and with Carausius the usurper in 286, to ascertain his era without recourse to Ireland'.[59] He was also among the first to question the late third-century incursion into Scotland by Carausius supposedly witnessed by Ossian himself. With mention of Carausius in Caledonia first found in an undated gloss in a single manuscript version of Nennius, a story of a Carausian alliance with the Caledonians also appears in the fantastical *Historia Regum Britanniae* of Geoffrey of Monmouth and was later elaborated (with a more patriotically Scottish slant) by Fordun and Boece.[60] Robert Sibbald combined these into a full-blown invasion of southern Scotland by the renegade emperor, with the conquered lands later handed back to their original occupants.[61] Laing proposed that this invasion had never actually taken place, and by the mid-nineteenth century these tales of Carausias' exploits in the north were correctly dismissed as nothing more than legend.[62]

Filling the void: the motivations of Bertram and Macpherson

As long, complicated texts filled with historical and pseudo-historical detail, and in the case of the *De Situ Britanniae* also written in an ancient language, the composition of these (in)famous works by Charles Bertram and James Macpherson undoubtedly required huge amounts of time, effort and knowledge. Both men cleverly contrived to disseminate their texts, and both successfully convinced many readers of their veracity. Bertram escaped almost unchallenged, and although Macpherson faced huge amounts of criticism during his lifetime, he remained steadfast in his claims regarding the authenticity of Ossian until his death in 1796. While their content and style might be markedly different, both the *De Situ Britanniae* and the poetry of Ossian can be viewed as part of a wider trend for forged works of history and literature that blossomed in the later eighteenth century. Anthony Grafton identifies an early modern taste for what he calls the 'forgery of nostalgia' in which national histories would be filled out with spurious material that often displays a romantic tone.[63] Ossian in particular can be related to an era of British forgeries such as the 'Rowley' poems by Thomas Chatterton and the Shakespearean papers cobbled together by William Henry Ireland that Nick Groom has associated with the rise of the Romantic movement.[64] That this was a time when the fakery of historical sources was becoming more common is clear: if the demand for new documentary material in Hume's great 'historical age' was outstripping supply, then there were, it appears, plenty of budding antiquarians, dealers and authors hoping to build a reputation (and perhaps a fortune) who were only too willing to fill the gap with their own phony concoctions.

Since neither Bertram nor Macpherson ever admitted any wrongdoing, we can only speculate as to their motives. Bertram's ambitions are perhaps the more puzzling, since he could hardly have hoped to gain fame and fortune from a manuscript describing the geography of Roman Britain. What he did achieve, however, was a close friendship with one of Britain's most respected scholars and a degree of respect from fellow antiquarians, ending up as an Honorary Fellow of the Society of Antiquaries in 1756. His belief that his new-found reputation would further enhance his career in the Danish royal household proved overambitious, however, and having lost his teaching post in 1762 he spent his final years reduced to penury and dreaming of a return to England.[65] And while Macpherson may well have been fighting to preserve his beloved Gaelic culture from the threat of Hanoverian oppression, it is surely no coincidence that his poems captured the current fashion for the sublime, their appeal to the general public leading to him becoming both rich and famous. Thanks partly to Ossian (but also due to his later career in politics) this humble son of a tenant farmer ended his days as laird of the Adam-designed Belleville House, his portrait painted by Reynolds and Romney and his remains eventually laid to rest in Westminster Abbey.

The one approach that both men shared was their use of the Roman invasions of Scotland in the formulation and dissemination of their works. Bertram's emphasis on the subject in his original letters as a bait to hook William Stukeley reveals that he viewed it as a highly contested area, a historical void waiting to be filled with dramatic revelations. He also correctly calculated that many would be satisfied to find that Scotland had been almost entirely subject to Rome, despite the centuries-old tradition that proposed otherwise. Analysis of the *De Situ Britanniae* has revealed the extent of its creator's research, with a knowledge of the works of Caesar and Tacitus as well as more recent scholarship by Camden, Horsley and Stukeley evident throughout. We have no way of knowing if Bertram ever read Stukeley's *Account of a Roman Temple*, which includes a remarkably similar representation of the limit of Roman power in the north; any similarities may be due to the fact that both authors took much inspiration from William Baxter's *Glossarium Antiquitatum Britannicarum*.[66] Stukeley would surely have recognised that the *De Situ Britanniae* seemed to confirm his own earlier conjectures, giving him even more reason to accept its authenticity without question.

That the poetry of Ossian was such a phenomenal popular success in the face of rampant ridicule is surely more thanks to its poetical and romantic attributes than its historical content. These, after all, are verses that, if Hugh Blair is to be believed, would leave the reader 'warmed with the sentiments of humanity, virtue and honour', and that possessed the power to 'to command, to transport, to melt the heart'.[67] For Macpherson, however, this historical content was crucial for their acceptance as authentic ancient texts, although its inclusion was only to lead to more questions and doubts; unlike Bertram, Macpherson's understanding of the Roman period was apparently restricted to a vague idea of Tacitus and an awareness of the by now largely obsolete legendary histories of Boece and Buchanan.

As Scotland's antiquarians entered the final decades of the eighteenth century, they remained sharply divided over their nation's Roman past. If anything, the source material now available was more confusing and inconsistent than ever. While some clung to those old tales of Caledonian resistance, others were delighted with the idea that their nation had after all been a Roman province (or indeed two Roman provinces), providing them with the kind of classical inheritance that they had previously been denied. Writing in 1876, just after the *De Situ Britanniae* had finally been debunked, John Hill Burton described the contradictory pulls that the subject inspired in the minds of many Scots:

> A very patriotic Scotsman might be expected to exult in seeing Richard of Cirencester swept from historical literature, since he represents Scotland as subdued and divided into provinces as far as Inverness, where he planted a municipium. It is an instance of the [positive] feeling already referred to about the Roman invasion, that, far from wishing to repudiate this new chapter in history, the most zealous Scottish antiquaries welcomed with delight the addition of the territories north of the Tay to the Roman acquisitions.[68]

But while the *De Situ Britanniae* may have established itself as one of the most important textual sources for late eighteenth-century scholars of ancient Scottish history, it was Ossian and his Caledonian heroes who had captured the hearts of the Scottish people. The impact of this discord on the historiography of the nation as the century reached its close will be revealed in the final chapter.

Notes

1. Sibbald, *Historical Inquiries*, p. 36; Roy, *Military Antiquities*, p. 94.
2. Bodl.MS.Eng.Lett.b.2, f. 6: Bertram to Stukeley, 23 August 1746. The quote ('no one lives without wrongdoing') is actually from the *Disticha Catonis*.
3. Bodl.MS.Eng.Lett.b.2, ff. 7–8: Bertram to Stukeley, 1747.
4. Bodl.MS.Eng.Lett.b.2, f. 10: Bertram to Stukeley, 10 November 1747.
5. Ibid.
6. Piggott, *William Stukeley*, p. 129.
7. Bodl.MS.Eng.Lett.b.2, f. 15: Bertram to Stukeley, 17 August 1748.
8. Bodl.MS.Eng.Lett.b.2, ff. 20-21: Bertram to Stukeley, 25 February 1749.
9. Stukeley, *An Account of Richard of Cirencester*, p. 12.
10. Bodl.MS.Eng.Lett.b.2, f. 23: Bertram to Stukeley, 12 May 1749.
11. Bertram, *The Description of Britain*, p. 56; ibid. p. 60.
12. Ibid. p. 57; ibid. p. 31.
13. Stukeley, *Itinerarium Curiosum*, Centuria II, p. 117; Bodl.MS.Top.gen.e.68, f. 2: Stukeley, 'The Itinerarium of Richard of Cirencester', 1750.
14. Bodl.MS.Eng.misc.d.451, f. 11: Stukeley, undated translation of the *De Situ Britanniae*.
15. Ibid. f. 13.
16. Stukeley, *Itinerarium Curiosum*, Centuria II, p. 133; Bodl.MS.Top.gen.e.68, ff. 4–5: Stukeley, 'The Itinerarium of Richard of Cirencester', 1750.
17. Stukeley, *The Medallic History of . . . Carausius*, p. 135.
18. Bodl.MS.Top.gen.e.67, ff. 20–23: 'Comment on Richardi Westmon.', 1749.
19. Bodl.533.7 G.42 fol.
20. The quote is from the *Aeneid* 1.278–9.

21. On the doubts expressed by some antiquarians, see: Sweet, *Antiquaries*, pp. 179–81.
22. NRS GD126/Box 28: Melville, 'Agricola's Camps', f. 43.
23. Roy, *Military Antiquities*, p. ix.
24. Pinkerton, *An Enquiry into the History of Scotland*, p. 12.
25. Blair, *A Critical Dissertation on the Poems of Ossian*, p. 32; ibid. p. 62.
26. Smiles, *The Image of Antiquity*, p. 64.
27. Boyd Haycock, *William Stukeley*, p. 234; Christie's, *A Catalogue of a Select, Well-Chosen, Valuable Library of Books, Maps &c.*, p. 7.
28. Shaw, *An Enquiry into the Authenticity of the Poems Ascribed to Ossian*, p. 35.
29. Ibid. p. 3.
30. Clark, *An Answer to Mr Shaw's Inquiry*, p. 5; ibid. p. 13.
31. On Macpherson's collation of Gaelic source material, see: McKean, 'The Fieldwork Legacy of James Macpherson'.
32. Shaw, *An Enquiry into the Authenticity of the Poems Ascribed to Ossian*, p. 32.
33. Stafford, *The Sublime Savage*, p. 101; ibid. pp. 136–7.
34. Shaw, *An Enquiry into the Authenticity of the Poems Ascribed to Ossian*, p. 5.
35. Macpherson, *Fingal*, Preface.
36. Mitchell, 'Landscape and the Sense of Place', p. 66; Henry, *The History of Great Britain*, p. 418.
37. Macpherson, *Fragments of Ancient Poetry*, p. iii.
38. Macpherson, *Fingal*, p. 87; ibid. p. 95.
39. Ibid. p. 93; ibid. p. 91; ibid. p. 83; ibid. p. 95.
40. Blackwell, *An Enquiry into the Life and Writings of Homer*, pp. 26–7.
41. Kidd, *Subverting Scotland's Past*, p. 228.
42. Macpherson, *Fingal*, p. 87.
43. Ibid. p. ix.
44. Ibid.
45. Haywood, *The Making of History*, p. 73.
46. For an analysis of the uses of geography in the poems, see: Mitchell, 'Landscape and the Sense of Place in the Poems of Ossian'.
47. Macpherson, *Fingal*, p. 93.
48. Ibid. p. 96.
49. Ibid. pp. 102–3.
50. Macpherson, *The Works of Ossian*, p. v.
51. Macpherson, *An Introduction to the History of Great Britain*, p. 41.
52. Ibid. p. 99.
53. Ibid. p. 101.
54. Ibid. p. 100.
55. Ibid. p. 103.
56. Ibid. p. 202.
57. Shaw, *An Enquiry into the Authenticity of the Poems Ascribed to Ossian*, p. 36; Pinkerton, *An Enquiry into the History of Scotland*, p. lxiv.
58. Gibbon, *The History of the Decline and Fall of the Roman Empire*, p. 152 n. 14.
59. Laing, *The History of Scotland*, p. 379.
60. On the dissemination of the legend of Carausius' dealings with the Caledonians, see: Casey, *Carausius and Allectus*, pp. 168–75.
61. Sibbald, *Historical Inquiries*, p. 23.
62. Laing, *The History of Scotland*, pp. 379–80; Stuart, *Caledonia Romana*, pp. 280–1.

63. Grafton, *Forgers and Critics*, p. 32.
64. Groom, *The Forger's Shadow*, p. 15.
65. Boyd Haycock, 'Charles Julius Bertram', p. 501.
66. For a brief discussion of Bertram's source materials, see: Piggott, *William Stukeley*, p. 136.
67. Blair, *A Critical Dissertation on the Poems of Ossian*, p. 74; ibid. p. 75.
68. Burton, *The History of Scotland*, p. 62.

9

After Ossian: changing interpretations of Roman Scotland

> The wall of Antoninus is now intirely demolished in many places, and the ground plowed where it stood; and . . . it is probable that, twenty years hence, few remains of it will be visible: The grounds still occupied by it will be more usefully employed; and instead of those memorials of ambition and war, succeeding generations will behold green fields and plentiful harvests, the produce of peace and industry.
>
> William Nimmo, *A General History of Stirlingshire*, 1777, p. 51–2

As Scotland's ancient history was reassessed in light of further research and fraudulent new sources, so the debate regarding the extent and impact of Roman activity in the region continued. If anything, later eighteenth-century attitudes towards the subject became even more entrenched and ebullient: as is often the case with something on the brink of demise, the chauvinistic and belligerent wrangling over just how Roman ancient Caledonia had actually been experienced a burst of energy in its final years. But while the intensity of the arguments had not yet waned, their scope and influence certainly did, as antiquarians became increasingly parochial, more concerned with the local than the national. Agricolamania was to remain a driving force in their research, particularly the endless (and ultimately fruitless) attempts to locate the elusive site of Mons Graupius.

The formation of antiquarian societies in the last decades of the eighteenth century may have ensured the popularity of the subject, but the new approaches to the past associated with Enlightenment scholarship marked a departure from, or more precisely a rejection of antiquarian methodology. Value was now placed on what Susan Manning calls the 'grand narratives of philosophic history', rather than the antiquarians' love of the tangible 'relic' and their 'sentimental and proprietorial responses, often of a very personal nature'.[1] While they remained interested in ancient Rome, with Adam Ferguson famously analysing the history and constitution of the Republic for the lessons they could teach modern states, Enlightenment scholars had no time for poring over maps and artefacts, and demonstrated little interest in the minutiae of Roman Britain. In the opening volume of his influential *History of England* (published in 1762, with numerous later reprints), David Hume stated his intention to 'briefly run over the events, which attended the conquest made by that empire, as belonging more to Roman than British [hi]story'.[2] For him, the subject, shadowy and disrupted, had little use in his survey of the evolution of the British nation. It is because of such attitudes that the antiquarians inhabited what Manning describes as 'a contested position at the margins of a self-consciously new historiography'.[3] Once at the forefront of attempts to formulate notions of Scotland and Scottishness both ancient and modern, they were now more than ever deemed to be eccentric dabblers obsessed with inconsequential geegaws who rarely ventured outside their own localities or concerned themselves with the bigger picture of national history.

Meanwhile, new trends in how Scots both viewed and presented themselves were also emerging, trends that would ultimately smother the interest in the nation's Roman heritage and replace it with a romantic nostalgia that was largely ahistorical. With its roots in the fantasies of Ossian, it is no coincidence that the growing admiration for the 'noble savage' coincided with a decline in the desire to establish Caledonia's classical credentials. Scotland, after all, now had its own ancient civilisation to celebrate, one that rivalled those of even Greece or Rome. Even more radical were suggestions that the loss of Scotland's classical heritage as a result of agricultural innovation was to be celebrated rather than mourned, its destruction symbolic of modernity's erasure of ancient tyranny and oppression.

Later eighteenth-century Romanist antiquarianism

Even in the wake of Ossian, the vision of a classical Caledonia securely within the bounds of the Roman Empire persisted into the later eighteenth century, largely thanks to the fake *De Situ Britanniae* attributed to Richard of Cirencester, but also at times demonstrating the ongoing influence of the decades-old scholarship of Sir Robert Sibbald. In his 1775 *History of the Province of Moray*, Lachlan Shaw proposed that many of the towns around the Firth of Forth were built on the sites of Roman military and civil settlements, a suggestion surely inspired by Sibbald's *Conjectures Concerning the Roman Ports, Colonies, and Forts, in the Firths*. Furthermore, Shaw claimed, the civilised state of southern Scotland in his own time was due to the lasting influence of Rome, while the lamentably barbaric conditions in the north could be blamed on its absence there:

> I have said, it was the misfortune of the Northern Countries, that the ROMANS were so little acquainted with them: for where-ever they settled, they softened the rough temper, and civilized the rude manners of the natives. They introduced letters, arts,

and sciences. They taught agriculture, and laid the foundations of cities and towns, navigation and commerce. Hence the many towns and villages, on both sides of the Frith of Forth, had their rise from the Roman colonies, forts and naval stations: and the foundation of the culture and fertility of the Lothians, was laid by their industry: While the Western coast, from the Clyde Northward, into which the Romans never entered, (thought better furnished by nature with bays, harbours and creeks) remained long uncivilised, without towns, trade or commerce.[4]

Elsewhere, a report in the 1789 edition of *Britannia* based on a letter written by landowner James Wedderburn to antiquarian Adam de Cardonnel, which described Roman remains discovered in Inveresk, strongly suggests that Scotland had been firmly under Roman control:

> By this post and the camp at Ardoch the Romans meant, at one time, to have considered the river Earn as their boundary, and covered the county of Fife completely: and they must have been in peaceable possession when they erected stone and brick buildings of imported materials . . . Beyond and to the northward of their posts they must also have extended to a high and settled authority.[5]

For Wedderburn, the fact that the Romans had put so much effort into constructing the apparently substantial buildings uncovered on his own property suggested that 'all Scotland was permanently subjected'.[6]

Perhaps the last concerted attempt to establish Scotland as an enduring element of the Roman Empire can be found in the first volume of *Caledonia*, published in 1807 by George Chalmers (Figure 9.1). Although he had emigrated to America in 1763 aged twenty, Chalmers' loyalist sympathies during the discontent that preceded the War of Independence forced him to return to Britain in 1775, and he eventually settled in London. He experienced a period of financial hardship, during which he produced several political (generally anti-American independence) tracts, but later secured paid posts that allowed him to devote more of his time to writing. Following the publication of his biography of Thomas Ruddiman, Chalmers turned his attention to the history of his home nation. The preface to the opening volume of *Caledonia* (two others would follow before the author's death in 1825, the final three planned by Chalmers were never completed) features a standard criticism of the myths and fables that had previously passed for Scottish history, as well as an attack on the 'vain credulity of the industrious antiquaries', which the author believed had hampered recent scholarship on the ancient past.[7] Chalmers regarded Scotland's Roman heritage as a key part of the national story, so he placed the subject at the very beginning of his work 'from its priority in time, as well as precedence in importance'.[8] Despite his criticism of antiquarians, he regularly cites Sibbald, Gordon, Horsley and Roy and reveals that the study of ancient remains had played a role in his own research, adding that the necessary inspection and surveying of Roman

Figure 9.1 George Chalmers, pencil and watercolour by Henry Edridge, 1809. (© National Portrait Gallery, London)

sites and roads had been carried out by other 'intelligent persons' who remain nameless.

In his description of Agricola's expeditions in Scotland Chalmers remains faithful to the account of Tacitus, but in what followed the general's return to

Rome he differs dramatically from previous conjectures. While it was (and still is) often assumed that a pithy phrase in Tacitus' *Histories*, '*perdomita Britannia et statim omissa*' (Britain was subdued and then immediately let go), together with a lack of subsequent references to Caledonia in ancient literary sources, demonstrates that the Roman victory in the north had been short-lived, Chalmers claimed that the Roman author was a 'querulous historian' who was not to be trusted.[9] Rather than being relinquished, he argued that the 'silence of history' proved that Caledonia had been completely subdued and held thanks to 'the power of the governors, and the weakness of the governed'.[10] The Roman walls, he proposed, gave a false idea of the limits of Roman power, and he suggested that, during the rule of Antoninus Pius, 'every inhabitant of North-Britain, who resided along the east coast, from the Tweed to the Murray Frith, might have claimed, like St. Paul, every privilege, which peculiarly belonged to a Roman citizen'.[11] The inspiration for this claim probably came from the *De Situ Britanniae*, although the fact that Chalmers was himself born in Fochabers in Moray no doubt encouraged his belief that the north-east had been settled by Rome.

The infrastructure of Roman roads found in Scotland, which the author describes in some detail in his fourth chapter, is also presented as evidence of Roman power in the region. Chalmers' discussion of other Roman remains includes mention of towns at Cramond and Camelon and a villa at Linlithgow, probably on the site now inhabited by the palace.[12] In his preface he also notes the recent discovery of a Roman bath at Moray (actually the Burghead Well, of unknown date but no longer thought to be Roman), another apparent sign of classical civilisation near the author's home town.[13] Despite his own Highland provenance, Chalmers was not convinced that the poems of Ossian could be used as a historical source, pointing out that 'heroic poetry requires not authentic history to support its elegant narratives', also reminding readers that the Gaelic in which the original verses were supposedly composed was not spoken until centuries after the events that they purported to describe.[14] Overall he displays little respect for the indigenous tribes of Caledonia, suggesting that they remained tranquil even after a partial Roman retreat from the region north of the Antonine Wall in the year 170 CE, so accustomed were they to imperial subjugation.[15] Indeed, his explanation of why the Romans left the Highlands is more reminiscent of the proposals of disdainful English antiquarians than his patriotic fellow Scots: 'The Romans relinquished the country, which experience had taught them to regard, neither as useful nor agreeable'.[16]

In his descriptions of Roman activity in Scotland, Chalmers' sympathies clearly lie with the invaders rather than the invaded. This pro-Roman/anti-Caledonian attitude is surely linked to his own political affiliations. Chalmers could be classed as a tory with a strong belief in upholding the Establishment. He spent most of his adult life in England and was also an enthusiastic supporter of the rapidly expanding British Empire. Throughout *Caledonia*, Scotland is referred to as 'North-Britain', even in its subtitle (*An Account, Historical and Topographical, of North Britain*). His approach certainly led to criticism, and although it is the work for which the author is now best remembered, it was received unfavourably during the nineteenth century. Alexander du Toit records that it was 'for many years regarded as dated, erroneous and even unoriginal', while an anonymous review in *The Annual Register* of 1807 harshly criticised Chalmers' abilities and writing style, also systematically deconstructing his conjectures regarding 'that part of his work which will probably draw most general attention', namely the Agricolan invasion.[17]

Regional antiquarianism

Although it was certainly facing growing levels of scorn and ridicule in an increasingly Enlightened world, antiquarianism remained popular amongst Scottish gentlemen. But while previous generations of its practitioners had been interested in the story of Scotland, in the latter part of the eighteenth century many focused more closely on their local history. Thanks to the fascination with Agricola and his battle against the Caledonians, Perthshire became a particular focus for much of the Romanist research during this period; the region was dotted with Roman remains and still held the potential for exciting new discoveries that might shed light on this most captivating (but also frustratingly intangible) historical campaign. The Antiquarian Society of Perth was founded in 1784 with the intention of promoting the study of local, national and international history both natural and human; a group of manuscripts relating to it, now held in Perth Museum, attests to a flurry of activity concerning the area's Roman heritage that lasted from the 1770s into the early 1800s. Produced by local residents possessed of varying degrees of knowledge and skill, this collection includes several carefully drawn plans of military sites such as Fendoch, Inchtuthil and Grassy Walls created during the late 1770s by John McOmie, a master at the Perth Academy and later secretary of the town's Antiquarian Society, as well as another of Glenmailen dating from 1789 by one Theodore McRonald.[18] McOmie presented three plans to the Society of Antiquaries of Scotland in 1785, including one of a supposed Roman wall and camp at Meikleour (this earthwork, often referred to as the Cleaven Dyke, is now recognised as a Neolithic cursus), noting on it that the monument 'surprises the Spectator with the greatness of the work, which none can doubt, of its having been built by the Roman Army' (Figure 9.2).[19] The following year he also received a plan and description of the Roman earthworks at Dalginross from an anonymous 'young gentleman residing in its neighbourhood' who wondered if they might be the 'camp possessed by Galgacus & recorded by Tacitus'.[20]

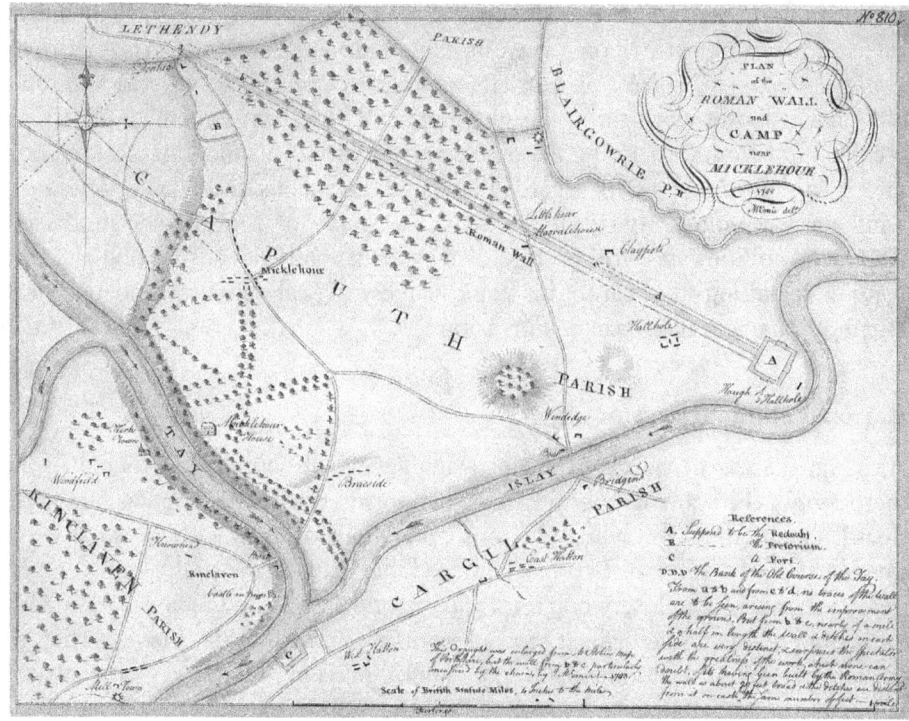

Figure 9.2 'The Roman Wall and Camp near Micklehour', manuscript map by John McOmie, 1785. (© National Museums Scotland: NMS Acc. 1737 (34))

Most of the sites recorded and described by these Perthshire antiquarians had already been discovered by Alexander Shand or William Roy, and some had also been accurately surveyed by Roy, although his work still remained unpublished. Another account of Dalginross written by the Rev. Mr McDiarmid of nearby Comrie in 1800 attempted to confirm Alexander Gordon's proposal that this was the location of Mons Graupius. McDiarmid's use of implausible Gaelic etymology and local folklore rather than Tacitus to reconstruct the events of the conflict, however, reveals the dubious quality of much of this sort of antiquarianism:

> In the first attack it is said the Romans were severely handled and routed at Blardearg, that is, the red or bloody field ... next we have Dailrannaich, or the plain of the loud cry, where it is said the second in command of the Roman army was killed. This loss tradition says forced Agricola himself to retreat and the town of Cuilt in Gaelic cuil-teichead is the Den of Retreat.[21]

McDiarmid also cites 'some intelligent old persons' from the area with whom he spoke in 1791, who claimed that 10,000 Romans had died in the battle rather than the 360 mentioned by Tacitus. While the Roman author predictably presented the battle as a decisive victory for Rome, McDiarmid was not so convinced:

> Tradition says that the Romans were overcome by the Old Heroes, and forced to retreat by Cultiwhey in Galic Cuiltachaidh, the den to which the fighting army retreated & where they last fought. Tacitus says Agricola returned with his army to Angus. But whither victorious or not it is certain no Roman General of army every visited the Moor of Dalginross a second time.[22]

In the first publication produced by the Society of Antiquaries of Scotland, founded in 1780 largely due to the efforts of David Erskine, 11th Earl of Buchan, the only essay on Roman Scotland ('On Agricola's Engagement with the Caledonians' by Robert Barclay) comprised yet another suggestion for the location of Mons Graupius, placing it near Stonehaven. The majority of new material on the subject of the Romans in Scotland in Gough's 1789 edition of *Britannia* relates to the county of Angus, with an essay by the Earl of Buchan on the fortifications that demonstrated Agricola's progress, an account of two Roman camps in Forfar by one Reverend Jameson as well as General's Melville's description of his investigations into Agricolan sites all included.[23] Roman remains also appear regularly in the first *Statistical Account of Scotland*, a huge nationwide project produced during the 1790s in which local worthies (generally men of the church) were sent a questionnaire containing 160 questions relating to local geography, antiquities, population, agriculture and industry; the replies were later edited and published in twenty-one volumes by Sir John Sinclair of Ulbster. This method of gathering information is the same as that used by Sir Robert Sibbald over a century previously, and the results were similarly infused with folklore and legend. Spurious etymology was often employed to conjure up Roman heritage, with the town of Lenzie near the Antonine Wall supposedly deriving its name from the Latin word *linea*; similarly Catter Mellie, the site of a supposed Roman camp outside Invergowrie, is 'certainly a corruption of Quatuor Mille', the Reverend Thomas Constable suggesting that this was a reference to either the number of troops stationed there or its distance from another camp.[24] The untrustworthy chronicles of Hector Boece are often cited, such as in the description of a battle site where the Scots and the Picts fought the Romans near Blairgowrie, while James Playfair's (probably incorrect) claim that the ditches surrounding the medieval abbey at Coupar Angus were Roman closely follows his account of the tomb of Queen Guinevere in a nearby church.[25] While some imagined a Roman heritage where there was none, others overlooked clear evidence of Roman activity: John Wood of Cramond completely ignores the parish's copious Roman remains, which had been regularly described in previous antiquarian publications (although he does discuss them extensively in his 1794 *Antient and Modern State of the Parish of Cramond*). It may demonstrate an awareness of the Romans in Scotland among the nation's elite, but the *Statistical Account* also reveals just how little impact the previous century's scholarship had made on the wider population. Outside antiquarian circles, it seems, local legends and the fabulous histories of Boece and Buchanan were more influential than the writings of Sibbald, Gordon and the like.

Flights of fancy were obviously not unusual amongst such parochial antiquarians. Perhaps the nadir of this trend for localised amateur antiquarianism was reached in 1823 with the publication of *Interesting Roman Antiquities Recently Discovered in Fife* by the Reverend Andrew Small of Edenshead. Small joined the long list of antiquarians who proposed a new location for Mons Graupius; in this case it just happened to be in the fields that surrounded his own home. He also describes five supposed Roman towns in Scotland and identifies various standing stones and rock formations around the Lomond Hills as Roman religious sites, believing the (in fact naturally occurring) rock known locally as the Bonnet Stane to be 'one of the greatest Roman antiquities in the kingdom'.[26] A helpful fold-out map is decorated with drawings of 'Roman' (actually Bronze Age) artefacts from the area and also precisely pinpoints not just the battle lines laid out by the Romans and Caledonians, but even the very spot where Aulus Atticus fell. Perhaps surprisingly for a man intent on finding Roman history in his own parish, Small is dismissive of Tacitus, often questioning his accuracy and also suggesting that Agricola won the battle 'through artifice and stratagem, rather than by valour'.[27] Dedicated to Lord Gray, then president of the Society of Antiquaries of Scotland, the book's long list of subscribers includes many local gentleman, but also features distinguished names such as George Chalmers and Walter Scott, while five copies were apparently also taken by the King. Their reaction to Small's proposals can only be imagined; a mocking review of it published a year later stated that, although it was far from dull, Small's work displayed a lack of scholarship, suggesting that 'the Author has been less watchful over his imagination than was required by the kind of service in which he was engaged'.[28]

The influence of Ossian

While some late eighteenth-century commentators clung on to notions of a truly classical Caledonia, the poems of Ossian also inspired a contradictory confidence in the heroic status of the ancient Caledonians, which at times slipped into strident anti-Roman sentiments. Uses of the powerful symbolism of Scotland's rejection of foreign dominance in patriotic rhetoric became more militant than ever in some quarters, as concerns regarding the barbaric nature of the indigenous tribes fell away, replaced by new Ossianic visions of a cultured race of eloquent bards and courtly lovers.

Murray Pittock places James Macpherson at the forefront of a new wave of Primitivism that hoped to preserve disappearing indigenous culture in a rapidly changing world.[29] A survey of attitudes towards the ancient inhabitants of Scotland in texts published around the time of the 'rediscovery' of Ossian and in the years that followed reveals a notable evolution, as a long-held admiration for their noble simplicity and great valour morphs into a notion that they were equal to or even better than their classical contemporaries. John Macpherson of Sleat (1710–65), a minister on Skye who was also a distinguished scholar, was particularly interested in the origins of Scotland's earliest inhabitants, and as a result became embroiled in the debates surrounding Ossianic poetry in the final years of his life. A committed supporter (but not a direct relation) of his namesake James, Macpherson of Sleat met the young poet in 1760 and assisted in his research by supplying him with written material and contacts. His own attitudes to the Caledonians can be deduced from his *Critical Dissertations on the Origin, Antiquities, Language, Government, Manners and Religion of the Ancient Caledonians*, published posthumously in 1768; its portrayal of the ancient tribes is one of unsophisticated people more skilled in war than anything else, with no understanding of commerce or agriculture, utterly ignorant of 'the refinements of luxury'.[30] While Macpherson of Sleat, a proud Highlander, intended to highlight positive aspects of the Caledonians, such as their hospitality and conjugal fidelity, he also admitted that it was impossible to know how far they were able to pursue intellectual endeavours.[31] Instead, he fell back on the reliable trope of indomitable resistance to invasion: 'Let history determine, whether they were ever conquered, or whether the Lords of mankind, the Romans, were so bravely repulsed by any other nation, except the Parthians of the East and the Germans of the West'.[32] An accompanying note quoting George Buchanan's famous claim that Scotland had halted the progress of Rome leaves the reader in no doubt as to which of these two possibilities was the more likely.

This image was to alter as the poems attributed to Ossian took hold of the public imagination, and a derisive attitude towards the Romans can also be detected during the same period. Despite his copious notes on Agricola's campaigns in the north and descriptions of the Roman remains to be found in Scotland, French visitor Louis de la Rochette expressed frustration that Scottish antiquarians such as Sibbald and Gordon had focused on the Romans at the expense of the Caledonians, and aimed to redress the balance by using the poems of Ossian to build a picture of the indigenous peoples.[33] A decade later one Scot displayed a disdain for the Romans more aggressive than anything that had come before. Serialised in *The Edinburgh Magazine and Review* in 1774–5 and published as a book in 1777, not long after John Anderson talked of 'the high idea which is commonly entertained of Roman greatness', local minister William Nimmo's *General History of Stirlingshire* roundly denounced Rome and its imperial ambitions. The author's descriptions of Roman sites in the region cite the *Itinerarium Septentrionale*, but his dismissal of these remains would surely have made even the staunchly patriotic Gordon balk:

> In fine, we are tempted to think, that those works we have been surveying were never intended for any great or lasting use. Notwithstanding all the parade which Tacitus makes, when he speaks of his father-in-law's transactions, we cannot see how such feeble barriers could secure the Roman conquests . . . What effect could a few fortifications of earth, as most of those were . . . have to repel so brave a people as the ancient Caledonians appear to have been?[34]

Nimmo describes the Roman wall in Scotland in some detail, citing its description in the poems of Ossian as a 'gathered heap' before denouncing it as 'a very feeble frontier'.[35] The Roman belief that such 'castles of mud, and walls of turf' could keep out the Caledonians was, he proposed, nothing short of vanity.[36] The vestiges of Rome still to be found in Stirlingshire are described here as 'the remains of an all-grasping, rapacious nation . . . animated by a malicious passion to pillage and enslave the rest of mankind'.[37] As we see in the epigraph to this chapter, Nimmo applauded the destruction of such classical relics. This sentiment is not dissimilar to one expressed in the anonymous *Traveller's Guide or, a Topographical Description of Scotland* of 1798, which records the loss of the Antonine Wall to the plough: 'Here we see the Caledonian trampling upon the ruins of Roman ambition, and unfettered commerce occupying the seat of imperious usurpation'.[38]

In a paper on Roman activity in northern Scotland delivered to the Society of Antiquaries of Scotland in 1787 (and finally published in their *Archaeologia Scotica* in 1822), the Reverend George Grant of Boharn optimistically claimed that the age of partisan patriotic history was over, proposing that the subject could now be better understood since 'prejudices of national vanity no longer will warp the judgement'.[39] In fact, political antiquarianism was still alive and well, and in some cases more virulent than before; even Grant himself felt compelled to 'gratify national pride' by emphasising the military strength of the Romans and playing down the duration of their influence in Scotland.[40] The negative attitudes towards Roman imperialism displayed by Nimmo set the standard for the decades that were to follow. In his *Galic Antiquities* of 1780, John Smith used the poems of Ossian, along with several classical sources, to establish what he believed to be the true nature of Scotland's ancient peoples, portraying their (remarkably modern) attitudes towards religion, philosophy, medicine and law, also suggesting that the lack of Roman influence meant that Scotland was the only place where traces of Celtic culture truly survived.[41] South of the border, Edward Gibbon, who had earlier described the tribes faced by Agricola as 'a troop of naked barbarians', tentatively accepted that the poems of Ossian revealed another side to the Caledonians.[42] In fact, in light of the new information included in these verses, Gibbon argued that Scotland's ancient inhabitants were perhaps more admirable than the decadent Romans:

> The parallel would be little to the advantage of the more civilised people, if we compared the unrelenting revenge of Severus with the generous clemency of Fingal; the timid and brutal cruelty of Caracalla, with the bravery, the tenderness, the elegant genius of Ossian; the mercenary chiefs who, from the motives of fear or interest, served under the Imperial standard, with the freeborn warriors who started to arms at the voice of the king of Morven; if, in a word, we contemplated the untutored Caledonians, glowing with the warm virtues of nature, and the degenerate Romans, polluted with the mean vices of wealth and slavery.[43]

If he remained unsure about the authenticity of Ossian's poems, Gibbon seems to have wanted to believe in them. Ultimately, he decided, negative views of the ancient Scots and Picts were probably encouraged by the exaggerations of their southern neighbours in later times.[44] Writing in 1794 in his spirited *Defence of the Scots Highlanders*, John Buchanan quoted in full Gibbon's favourable comparison of the Caledonians with the Severans.[45] He recognised that Tacitus was the 'sure standard to be depended upon by moderns', but claimed that such an approach was flawed, and cast his own doubts upon the Roman author's accuracy.[46] A firm supporter of the authenticity of Ossian, Buchanan was not averse to using the *Agricola* when it suited his ambitions to frame the Caledonians in a positive light: 'And it is clear, from the speech of Galgacus, that their manners in these days, were no less refined than that of the Romans, who were rude enough to call them barbarians in common with all other nations, who would not submit to these tyrannical people'.[47]

In the final decades of the eighteenth century, that ancient battle between the plucky Caledonians and the rapacious Romans was still being replayed in Scottish minds; thanks to Ossian it was the Caledonians who were now consistently coming out on top. The imagery of a Scottish rejection of Roman oppression endured in the nation's poetry too. Robert Fergusson (1750–1774) was much influenced by Allan Ramsay, displaying a similar interest in vernacular Scots poetry; unlike Ramsay, however, Fergusson was also an accomplished classicist whose works demonstrate a knowledge of Juvenal, Horace, Virgil and the Scottish Latinists.[48] Several of his poems refer to Caledonia's repulsion of Rome, with his *Elegy, On the Death of Scots Music* lamenting the loss of old traditions in the face of foreign influence and recalling a time when Scots were more willing to fight for their cultural inheritance:

> O Scotland! That cou'd yence afford
> To bang the pith of Roman sword,
> Winna your sons, wi' joint accord,

> To battle speed,
> And fight till Music be restor'd,
> Which now lies dead?[49]

Thomas Mercer's poem *Arthur's Seat*, published in 1774 in his *Poems: By the Author of the Sentimental Sailor*, takes the readers on a fantastical journey through Scotland's past and combines the imagery of George Buchanan with the language of Ossian to describe the Antonine Wall as a place where 'gather'd heap around / Marks of Roman power the bound'.[50] The subject was also mined by Robert Burns, whose typically nostalgic ballad entitled *Caledonia*, written in 1789, imagines the nation personified as a female deity who stood up to Roman attack, with predictable results:

> Long quiet she reign'd; till thitherward steers
> A flight of bold eagles from Adria's strand:
> Repeated, successive, for many long years,
> They darken'd the air, and they plunder'd the land:
> Their pounces were murder, and terror their cry,
> They'd conquer'd and ruin'd a world beside;
> She took to her hills, and her arrows let fly,
> The daring invaders they fled or they died.[51]

New approaches to Scottish history

Many of the men who indulged in antiquarianism in the final years of the century were driven more by their imaginations than their historical knowledge, an approach that sometimes resulted in fanciful portrayals of the past. A prime example of such attitudes can be found in a 1785 manuscript now in the Perth Museum. Originally written for the Antiquarian Society of Perth, the text describes a supposedly Roman sword found in the Firth of Forth, apparently 'with part of a human scull fixed on its point', which one Mr Coldstream of Crieff had donated to the Society's museum. The Roman provenance of the weapon is established by comparisons with two other swords illustrated in the *Itinerarium Septentrionale* (neither of which are now thought to be Roman). While the author of the piece admits that conjecture is required in reconstructing its history, the ensuing tale goes beyond the bounds of scholarship and into the realms of pure fantasy, relying on stock characters of a noble Caledonian and a treacherous Roman in the process:

> Perhaps in some of the skirmishes between the Romans and Caledonians, on the banks of the Forth, a Legionary soldier having slain his adversary, might, in the wantonness of cruelty and insult, cut off his Head, and pitch it in triumph on the point of his sword; But while thus indulging the barbarous pride of victory, might meet with

some brave Caledonian eager to revenge (perhaps) the cause of his friend: and the haughty Roman, unable to maintain an unequal combat, might rather choose to commit his bloody Trophy to the adjacent river, than suffer the mortification of seeing it fall into the hands of the victor. But in points of the kind every one is at liberty to frame his own conjecture.[52]

The source of this romantic, imaginative approach, which saw Scots attempt to create an intimate personal connection with the past, is surely the poetry of Ossian. Elsewhere, despite evidence of a more positive attitude towards the Highlanders, a pessimistic and sombre tone can be detected in Scottish historiography. It has often been noted that Ossianic poems tend to look back to a better time, with Hugh Blair highlighting their 'tender melancholy'.[53] Like Ossian himself, readers were encouraged to pine for past glories, a Golden Age of redoubtable Scottish heroes. Men like Sibbald, Gordon and Clerk may have seen their studies as a way to elevate the current state of Scotland by promoting its admirable history, but Scots in the post-Ossian age tended to be less optimistic, viewing their nation's past as undoubtedly better, but now ultimately lost. Although, as Luke Gibbons notes, the Irish sometimes managed to harness a more positive, even revolutionary sense of nationalism in their bid to reclaim Ossianic mythology, the Scots preferred to revel in the air of 'resignation and melancholy' created by Macpherson.[54]

That such a feeling also infected later eighteenth-century historiography is demonstrated in the writings of the Earl of Buchan. A fanatical antiquarian who was widely regarded as a crashing bore (Walter Scott famously described him as 'a person whose immense vanity, bordering on insanity, obscured, or rather eclipsed, very considerable talents'), Buchan dedicated his life to restoring his family's finances and became something of a political campaigner, but spent his later years in retirement studying Scotland's antiquities.[55] In general, Buchan's attitudes towards ancient Rome display an ambivalence similar to that of Sir John Clerk, but lacking Clerk's pragmatism. He recommended that the emotions of young students should be aroused by reading of 'the death of Brutus, Cato, Helvidius Priscus, Arulenus Rusticus, Thrasea Poetus and of Arria' rather than modern novels or fairy tales, and he encouraged the pupils of Edinburgh High School to 'not allow your attachment to the classics ... to abate'.[56]

In one essay, published in *The Bee* on 11 August 1791, Buchan even imagined himself a Roman, explaining that the name of his home at Dryburgh signified 'in the language of old Pictland, the Brow of Oaks; so that were I Roman, I would call this my Quereinian Villa'; in a longer version of the same letter published posthumously he also speculated that the discovery of Roman coins and what he believed to be 'fragments of Roman buildings' on his estate marked the location of a '*praetorian* residence'.[57] As already noted, he wrote about the endeavours of Agricola in Scotland, but unlike men such as Clerk and Shand, Buchan's approach to writing history was often distinctly whimsical and romanticised. Perhaps inspired by a tour of the Highlands he had made in 1761, he expressed a close spiritual and physical bond with the ancient Caledonians: 'I studied the language and manners of the Gael, examined the remains of their rude antiquities and with the speech of Galgacus in my hand adored the Spirit of my Ancestors on the footsteps of their Glory'.[58]

Two letters written by Buchan (published under his pen name 'Albanicus') that appear in the *Bibliotheca Topographica Britannica* of 1786 demonstrate both his interest in Agricola and his yearning for a seemingly lost Scotland. The first reveals the author's dissatisfaction with the current condition of the nation, describing it as a 'neglected country, now become a dispirited province of the British Union' and proposing nostalgia as the only solace: 'I turn with aversion from the filthy picture that is before my eyes, and look back for consolation at the times which are past'.[59] The second letter ends on a remarkably romantic note, the Earl's imagination fired by visions of a centuries-old battle for liberty:

> I own . . . that when I shall again survey the hill where the brave Galgacus fought, I shall be apt to throw off my shoes, and say the ground on which I stand is consecrated to the fervour of our patriotism; I shall hear the harangues of Galgacus and of Agricola sounding in my ears with the eloquence of Tacitus; and, animated with the imaginary clashing of hostile shields, I shall exclaim, *My ancestors were defeated, but not subdued.*[60]

In his emotive account of historical events, his animated style and his encounter with ghosts of a glorious past, Buchan's words show a clear Ossianic influence. Stephen Bann identifies such a subjective relationship with the past as a symptom of new romantic tendencies in historiography.[61] Whether it was James Macpherson mourning the disappearance of Gaelic culture or Buchan bemoaning the once-proud nation's dwindling power, a sense of loss and regret haunts later eighteenth-century depictions of Scotland's early history.

Changing visions of Scotland

Outside the ivory towers of the antiquarian and literary worlds, the way in which Scotland past and present was perceived and packaged, both at home and abroad, was also changing. These changes are exemplified by developments at Penicuik House, the home which Sir John Clerk had filled with Roman antiquities and surrounded with a park remodelled to resemble a classical Elysium. On Baron Clerk's death in 1755 the estate passed to his son James, who soon initiated a project of major improvements including a new, grander house in the Palladian style. The mansion's opulent decoration included marble copies of famous classical sculptures ordered from Rome, but the niches to either side of the main entrance were filled not with Roman gods or heroes, but rather with two Caledonian druids. In 1767 aspiring young artist Alexander Runciman was sent to Italy at Sir James' expense to prepare plans for Penicuik's painted ceilings, with initial ideas including decorative elements inspired by the grotesques found in the Baths of Titus.[62] A Homeric subject was also proposed, but at some point the plans changed, apparently more at the behest of the artist than his patron; the saloon ceiling, completed by the end of 1772, portrayed scenes from the poems of Ossian, the room itself becoming known as 'Ossian's Hall'.[63] While his father had remained suspicious of such 'barbarians with no claim to civilisation whatever', Sir James was to become closely associated with Macpherson's version of ancient Caledonia. In January 1774 a jaunty reel entitled *Ossian's Hall*, composed by Daniel Dow and dedicated to Clerk himself, was printed in *The Edinburgh Magazine and Review*.[64]

Grenier identifies a 'steady trickle' of visitors to Scotland in the third quarter of the eighteenth century, but numbers had increased to such an extent by the 1790s that it could by then be termed 'the foundations of a tourist industry'.[65] She also highlights the importance of the reports and reminiscences of these visitors in shaping perceptions of the nation and its history, particularly south of the border: 'Whether they were scenic tourists, improvers, or antiquarians, those who introduced Scotland to the English public also defined Scotland'.[66] The books written by and for such travellers also give a sense of a new conceptualisation of the nation. Thomas Pennant, whose two journeys through Scotland in 1769 and 1772 were written up and first published in 1771 and 1774 respectively, made visits to Roman sites on both these epic trips. The most famous remains of the Roman incursions such as the forts and camps at Middleby, Burnswark and Ardoch, the carved stones at Glasgow University, the Antonine Wall, and even the site of the long-lost Arthur's O'on were included in his books, alongside countless medieval ruins and other historical and natural curiosities.[67] And while Keppie notes a sense of 'the rational giving way to the romantic' in Pennant's works, what was to follow would take this even further.[68]

Publications such as London-born Francis Grose's 1797 *Antiquities of Scotland*, a much larger and more lavishly illustrated affair than Pennant's guides, expressed no interest in the Roman remains in Scotland aside from a brief mention in the introduction of the recent publication of works by Melville and Roy.[69] As illustrations became more important, the scholarly maps and plans of Roman sites favoured by Pennant were dropped in favour of the dramatic imagery of overgrown castles and crumbling abbeys. The title page of Grose's book perfectly encapsulates this novel approach to Scotland's heritage; an illustration shows a tourist accompanied by a kilted guide standing before a Pictish carved stone, while across a loch the silhouette of a castle can be seen at the foot of a craggy mountain. Below it appear the following words:

> Let us explore the ruin'd Abbeys Choir: The Sculptur'd Tombs o'ergrown with shrubs & brambles. Or view the castle of some Ancient Thane. It's fretted roof & windows of rich Tracery, 'Midst broken arches, graves & gloomy vaults. It's Hall, its Dungeons & Embattled Towers Mantled with Ivy.

Even native authors with a knowledge of Roman Scotland seemed to feel that the subject would hold little interest for visitors. Adam de Cardonnel (whose thoughts on the Roman remains discovered at Inveresk were to be posthumously printed in the *Archaeologia Scotica* of 1822) wrote a guidebook entitled *Picturesque Antiquities of Scotland* that, besides passing mention of a Roman fort near Moffat (presumably Milton), generally stuck to the now customary list of 'Churches, Religious Houses and Castles . . . mostly in ruins'.[70] Scotland's historical material culture was no longer the preserve of scholars, and the fading remains of Roman Scotland that had so entranced generations of antiquarians were now deemed of little value by an emerging breed of guidebook writers. Offering limited potential for captivating illustrations, such sites were thus largely overlooked by a growing international audience.

The direct impact of the spectacular popularity of Ossian on Scottish tourism can also be detected around this time. Visitors wanted to confirm for themselves the authenticity of the poems by searching out locations related to them, while the very mood of the poetry inspired admiration for the windswept, mountainous Highland landscape, once denigrated as a barren place that no Roman would wish to conquer, now appreciated as the embodiment of the sublime and picturesque.[71] Some canny Highlanders took advantage of the craze by creating specious links between Scottish places and the events described by Ossian, with tales told by local guides leading, for example, to the international celebrity of Fingal's Cave on Staffa.[72] Recent structures that referenced the bard also became popular. On a visit to Scotland in 1788, one Elisabeth Diggle from Kent wrote to her sister of a visit to Penicuik House, a 'sweetly romantic' place she remembered not as a museum of Roman antiquities, but rather 'chiefly remarkable for a hall with the sides and ceiling painted, the subjects entirely from the poems of Ossian'.[73] Just a few days later she was in Perthshire admiring another 'Ossian's Hall', this one a folly built by the Duke of Atholl above a rocky waterfall in which a portrait of the bard could be rolled back by a hidden mechanism to reveal a mirrored room and the cascade beyond.[74]

For many early nineteenth-century commentators, both south of the border and further afield, the Highlands became a synecdoche for Scotland. Ossian fanatic Napoleon not only possessed a finely-bound copy of the poems, held at Fontainebleau, but also carried a copy as part of his large travelling library and kept a similarly decorative volume of Samuel Johnson's *Journey to the Western Isles of Scotland* in the library at Malmaison.[75] Although he arrived in Scotland sceptical of Ossian, French traveller Charles Nodier's mind was changed by what he found there, as he explains in his *Promenade de Dieppe aux Montagnes d' Écosse,* published in France in 1821 and translated into English a year later.[76] His description of his arrival across the border into Scotland also exaggerates the landscape to highlight its difference from England, noting how it 'becomes more austere and more varied; the ridges of the mountains appear sharper on the horizon, their profiles are more rude, more whimsical; terrible ravines cut the ground on both sides of the road to a great depth'.[77]

This new image of Scotland famously reached its zenith in 1822 with the visit of George IV to Edinburgh, a spectacle swathed in tartan and clan nostalgia that was largely choreographed by Walter Scott. Although Scott included numerous items believed to be Roman in his antiquarian collection and was apparently delighted to discover supposed Roman remains on land he bought in the Borders, he had little time for the Romans when it came to writing national history; indeed, he states in his *History of Scotland* that 'the history of every modern European nation must commence with the decay of the Roman Empire' and includes only a cursory (but suitably patriotic) description of the Roman incursions.[78] While he is often blamed for the nineteenth-century wave of 'Tartanism' and 'Balmoralisation' that would overwhelm previous notions of Scottish national identity, Scott was actually following a trend that had already been developing for decades; as James Coleman points out, 'the adoption of the Highlands as somehow representing Scotland as a whole has its roots in the Ossianic cult of the eighteenth century'.[79] These visions of Scotland's past were no less fanciful than those that had preceded it, but they were certainly less politicised and less threatening to the Establishment. Even when the poems of Ossian finally fell out of fashion, the imagery that they had inspired persisted.

The final decades of the eighteenth century saw a new mood engulf Scotland. Admiration for the classical (or at least the Roman), now regarded as rather staid and old fashioned, was replaced by the thrill of the romantic and the sublime. Although they are thinking predominantly of literature, Stafford and Gaskill propose that a transition from the classical to the romantic coincided with the lifespan of James Macpherson; as we have seen, a similar change in Scottish historiography occurred over the same period.[80] And just as the scepticism regarding the authenticity of the poems of Ossian did little to dent their popular success, so too the heroic picture they painted of Scotland's past was to survive even after their historicity had been largely discredited. James Macpherson's sophisticated fusion of literature, history and pseudo-history encouraged a more emotional and subjective response to antiquity. In earlier times of political change and insecurity, a number of notable Scots had focused their attention on the powerful empire of Rome, intending to link their nation, and by extension themselves, with its impressive cultural and military achievements. As Scotland become more confident and recognisably civilised itself, its capital city in the process of being transformed by a neo-classical New Town, its streets thronging with philosophers, scientists, writers and artists, so her people turned towards the primitive, searching for a time of simple nobility and a place of wide, open landscapes. As the Conclusion will demonstrate, Roman Scotland was to further fade from the public consciousness during the nineteenth century, to be replaced by more satisfying, less contentious episodes in the nation's long and eventful history, tales that could be more easily inserted into patriotic depictions of Scotland's distinguished past.

Notes

1. Manning, 'Antiquarianism, the Scottish Science of Man, and the Emergence of Modern Disciplinarity', p. 60; ibid. p. 63.
2. Hume, *History of England*, p. 2.
3. Manning, 'Antiquarianism, the Scottish Science of Man, and the Emergence of Modern Disciplinarity', p. 63.
4. Shaw, *The History of the Province of Moray*, pp. 2–3.
5. Gough, *Britannia*, p. 311.
6. Ibid.
7. Chalmers, *Caledonia*, p. iii.
8. Ibid. p. viii.
9. Tacitus, *Histories* 1.2; Chalmers, *Caledonia*, p. 115.
10. Ibid.; ibid. p. 183.
11. Ibid. p. 116.
12. Ibid. p. 166; ibid. p. 170.
13. Ibid. p. viii.
14. Ibid. p. 189.
15. Ibid. pp. 183–4.
16. Ibid. p. 183.
17. du Toit, 'George Chalmers', p. 871; *The Annual Register*, pp. 1003–4.
18. PM P.86: McOmie, 'A Plan of the Roman Camp at Fendoch', 1778; PM P.87: McOmie, 'Roman Fortifications Near Delvin House, Stormont, Perthshire', c.1780; PM P.88: McOmie, 'A Plan of the Roman Camp at Grassywell near Scoon', 1778; PM P.85: McRonald, 'An Accurate Plan of Part of Aberdeenshire Exhibiting the Roman Camp Near the Farm of Glenmailen', 1789.
19. NMS Acc. 1737 (34): McOmie, 'Plan of the Roman Wall and Camp near Micklehour', 1785.
20. PM 300: 'Plan & Description of the Roman Camp at Dalginross', 1786.
21. PM 307: 'Revd. Mr McDiarmid's Account of the Camp at Dalginross', 1800.
22. Ibid.
23. Gough, *Britannia*, pp. 409–17.
24. Sinclair, *Statistical Account of Scotland*, Vol. 2, p. 276; ibid. Vol. 13, p. 115.
25. Ibid. Vol. 13, p. 536; ibid. Vol. 1, p. 509: ibid. p. 506.

26. Small, *Interesting Roman Antiquities Recently Discovered in Fife*, p. 101.
27. Ibid. p. 71.
28. *The Eclectic Review*, pp. 527–30.
29. Pittock, *Inventing and Resisting Britain*, p. 153.
30. Macpherson, *Critical Dissertations*, p. 145; ibid. p. 131.
31. Ibid. p. 136; ibid. p. 139; ibid. p. 141.
32. Ibid. pp. 129–30.
33. NLS MS 3803, f. 27: de la Rochette, untitled notes; ibid. ff. 30–1.
34. Nimmo, *A General History of Stirlingshire*, p. 17.
35. Ibid. p. 39.
36. Ibid. p. 46.
37. Ibid. pp. 29–30.
38. *The Traveller's Guide*, p. 156.
39. Grant, 'Memoir Concerning the Roman Progress in Scotland', p. 32.
40. Ibid. p. 42.
41. Smith, *Galic Antiquities*, pp. 2–3.
42. Gibbon, *The History of the Decline and Fall of the Roman Empire*, p. 34.
43. Ibid. p. 152.
44. Ibid. p. 1000.
45. Buchanan, *A Defence of the Scots Highlanders*, p. 249.
46. Ibid. p. 122.
47. Ibid. p. 141.
48. Freeman, *Robert Fergusson and the Scots Humanist Compromise*, p. 23.
49. Fergusson, *The Works of Robert Fergusson*, p. 10.
50. Mercer, *Poems*, p. 17.
51. Burns, *The Works of Robert Burns*, p. 118.
52. PM 272: 'Mr Dowes Account of the Roman Weapon Communicated by Mr Coldstream of Crief', 1785.
53. Blair, *A Critical Dissertation on the Poems of Ossian*, p. 15.
54. Gibbons, 'From Ossian to O'Carolan', p. 236.
55. Scott quoted in: Cant, 'David Steuart Erskine, 11th Earl of Buchan', p. 26.
56. Erskine, *Letter from the Earl of Buchan to his Brother the Hon. Thomas Erskine*, p. 6; ibid. p. 12.
57. *The Bee*, Vol. 4, p. 161; Erskine, *The Anonymous and Fugitive Essays of the Earl of Buchan*, p. 100.
58. Buchan quoted in: Maxwell, *A Battle Lost*, p. 72.
59. Nichols, *Bibliotheca Topographica Britannica*, Vol. 5, p. 6; ibid. p. 1.
60. Ibid. pp. 14–15.
61. For his discussion of subjective approaches to the past, see: Bann, *Romanticism and the Rise of History*, pp. 79–101.
62. Booth, 'The Early Career of Alexander Runciman', pp. 336–7.
63. Macmillan, '"Truly National Designs"', p. 93.
64. *The Edinburgh Magazine and Review*, p. 140.
65. Grenier, *Tourism and Identity in Scotland*, pp. 16–17.
66. Ibid. p. 29.
67. Pennant, *A Tour in Scotland . . . Part I*, pp. 102–4; ibid. pp. 157–8; Pennant, *A Tour in Scotland . . . Part II*, pp. 101–3; ibid. p. 230; ibid. pp. 228–9.
68. Keppie, *The Antiquarian Rediscovery of the Antonine Wall*, p. 104.

69. Grose, *Antiquities of Scotland*, p. i.
70. de Cardonnel, *Picturesque Antiquities of Scotland*, Vol. 2, Auchincass Castle; ibid. Vol 1, p. iii.
71. For a discussion on new attitudes towards the Highland landscape, see: Grenier, *Tourism and Identity in Scotland*, pp. 21–3.
72. Ibid. p. 31.
73. Durie, *Travels in Scotland*, p. 24.
74. Ibid. pp. 25–6.
75. Brown, *Rax Me That Buik*, p. 112.
76. Nodier, *Promenade from Dieppe to the Mountains of Scotland*, pp. 163–5.
77. Ibid. p. 73.
78. Brown, 'Introduction', pp. xiv–v; Scott, *The History of Scotland*, p. 2.
79. Coleman, *Remembering the Past in Nineteenth-Century Scotland*, p. 23.
80. Stafford and Gaskill, 'Editors' Preface', p. xii.

Conclusion

> The footmark of the Roman on the soil of England is indelible... The history of the Scoto-Roman invasion is altogether different from this. It is a mere episode which might be altogether omitted without very greatly marring the integrity and completeness of the national annals.
> Daniel Wilson, *The Archaeology and Prehistoric Annals of Scotland*, 1851, p. 364

Although it is always more difficult to demonstrate an absence than a presence, a survey of nineteenth-century Scottish historiography, literature and popular culture exposes a distinct lack of interest in Roman Scotland. After Chalmers' bid to reclaim the nation's classical heritage, serious scholarly discussions (which clearly excludes eccentric oddities like Andrew Small's *Interesting Roman Antiquities Recently Discovered in Fife* discussed in the previous chapter) were to be few and far between over the following decades. The ways in which Scots saw themselves, also how they (and indeed all Britons) thought about Rome, were changing. As Rosemary Sweet points out, 'the admiration for all things Roman . . . no longer commanded the same position of intellectual dominance that had characterised the antiquarian world of the early eighteenth century'; her suggestion that 'by the early nineteenth century, the study of Roman antiquities had been consolidated', however, can be comfortably applied to England, but less convincingly to Scotland.[1]

Much recent scholarship on Romanist antiquarianism focuses exclusively on the long eighteenth century and has little interest in what came directly after. Richard Hingley's *The Recovery of Roman Britain* continues into the following century, but makes no mention of Scotland after the 1793 publication of William Roy's *Military Antiquities of the Romans in Britain*; thereafter Hingley's references to 'Roman Britain', like those of the nineteenth-century historians he discusses, actually mean Roman England. Keppie's *The Antiquarian Rediscovery of the Antonine Wall* explores attitudes towards Scotland's largest Roman monument right up until the first decade of the twentieth century, but the relatively small amount of material it contains on the first half of the nineteenth century is largely devoted to the damage caused by the construction of the Edinburgh to Glasgow railway, the wall's location in the increasingly industrialised central belt leading to much of it being swept away over the subsequent decades.[2] A drop in the status of the Roman stones kept at Glasgow University has already been noted towards the end of Chapter 5. Keppie also highlights their absence from visitors' accounts of their new home, the Hunterian Museum, which opened in 1807.[3] Apparently overshadowed by the collection donated by Dr William Hunter, which prompted the construction of a larger building and inspired the museum's new name but was predominantly dedicated to medicine and anatomy, the Roman stones were also overlooked by the new generation of professors in charge of the institution. One anecdote regarding an addition to the collection confirms that this attitude continued even after the stones were moved yet again to the Hunterian's present location at Gilmorehill. A newly donated Roman inscribed stone was delivered to the basement of the museum in 1871, but its arrival was not reported to the Keeper, Dr Young. It therefore languished in the joiner's workshop, only to be rediscovered when the area was cleared twenty-eight years later.[4] These carved Roman stones, the pride of Glasgow's eighteenth-century professors, were obviously no longer a priority to their Victorian counterparts.

Scottish opinion on the impact of Rome in the north remained divided, but the sentiments that it inspired were certainly less intense. The first nineteenth-century monograph on Roman Scotland would not appear until 1845, when Glaswegian Robert Stuart's *Caledonia Romana* was first published. Although he had little previous antiquarian experience, the author was inspired by a visit to the collection of banker and amateur historian John Buchanan, which contained several inscribed altars alongside other Roman antiquities of a Scottish provenance. Stuart was made aware of the lack of recent publications on the subject, with a biographical note in the second (posthumous) edition of *Caledonia Romana* describing how 'Mr Buchanan remarked that . . . it was surprising that no one, during nearly a century, had written on "the Roman Antiquities of Scotland", and the wish was expressed that some one, competent to the task, would write a book'.[5] The resulting tome, composed in a style recently described as 'colourful and verbose, in the flowery manner of the Victorian age', seems to have been aimed at a wide, non-specialist audience.[6] The appearance of that second edition seven years after the initial publication suggests that there was certainly a taste for such material.

No major discoveries having been made in the preceding decades, *Caledonia Romana* largely treads familiar ground in terms of the sites and artefacts that it covers. Its author also shows himself to be well-versed in eighteenth-century antiquarian texts. Compared to those of the previous century, however, Stuart's portrayal of Roman Scotland is distinctly un-partisan and shows few signs of patriotic intent, being more concerned with recording the material remains than describing the historical events. His depiction of the ancient Caledonian is more balanced than those of his predecessors: 'He may not have been quite the savage that Xiphiline has represented; but, without doubt, his mode of life was deeply tinged with the shades of original barbarism'.[7] Similarly, his attitude towards Rome was objective enough to allow mockery of the eighteenth-century obsession with Arthur's O'on.[8] Given his reliance on the works of Sibbald and Chalmers, as well as his belief in the authenticity of the *De Situ Britanniae*, it was inevitable that Stuart would propose the existence of several 'provincial towns, which sprung up in this country under the influence of Italian civilization'; he also talks of 'Romanized Caledonians', reasonably suggesting that many of the Roman forts in Scotland would have been abutted by civil settlements, believing that the poor preservation of such sites explained the fact that no physical remains of them had so far been discovered.[9] Stuart was certainly inclined to whimsy, particularly in imaging the thoughts and reactions of the Caledonian to Roman invasion (describing his 'fire-lit, joyful eye' and his 'hasty, unreflecting spirit').[10] In general, however, he preferred factual descriptions of antiquities to historical conjecture. His response to the question of how successful the Caledonians were at reclaiming their lost territory after the recall of Agricola, for example, is telling: 'The question is one that cannot now be decided; nor is it indeed of any material importance'.[11]

Meanwhile, Daniel Wilson included the Roman invasions of Scotland in his 1851 *Archaeology and Prehistoric Annals of Scotland*, but felt no particular draw towards the subject, arguing that while the Romans civilised England and its inhabitants and 'left them a totally different people than they had found them', their impact on Scotland had been negligible.[12] As the epigraph to this Conclusion reveals, Wilson believed that the Roman period had little importance for the overall narrative of Scottish history. While he suggested that English archaeologists had much to discover concerning the Roman heritage of their nation, he concluded that Roman Scotland had been wrung dry and thus deserved no more attention:

> Still the field of Anglo-Roman antiquities is an ample one, and therefore well-merited to be explored. But when Scottish archaeologists, following their [the English antiquarians] example, fall to discussing the weary battle of Mons Grampius . . . and the like threadbare questions, they are but thrashing straw from which the very chaff has long since been gleaned to the last husk, and can only bring well-deserved ridicule on their pursuits'.[13]

In the first volume of his 1867 *History of Scotland From Agricola's Invasion to the Revolution of 1688*, Aberdeen-born advocate and historian John Hill Burton was equally critical of what he described on his contents page as the 'useless search after Mons Grampius'.[14] The book includes a standard account of Roman endeavours in Scotland, and although the author admits to having been duped by the *De Situ Britanniae*, by the time of writing he recognised it as a forgery.[15] Burton nevertheless proposed that the south of the country had been civilised by the Romans for a while at least, producing as evidence extensive quotes from the (now almost 150-year-old) *Itinerarium Septentrionale* that describe supposedly Roman remains in the region around Camelon.[16] He also noted the quantity of military sites in the north-east, citing the scholarship of William Roy and suggesting that this was a consequence of the long contest between Rome and the Caledonians to secure the region.[17] But while Burton viewed the Roman period as a key part of Scotland's story and thought that the territory between the walls had been fully conquered, he was also dismissive of its material remains, stating that the majority of Roman sculptures found there were 'more ambitious than successful' and that 'there is not one specimen of the beautifully tessellated floorings found in the south of England, where they testify to a people living in luxurious elegance'.[18]

The first decades of the nineteenth century also saw an increased interest in the culture and history of ancient Greece, and the suggestion that Greece replaced Rome in Victorian British minds has become something of a commonplace in recent years.[19] The suspicion of ancient Athens and its democratic system demonstrated in the writings of late eighteenth-century Scottish Historiographer Royal John Gillies was certainly overcome, and the idea that Edinburgh was the 'Athens of the North' (perhaps initiated by poet and artist Hugh William Williams although, as Iain Gordon Brown has discovered, its origins are actually hard to pin down) became widespread during the 1820s.[20] The conceit of Edinburgh as a new Athens was clearly referenced in the very architecture of the expanding city, most evidently in Thomas Hamilton's Royal High School and William Henry Playfair's Royal Institution (now the Royal Scottish Academy) and National Gallery buildings, completed in 1829, 1836 and 1859 respectively; also in the less successful National Monument, a grandiose facsimile of the Parthenon atop Calton Hill that was left unfinished due to lack of funds in 1829. Books dedicated to describing and illustrating the city, such as Robert Mudie's *The Modern Athens* of 1825 and John Britton's *Modern Athens!* of 1829 (with illustrations by Thomas Shepherd), demonstrated a continuing desire to associate Scotland with the classical past, although it was now a foreign past with no direct links to the history of the nation itself.

Nineteenth-century approaches to Roman England

A rise in philhellenism can also be detected in England, but, as Vance and Wallace suggest, a fascination with Rome also persisted into the nineteenth century, largely thanks to the nation's own position within the ancient empire and the visible reminders of it that survived there.[21] Many inhabitants of England clearly relished their Roman heritage. Hingley identifies a focus among later eighteenth-century English antiquarians on the civil (as opposed to the military) aspects of Roman Britain alongside a tendency to suggest that the indigenous Britons had widely adopted Roman culture.[22]

The first two decades of the nineteenth century saw the publication of several lavishly-illustrated books by Samuel Lysons that recorded the discovery of impressive Roman mosaics and sculptures in the south and placed them within the context of their more celebrated continental equivalents, presenting them as proof that Britain had been no remote backwater, but rather a sophisticated and cosmopolitan part of the Roman world. Sarah Scott proposes that Lysons' work 'placed Britain firmly within a pan-European classical tradition', but it is worth noting that all of the sites that he studied were in England, and most of them in the extreme south.[23] Roman relics also appeared in illustrated guidebooks: the first (and ultimately the only) volume of *Britannia Delineata*, published in folio in 1822 by Charles Hullmandel and dedicated to Kent, includes images and descriptions of both the Roman 'station' of Reculver and the Roman lighthouse at Dover as well as the suggestion that Folkestone had once been a Roman colony. Restrictions on European travel during the Napoleonic Wars and the introduction of the railways further encouraged English tourists to discover and interact with their own classical past.[24] During his tour of Britain, which he would write up and publish in 1825 as the *Historical and Literary Tour of a Foreigner in England and Scotland*, Frenchman Amédée Pichot noticed how keen the residents of York were to show off the Roman relics in their city, some even comparing it to Rome itself, believing, Pichot deduced, 'in the fancy that there still lingers some drops of Roman blood in the pulses of their hearts'.[25] It is perhaps as a result of such enthusiasm, combined with widespread urban development, that high-profile excavations of Roman remains were to take place over the following decades in Cirencester, St Albans and Silchester amongst numerous other sites, with the discoveries at Cirencester attracting much interest in the national press.[26] As Virginia Hoselitz notes, while the classical texts tended to relate Roman military exploits, the material remains of towns and villas being unearthed in England presented a more peaceful and civilised picture of ancient Britannia.[27]

English nineteenth-century descriptions of Roman Britain often neglected the lands north of Hadrian's Wall altogether, since that troublesome region had no place in attempts to demonstrate that these islands had been just as civilised as the rest of the empire. Such an attitude was to last much of the century. Henry Charles Coote's *The Romans of Britain* of 1878, which aimed to prove that a Roman-style constitution had endured even after the Roman

Empire itself had collapsed, uses the term 'Britain' and 'England' interchangeably when referring to both the ancient and modern state, but understands them both to mean the region south of Hadrian's Wall. Hingley not only suggests that Coote was one of several authors around this time who intended to locate a 'Roman racial origin for aspects of English society', but also highlights the book's widespread influence on later generations.[28] Even Thomas Wright, whose 1852 book *The Celt, the Roman and the Saxon* included the unusual claim that both Scotland and Ireland had been conquered by Rome, includes only a brief mention of one Scottish monument (the Antonine Wall) in his extensive description of Romano-British material culture.[29] Only works that took a narrative approach to Roman history, such as Harry Scarth's *Roman Britain* of 1883, would spend much time discussing the Scottish incursions. For those more interested in Roman culture and its role in the evolution of modern Britain, the invasions of the north and the military remains that survived there served no useful purpose.

The profile of Hadrian's Wall itself also influenced how Britons thought about their ancient past. Regular organised walking 'pilgrimages' along the frontier began in 1849. Two years later John Collingwood Bruce published *The Roman Wall*, which was followed in 1863 by his smaller portable 'wallet-book' suitable for walkers and tourists. Its growing fame, along with the fading interest in the Roman remains further north, no doubt entrenched perceptions that it was this wall that represented the furthest limits of Roman power in Britain. In a paper delivered in 1860, Collingwood Bruce claimed that the Roman antiquities found in Britain revealed a distinct north/south divide, with those to the south demonstrating evidence of 'security and luxury', while those to the north were almost exclusively military, evidence of ongoing battles between Rome and Caledonia.[30] Ultimately, for Victorians intent on locating signs of a civilised ancient Britannia and thus establishing their own classical inheritance, the north of England was of little interest and Scotland completely irrelevant. By the early twentieth century these ideas seemed set in stone: in his influential lecture to the British Academy entitled *The Romanization of Roman Britain*, published in 1905, Francis Haverfield split Roman Britain into two zones, its southern reaches civil, its northern regions a military zone, Hadrian's Wall as its frontier and Scotland nowhere to be seen.

Classical Caledonia: a study in historical failure

In its description of the confusion, arguments, misunderstandings, misinterpretations and outright forgeries that characterise the early modern struggle to understand Scotland's distant past, *Classical Caledonia* has gone some way towards explaining why the rise and fall of Roman Scotland as an aspect of the national story was so dramatic. Ancient Scotland presented something of a conundrum for eighteenth-century antiquarians and commentators. Paradoxically, the more they studied it, the more unintelligible and contradictory it seemed to become. Challenging the existing notion of Caledonia's repulsion of foreign invasion in the late seventeenth and early eighteenth centuries, Sir Robert Sibbald and William Stukeley were the first of many who would be swayed by their admiration for Rome into imagining southern Scotland and beyond as a Roman province filled with symbols of imperial power and classical civility. Such ideas endured throughout the eighteenth century and were further encouraged by the widespread acceptance of the fake *De Situ Britanniae*, particularly amongst the Agricolamaniacs, who saw themselves as following in Roman footsteps and were determined to find traces of Rome wherever they could. But the persistent belief in a Caledonian resistance of Rome, bolstered by a new-found confidence in the nation's indigenous peoples based on the poems of Ossian, continually overshadowed aspirations to locate a classical heritage for Scotland. Scholarship declined towards the end of the century as both sides of the argument descended once again into myth and fancy.

There can be no doubt that patriotism was a defining feature of the eighteenth-century interpretation and manipulation of Scotland's Roman history. Many, if not most, of the antiquarians discussed in this book would certainly have seen themselves as committed patriots, proud of their origins and determined to present their home nation in the best possible light. But more personal desires were also at play. In his 1985 book *The Past is a Foreign Country*, David Lowenthal examines the ways in which history has been approached, appropriated and possessed. He assesses fictional representations of time travel, noting that the yearning to repossess and literally revisit the past is a staple of imaginative literature.[31] In their vivid portrayals of ancient Caledonia, our antiquarians seem to demonstrate that they similarly wanted to repossess their nation's earliest history. Each of them created a past that he himself would have preferred to inhabit, imagining a place and time in which he would feel at home: erudite virtuosi, statesmen and imperialists like Sir Robert Sibbald, Sir John Clerk and George Chalmers craved an ancient Scotland filled with civilised towns and classical villas overseen by a stable Roman government; Hanoverian soldiers General Robert Melville and Major-General William Roy focused on a victorious Roman invasion that demonstrated admirable military tactics; political, religious and cultural outsiders such as Patrick Abercromby, Alexander Gordon and James Macpherson portrayed embattled Caledonians bravely and successfully defending their liberty in the face of hostile attack from a more powerful enemy. The forged and manipulated sources that satisfied such appetites, most notably the *De Situ Britanniae* and the poems of Ossian, suggest that such desires were recognised and exploited at the time.

Confirmation bias also played a role in these early modern visions of Caledonia, each commentator subconsciously interpreting the evidence to fit his own preconceptions and expectations. The fact that each of these factions sought something different from Scotland's earliest history produced an unsettled, unresolved view of the past, one which changed from generation to generation. That such a volatile and inconsistent narrative is ultimately useless as national history is highlighted by Lowenthal, who believes that 'we need a stable past to validate tradition, to confirm our own identity, and to make sense of the present. How can we rely on a past that is fluid and alterable?'[32]

By the end of the eighteenth century, no clear consensus had been reached on how important the Romans had been in the development of the Scottish nation, while the limited written and material sources continued to baffle and confuse. The idea that the Romans had established a province in the north lingered, but the signs of elegant classical culture such as the luxurious villas that were being unearthed in England were notable by their absence in the region beyond Hadrian's Wall. While Scotland's Roman military monuments were undoubtedly impressive, the sculptures and other material remains found in and around them generally failed to live up to the high ideas of Rome widely held in the eighteenth century. Meanwhile, any credible evidence for the much-vaunted Caledonian rejection of Rome proved elusive. They might have been widely admired by early modern Scots, but to admit that the Romans had conquered Scotland meant trashing centuries of tradition and recognising the inferiority of one's own nation. On the other hand, to laud Caledonian ancestors who, although certainly brave, were also unavoidably barbaric, proved too much for some genteel eighteenth-century Scots.

Roman Scotland had turned out to be a historiographical dead end. Just as happened in other areas of British historiography, the history of Roman Britain came to mean more precisely the history of Roman England, with the on/off occupation of Scotland playing no role in descriptions of 'Romanisation' and associated discussions on the constitutional evolution of the modern British nation.[33] Even as Scotland itself, with its emerging cities forming imperial hubs, its neoclassical architecture and its world-renowned thinkers, began to reflect early modern visions of ancient Rome, nostalgic Scots increasingly looked elsewhere for their historical identity. Primitivism emerged in the later eighteenth century as something to aspire to rather than to denigrate and, as Scots became more selective when it came to the historical figures they viewed as national heroes, so Roman Scotland was sidelined. Many ignored it, some dismissed it as an inconsequential footnote and even the relatively few Victorian Scots who viewed the Roman period as an important aspect of their nation's story display none of the patriotic fire of their eighteenth-century predecessors; its lack of a clear, reliable narrative combined with ambiguous sources and the constant contradictions and discord that its study induced hardly made for inspirational national history.

Modern attitudes to patriotic Scottish history

Sophie Thomas notes that the Romantic era heralded a more widespread interest in history that rendered it 'available and meaningful to a mass reading and viewing public', opening the subject up to non-elites.[34] Roman Scotland seemed to hold a limited interest for this new audience. As the nineteenth century progressed, the Romans and Caledonians faded from the Scottish imagination and patriotic interpretations of Agricola and Calgacus all but disappear. It should not be thought, however, that patriotic history was a thing of the past, even in these days when Scots had become more accustomed (or resigned) to the idea of a British union. In fact, Scottish patriotism simply found other historical episodes to celebrate. While the Germans and the French turned to their own indigenous heroes who had resisted Rome in their creation of a national identity, it was fourteenth-century anti-English freedom fighters who inspired nineteenth-century Scots. The growing status of William Wallace and Robert the Bruce is charted in James Coleman's recent book *Remembering the Past in Nineteenth-Century Scotland*. Coleman compares the nineteenth-century impetus to build memorials to Hermann and Vercingetorix (particularly the imposing *Hermannsdenkmal* monument constructed in the Teutoburg Forest between 1838 and 1875 and the sculpture of Vercingetorix commissioned by Napoleon III that was erected on Mont Auxois in 1865) with similar patriotic endeavours in Scotland, but since public commemoration of Calgacus was non-existent at this time, he makes comparisons instead with the Victorian monuments dedicated to William Wallace.[35] In England, meanwhile, a growing admiration for Boudica in the later nineteenth century is demonstrated by the striking sculptural portrayal of the warrior queen with her daughters modelled by Thomas Thornycroft between 1856 and 1871 and finally cast in bronze during the 1890s. The fact that Boudica's name, like that of the reigning queen, signified victory only added to her heroic status.[36] Those colossal monuments to rebel tribal leaders in Germany and France were situated near what was then believed to be the ancient battle sites where they had faced the might of Rome. But where would such a memorial to Calgacus even be located? The veneration of Vercingetorix and Boudica demonstrates that even losers could be idolised; Calgacus was surely neglected because Scotland had better heroes in her historical arsenal, warriors who were either more successful or more fully formed, or both. Once it became clear that Calgacus' famous speech was probably a Tacitean literary construct, what was left of him to celebrate? Why employ a lost (in both senses of the word) battle between Caledonia and Rome as an analogy for Scotland's struggle to retain a national identity distinct from that of England when glorious medieval Scottish victories against the English could be invoked?

Colin Kidd has written extensively about the collapse of a coherent Scottish historiography during the later eighteenth and early nineteenth centuries, identifying in particular the decline of a satisfying patriotic narrative. He also observes the evolution of a 'bowdlerised historical canon: a very loose collection of incidents without a plot or unifying thread of constitutional development'.[37] These incidents tended to be distinctly romantic and included the courageous resistance to English invasion of Bruce and Wallace, the dramatic adventures of Mary Queen of Scots and the ill-fated efforts of Bonnie Prince Charlie to regain the British throne for the Stuarts. Coleman argues that Scots were as eager as any other European nation to demonstrate their distinctiveness and distinction through historical precedent and call up the ghosts of long-dead historical personalities in the process, even suggesting that Scotland had a 'surfeit' of focal points that could be employed to define her national story.[38] In some respects, the courageous last stand of Calgacus would fit perfectly into this group of (mostly doomed) historical heroes, but neither the invading Romans nor those Caledonians who opposed them would secure a place in this emerging canon.

Once a subject that had enthused generations of antiquarians, historians, political agitators, poets and schoolboys, Roman Scotland faded from view for decades, only to re-emerge briefly towards the close of the nineteenth century as Britain turned again to ancient Rome in attempts to justify its new imperial identity. By then, improved archaeological techniques allowed academics such as George MacDonald and enthusiastic amateurs like James Curle to reveal and more fully understand the often subtle and ambiguous material remains of the Roman invasions. Excavations focused particularly on the Antonine Wall and were often carried out by local groups such as the Glasgow Archaeological Society; Hingley suggests that these investigations into Scotland's Roman frontier also informed contemporary frontier policy for the British Empire.[39] In 1898 a new frieze by English-born but Edinburgh-bred artist William Brassey Hole, which depicted 155 figures generally referred to as 'notable Scots', was unveiled in the lobby of the National Portrait Gallery and Museum of Antiquities in the Scottish capital. Calgacus appears, of course, alongside an unnamed druid, but these Caledonians are heavily outnumbered by the Roman contingent comprising Theodosius, Septimius Severus, Antoninus Pius, Lollius Urbicus, Hadrian, Agricola and even Tacitus himself. As Britain reached its peak as a world power, the citizens of Edinburgh were apparently happy to celebrate the imperial achievements of these Romans, who were effectively nominated honorary Scots. The focus of this Romanist resurgence was almost exclusively military, and by the early twentieth century any idea of a classical Caledonia had evaporated. In the introduction to *In Roman Scotland*, published in 1927, Jessie Mothersole warns her readers that 'it is for the remains of forts and of temporary camps that we must look, and not for signs of Romanized civil life, such as are common in the south'.[40]

Nowadays Roman Scotland seems to have slipped out of the national consciousness yet again. Many apparently still believe Hadrian's Wall to be the final endpoint of the Roman Empire. Volunteers at the Trimontium Museum in Melrose, which displays the finds from the nearby Roman fort at Newstead, have become accustomed to visitors expressing their surprise that the Romans made it to Scotland at all.[41] Despite its 2008 inscription as a UNESCO World Heritage site and a recent National Lottery Heritage Fund grant intended to promote awareness of the monument, the Antonine Wall remains overshadowed by its world-famous Hadrianic predecessor. Evidence of that Caledonian resistance remains elusive, while the discovery of Roman objects at Iron Age sites in Scotland suggests that some of its ancient inhabitants were not quite as resistant to the Roman way of life as our early modern antiquarians liked to believe, or even that they accepted payment from Rome in return for their good behaviour.[42] James Fraser has described the lingering idea of a brave Caledonian resistance as 'an utter fairy tale', proposing than any disruption caused by the tribes was motivated more by a desire for bribery than any virtuous defence of liberty.[43] While scholars discuss the sources, formulation and dissemination of Macpherson's Ossianic poetry, the turgid, impenetrable verses themselves are rarely read outside academic circles. Archaeological work continues and the search for Mons Graupius goes on, but the period holds little resonance for the wider public. In fact, if big-budget films and television series are anything to go by, the characters from Scottish history that inspire the most admiration at home and abroad have remained unchanged since the nineteenth century, with William Wallace (*Braveheart*, 1995), Robert the Bruce (*Outlaw King*, 2018), Mary Stuart (*Mary Queen of Scots*, 2019) and the Jacobites (*Outlander*, 2014 onwards) still taking the leading roles. Even at a time when Scotland's position within the British union is once again being questioned, Calgacus and Fingal remain largely forgotten; but fragments of their DNA survive, perhaps, in the proud pipers and kilted musclemen who decorate countless porridge packets and shortbread tins around the globe, these nameless, Highland-esque symbols of a modern 'Scotland the Brave'.

Notes

1. Sweet, *Antiquaries*, p. 186.
2. Keppie, *The Antiquarian Rediscovery of the Antonine Wall*, pp. 115–17.
3. Keppie, *Roman Inscribed and Sculptured Stones*, p. 34.
4. Ibid. p. 38. The stone is RIB 2184.

5. Stuart, *Caledonia Romana*, p. x.
6. Keppie, *The Antiquarian Rediscovery of the Antonine Wall*, p. 118.
7. Stuart, *Caledonia Romana*, p. 31.
8. Ibid. p. 184.
9. Ibid. p. 119; ibid. p. 120.
10. Ibid. p. 104.
11. Ibid.
12. Wilson, *The Archaeology and Prehistoric Annals of Scotland*, p. 363.
13. Ibid. p. 379.
14. Burton, *The History of Scotland*, p. v.
15. Ibid. pp. 61–2 n. 1.
16. Ibid. pp. 66–70.
17. Ibid. pp. 74–6.
18. Ibid. p. 51; ibid. p. 53.
19. For more on the importance of Greece rather than Rome in the nineteenth-century British imagination, see: Turner, 'Why the Greeks and Not the Romans in Victorian Britain'.
20. On Gillies' negative attitudes towards the political system of ancient Athens, see: Turner, *The Greek Heritage in Victorian Britain*, p. 189; Devine, *The Scottish Nation*, p. 329; Brown, *Rax Me That Buik*, p. 85.
21. Vance and Wallace, 'Introduction', p. 6.
22. Hingley, *The Recovery of Roman Britain*, p. 225.
23. Scott, 'Britain in the Classical World', p. 294.
24. Vance, *The Victorians and Ancient Rome*, p. 23.
25. Pichot, *Historical and Literary Tour*, p. 246.
26. Hoselitz, *Imagining Roman Britain*, p. 95.
27. Ibid. pp. 172–3.
28. Hingley, *Roman Officers and English Gentlemen*, p. 69.
29. Wright, *The Celt, the Roman and the Saxon*, p. 39; ibid, p. 101.
30. Hoselitz, *Imagining Roman Britain*, p. 172.
31. Lowenthal, *The Past is a Foreign Country*, pp. 13–21.
32. Ibid. p. 263.
33. On the Enlightenment and nineteenth-century sidelining of Scotland in British historiography, see: Kidd, '"The Strange Death of Scottish History" Revisited', pp. 86–90.
34. Thomas, *Romanticism and Visuality*, p. 48.
35. Coleman, *Remembering the Past in Nineteenth-Century Scotland*, pp. 64–9.
36. Hingley, *Roman Officers and English Gentlemen*, p. 77.
37. Kidd, 'The Canon of Patriotic Landmarks in Scottish History', p. 7.
38. Coleman, *Remembering the Past in Nineteenth-Century Scotland*, p. 20.
39. Hingley, *Roman Officers and English Gentlemen*, p. 42.
40. Mothersole, *In Roman Scotland*, p. v.
41. *The Trimontium Trumpet*, p. 6.
42. Harding, *The Iron Age in Northern Britain*, pp. 192–5.
43. Fraser, *Caledonia to Pictland*, p. 30; ibid. p. 25.

Bibliography

Manuscript abbreviations

Bodl. – Bodleian Libraries
EUL – Edinburgh University Library
NLS – National Library of Scotland
NMS – National Museums Scotland Library
NRS – National Records of Scotland
PM – Perth Museum
RA – Royal Archives
SUL – Strathclyde University Library

Printed sources

Abercromby, Patrick, *The Martial Atchievements of the Scots Nation*, Volume 1 (Edinburgh, 1711)
Adam, Alexander, *Roman Antiquities: or, A Description of the Manners and Customs of the Romans* (Edinburgh, 1791)
Adamson, Henry, *The Muses Threnodie, or, Mirthfull Mournings, on the Death of Master Gall* (Perth, 1774)
Allan, David, 'A Commendation of the Private Countrey Life: Philosophy and the Garden in Seventeenth Century Scotland', *Garden History*, 25.1 (1997), pp. 59–80
———, *Virtue, Learning and the Scottish Enlightenment: Ideas of Scholarship in Early Modern History* (Edinburgh: Edinburgh University Press, 1993)
An Elegye Upon the Never Enough to Be Lamented Decease of That Antient Illustrious and Venerable Lady Princess Scocia (Edinburgh, 1707)
Andrews, Corey, *Literary Nationalism in Eighteenth-Century Scottish Club Poetry* (Lewiston; Lampeter: Edwin Mellen Press, 2004)
Ayres, Philip, *Classical Culture and the Idea of Rome in Eighteenth-Century England* (Cambridge: Cambridge University Press, 1997)

Bacon, Francis, *A Brief Discourse of the Happy Union in the Kingdoms of Scotland and England* (London, 1700)

Baigent, Elizabeth, 'William Roy', in *The Oxford Dictionary of National Biography*, Volume 48 (Oxford: Oxford University Press, 2004), pp. 50–53

Balfour-Melville, Evan, 'A Biographical Sketch of General Robert Melville of Strathkinness Written by His Secretary', *The Scottish Historical Review*, 14.54 (1917), pp. 116–46

Bann, Stephen, *Romanticism and the Rise of History* (New York: Twayne Publishers, 1995)

Barclay, Robert, 'On Agricola's Engagement with the Caledonians, Under Their Leader, Galgacus', *Archaeologia Scotica*, 1 (1792), pp. 565–9

Baxter, William, *Glossarium Antiquitatum Britannicarum* (London, 1733)

Beattie, James, *Essays. On Poetry and Music, as They Affect the Mind. On Laughter, and Ludicrous Composition. On the Utility of Classical Learning* (Edinburgh, 1776)

Bellenden, John, *The Works of John Bellenden*, Volume 1 (Edinburgh: W. & C. Tait, 1821)

Benario, Herbert W., 'Gordon's Tacitus', *The Classical Journal*, 72.2 (1976), pp. 107–14

Bertram, Charles, *The Description of Britain* (London: J. Wright & Co., 1809)

Bibliotheca Sibbaldiana: or, A Catalogue of Curious and Valuable Books . . . To Be Sold by Way of Auction, on Tuesday the 5th of February 1723 (Edinburgh, 1722)

Blackwell, Thomas, *An Enquiry into the Life and Writings of Homer* (London, 1735)

Blair, Hugh, *A Critical Dissertation on the Poems of Ossian, the Son of Fingal* (London, 1763)

Booth, Susan, 'The Early Career of Alexander Runciman and His Relations with Sir James Clerk of Penicuik', *Journal of the Warburg and Courtauld Institutes*, 32 (1969), pp. 332–43

Bosanquet, Robert C., 'John Horsley and His Times', *Archaeologia Aeliana*, 4, 10 (1933), pp. 58–81

Boswell, James, *The Life of Samuel Johnson*, Volume 1 (London, 1791)

Bowie, Karin, 'New Perspectives on Pre-Union Scotland', in *The Oxford Handbook of Modern Scottish History*, ed. by Tom M. Devine and Jenny Wormald (Oxford: Oxford University Press, 2012), pp. 303–19

———, *Scottish Public Opinion and the Anglo-Scottish Union, 1699–1707* (London: Boydell Press, 2007)

Boyd Haycock, David, 'Charles Julius Bertram', in *The Oxford Dictionary of National Biography*, Volume 5 (Oxford: Oxford University Press, 2004), pp. 500–2

———, *William Stukeley: Science, Religion, and Archaeology in Eighteenth-Century England* (Woodbridge: Boydell Press, 2002)

Boyse, Samuel, *Translations and Poems, Written on Several Occasions* (London, 1738)

Britton, John, *Modern Athens! Displayed in a Series of Views* (London: Jones & Co., 1829)

Broun, Dauvit, 'The Picts' Place in Kingship's Past Before John of Fordun', in *Scottish History: The Power of the Past*, ed. by Richard J. Finlay and Edward J. Cowan (Edinburgh: Edinburgh University Press, 2002), pp. 11–28

Brown, Iain Gordon, 'Alexander Gordon', in *The Oxford Dictionary of National Biography*, Volume 22 (Oxford: Oxford University Press, 2004), pp. 851–5

———, 'Archaeological Publication in the First Half of the Eighteenth Century', in *The Edinburgh History of the Book in Scotland*, Volume 2, ed. by Stephen W. Brown and Warren McDougall (Edinburgh: Edinburgh University Press, 2012)

———, 'Introduction', in *Abbotsford and Sir Walter Scott: The Image and the Influence* (Edinburgh: Society of Antiquaries of Scotland, 2003), pp. xiii–xvii

———, 'Modern Rome and Ancient Caledonia', in *The History of Scottish Literature, Volume 2 1660–1800*, ed. by Andrew Hook (Aberdeen: Aberdeen University Press, 1987), pp. 33–48

———, *Poet & Painter: Allan Ramsay, Father and Son, 1684–1784* (Edinburgh: National Library of Scotland, 1984)

———, *Rax Me That Buik: Highlights from the Collections of the National Library of Scotland* (London: Scala, 2010)

———, *Sir John Clerk of Penicuik (1676–1755): Aspects of a Virtuoso Life* (University of Cambridge: Unpublished PhD thesis, 1980)

———, *The Hobby-Horsical Antiquary: A Scottish Character, 1640–1830* (Edinburgh: National Library of Scotland, 1980)

———, 'The Penicuik Copy of Alexander Gordon's Itinerarium Septentrionale', *The Journal of the Edinburgh Bibliographical Society*, 6 (2011), pp. 56–73

———, '"This Old Magazine of Antiquities": The Advocates' Library as National Museum', in *The Encouragement of Learning: Scotland's National Library, 1689–1989*, ed. by Patrick Cadell and Ann Matheson (Edinburgh: Her Majesty's Stationery Office, 1989), pp. 149–85

Brown, Iain Gordon, and Alan Montgomery, 'The "Roman Heads" at the Netherbow in Edinburgh: A Case of Antiquarian Wishful Thinking in the 18th and 19th Centuries', *Proceedings of the Society of Antiquaries of Scotland*, 146 (2017), pp. 253–74

Brown, Keith M., 'Scottish Identity in the Seventeenth Century', in *British Consciousness and Identity: The Making of Britain, 1533–1707*, ed. by Brendan Bradshaw and Peter Roberts (Cambridge: Cambridge University Press, 1998), pp. 236–58

Bruce, John Collingwood, *The Roman Wall* (London: John Russell Smith, 1851)

Buchanan, George, *George Buchanan: The Political Poetry*, ed. by Paul J. McGinnis and Arthur H. Williamson (Edinburgh: Scottish History Society, 1995)

———, *The History of Scotland* (London, 1690)

Buchanan, John Lanne, *A Defence of the Scots Highlanders, in General and Some Learned Characters, in Particular: With a New and Satisfactory Account of the Picts, Scots, Fingal, Ossian, and His Poems* (London, 1794)

Burns, Robert, *The Works of Robert Burns: With an Account of His Life, and a Criticism on His Writings* (New York: W. Borradaile, 1826)

Burt, Edmund, *Burt's Letters from the North of Scotland* (Edinburgh: Birlinn, 2005)
Burton, John Hill, *The History of Scotland From Agricola's Invasion to the Revolution of 1688*, Volume 1 (Edinburgh; London: W. Blackwood, 1867)
Bushnell, Rebecca, 'George Buchanan, James VI and Neoclassicism', in *Scots and Britons: Scottish Political Thought and the Union of 1603*, ed. by Roger A. Mason (Cambridge: Cambridge University Press, 1994), pp. 91–111
Camden, William, *Britain, or a Chorographicall Description of the Most Flourishing Kingdoms, England, Scotland, and Ireland* . . . (London, 1610)
Cant, Ronald G., 'David Steuart Erskine, 11th Earl of Buchan: Founder of the Society of Antiquaries of Scotland', in *The Scottish Antiquarian Tradition*, ed. by Alan S. Bell (Edinburgh: John Donald, 1981), pp. 1–30
de Cardonnel, Adam, *Picturesque Antiquities of Scotland*, Volume 1 (London, 1788)
———, *Picturesque Antiquities of Scotland*, Volume 2 (London, 1793)
Casey, P. J., *Carausius and Allectus: The British Usurpers* (London: Batsford, 1994)
Castell, Robert, *The Villas of the Ancients Illustrated* (London, 1728)
Catalogue of the National Museum of Antiquities of Scotland, (Edinburgh: Printed for the Society of Antiquaries of Scotland, 1892)
Chalmers, George, *Caledonia, or, An Account Historical and Topographical of North Britain*, Volume 1 (London: T. Cadell, 1807)
Chamberlayne, John, *Magnae Britanniae Notitia: or, The Present State of Great-Britain* (London, 1716)
Chambers, Robert, *A Biographical Dictionary of Eminent Scotsmen*, Volume 3 (Glasgow: Blackie & Son, 1855)
Christie's, *A Catalogue of a Select, Well-Chosen, Valuable Library of Books, Maps &c . . . Also a Capital Collection of Astronomical and Mathematical Instruments . . . Late the Property of General Roy, Decd.* (London, 1790)
Clark, James, *Scotland's Speech to Her Sons* (Edinburgh?, 1706)
Clark, John, *An Answer to Mr Shaw's Inquiry into the Authenticity of the Poems Ascribed to Ossian* (Edinburgh, 1781)
Clarke, Katherine, 'An Island Nation: Re-Reading Tacitus' Agricola', *The Journal of Roman Studies*, 91 (2001), pp. 94–112
Clarke, Martin L., *Classical Education in Britain, 1500–1900* (Cambridge: Cambridge University Press, 1959)
Clerk, Sir John, *A Letter to a Friend, Giving an Account How the Treaty of Union Has Been Received Here* (Edinburgh, 1706)
———, *An Enquiry into the Roman Stylus* (Edinburgh?, 1704)
———, *Dissertatio de Monumentis Quibusdam Romanis in Boreali Magnae Britanniae Parte, Detectis, Anno MDCCXXXI* (Edinburgh, 1750)
———, *Dissertatio de Stylis Veterum, et Diversis Chartarum Generibus* (Edinburgh?, 1731)
———, *History of the Union of Scotland and England*, ed. by Douglas Duncan (Edinburgh: Scottish History Society, 1993)
———, *Memoirs of the Life of Sir John Clerk of Penicuik*, ed. by John Miller Gray (Edinburgh: Scottish History Society, 1892)

Coleman, James J., *Remembering the Past in Nineteenth-Century Scotland: Commemoration, Nationality and Memory* (Edinburgh: Edinburgh University Press, 2014)
Constantine, Mary-Ann, 'Heart of Darkness: Thomas Pennant and Roman Britain', in *Enlightenment Travel and British Identities*, ed. by Mary-Ann Constantine and Nigel Leask (London: Anthem Press, 2017), pp. 65–84
Cooper, Scott, 'Sir John Clerk's Garden at Penicuik', *Architectural Heritage*, 13.1 (2002), pp. 47–62
Coote, Henry Charles, *The Romans of Britain* (London: F. Norgate, 1878)
Cornish, Rory T., 'Robert Melville', in *The Oxford Dictionary of National Biography*, Volume 37 (Oxford: Oxford University Press, 2004), pp. 787–8
Dallas, George, *A System of Stiles: As Now Practised Within the Kingdom of Scotland, Reduced to a Clear Method* (Edinburgh, 1774)
Dalrymple, Viscount Stair, James, *The Institutions of the Law of Scotland* (Edinburgh, 1681)
Davidson, Neil, *The Origins of Scottish Nationhood* (London; Sterling, VA: Pluto Press, 2000)
Dawson, Jane, 'The Gaidhealtachd and the Emergence of the Scottish Highlands', in *British Consciousness and Identity: The Making of Britain, 1533–1707*, ed. by Brendan Bradshaw and Peter Roberts (Cambridge: Cambridge University Press, 1998), pp. 259–300
Defoe, Daniel, *The History of the Union of Great Britain* (Edinburgh, 1709)
Devine, Tom M., *The Scottish Nation: A Modern History* (London: Penguin Books, 2012)
Dio, Cassius, *Roman History*, Volume 9, ed. by Herbert Baldwin Foster, trans. by Earnest Cary (Cambridge, MA; London: Harvard University Press; William Heinemann, 1982)
Donaldson, Iain, 'The Sale Catalogue of Sir Robert Sibbald's Last Library', *The Journal of the Royal College of Physicians of Edinburgh*, 40.1 (2010), pp. 86–7
Duncan, Douglas, 'Introduction', in *History of the Union of Scotland and England* (Edinburgh: Scottish History Society, 1993), pp. 1–29
Duncan, William, *The Commentaries of Caesar, Translated into English ... To Which Is Prefixed a Discourse Concerning the Roman Art of War* (London, 1753)
Durie, Alastair J., *Travels in Scotland, 1788–1881: A Selection from Contemporary Tourist Journals* (Edinburgh: Scottish History Society/The Boydell Press, 2012)
Emerson, Roger L., 'Scottish Cultural Change 1660–1710', in *A Union for Empire: Political Thought and the British Union of 1707*, ed. by John Robertson (Cambridge: Cambridge University Press, 1995), pp. 121–44
———, 'Sir Robert Sibbald, Kt, The Royal Society of Scotland and the Origins of the Scottish Enlightenment', *Annals of Science*, 45.1 (1988), pp. 41–72
Erskine, 11th Earl of Buchan, David Steuart, *Letter from the Earl of Buchan to His Brother, the Hon. Thomas Erskine, Counsellor at Law; On the Subject of Education* (Edinburgh, 1782)

———, *The Anonymous and Fugitive Essays of the Earl of Buchan*, Volume 1 (Edinburgh: J. Ruthven & Co., 1812)
Ferguson, William, *The Identity of the Scottish Nation: An Historic Quest* (Edinburgh: Edinburgh University Press, 1998)
Fergusson, Robert, *The Works of Robert Fergusson, with the Life of the Author and an Essay on His Genius and Writings*, ed. by Alexander Balloch Grossart (London, Edinburgh and Dublin: A. Fullarton & Co., 1851)
Forbes, William, *The True Scots Genius, Reviving. A Poem. Written upon Occasion of the Resolve Past in Parliament, the 17th of July 1704* (Edinburgh, 1704)
Fordun, John, *Chronicle of the Scottish Nation*, ed. by William F. Skene, trans. by Felix J. H. Skene (Edinburgh: Edmonston and Douglas, 1872)
Fraser, James, *Caledonia to Pictland: Scotland to 795* (Edinburgh: Edinburgh University Press, 2009)
Freeman, F. W., *Robert Fergusson and the Scots Humanist Compromise* (Edinburgh: Edinburgh University Press, 1984)
Fulvius, Andreas, *L'Antichità di Roma* (Venice, 1588)
Gardiner, R. A., 'William Roy, Surveyor and Antiquary', *The Geographical Journal*, 143.3 (1977), pp. 439–50
Gibbon, Edward, *The History of the Decline and Fall of the Roman Empire*, Volume 1, ed. by David Womersley (London; New York: Penguin Books, 1995)
Gibbons, Luke, 'From Ossian to O'Carolan: The Bard as Separatist Symbol', in *From Gaelic to Romantic: Ossianic Translations*, ed. by Fiona Stafford and Howard Gaskill (Amsterdam: Rodopi, 1998), pp. 226–51
Gibson, Edmund, ed., *Britannia: or, A Chorographical Description of Great Britain and Ireland* (London, 1695)
Gordon, Alexander, *Additions and Corrections, By Way of Supplement, to the Itinerarium Septentrionale* (London, 1732)
———, *Itinerarium Septentrionale: or, A Journey Thro' Most of the Counties in Scotland, and Those in the North of England* (London, 1726)
———, *Proposals for Printing, by Subscription, a Book, Intitled, Itinerarium Septentrionale* (London?, 1725)
Gordon, Thomas, *The Life of Agricola. By Tacitus. With an Account of the Situation, Climate, and People of Britain* (Glasgow, 1763)
Gough, Richard, ed., *Britannia: or, A Chorographical Description of the Flourishing Kingdoms of England, Scotland and Ireland*, Volume 3 (London, 1789)
Grafton, Anthony, *Forgers and Critics: Creativity and Duplicity in Western Scholarship* (Princeton: Princeton University Press, 1990)
Grant, John, 'Memoir Concerning the Roman Progress in Scotland to the North of the Grampian Hills', *Archaeologia Scotica*, 2 (1822), pp. 31–42
Grenier, Katherine Haldane, *Tourism and Identity in Scotland, 1770–1914: Creating Caledonia* (Aldershot: Ashgate, 2005)
Groom, Nick, *The Forger's Shadow: How Forgery Changed the Course of Literature* (London: Picador, 2002)
Grose, Francis, *The Antiquities of Scotland*, Volume 1 (London, 1797)

Guide to the City and County of Perth (Perth, 1805)

Harding, Dennis W., *The Iron Age in Northern Britain: Celts and Romans, Natives and Invaders* (London: Routledge, 2004)

Haskell, Francis, *History and Its Images: Art and the Interpretation of the Past* (New Haven: Yale University Press, 1993)

Haverfield, Francis, 'Sir Robert Sibbald's "Directions for His Honoured Friend Mr. Llwyd How to Trace and Remarke the Vestiges of the Roman Wall Betwixt Forth and Clyde"', *Proceedings of the Society of Antiquaries of Scotland*, 44 (1910), pp. 319–27

——, *The Romanization of Roman Britain* (London, Published for the British Academy by H. Frowde, 1905)

Haywood, Ian, *The Making of History: A Study of the Literary Forgeries of James Macpherson and Thomas Chatterton in Relation to Eighteenth-Century Ideas of History and Fiction* (Rutherford; London: Fairleigh Dickinson University Press, 1986)

Henry, Robert, *The History of Great Britain From the First Invasion by the Romans Under Julius Caesar*, Volume 1 (London, 1771)

Hingley, Richard, *Hadrian's Wall: A Life* (Oxford: Oxford University Press, 2012)

——, *Roman Officers and English Gentlemen: The Imperial Origins of Roman Archaeology* (London: Routledge, 2000)

——, *The Recovery of Roman Britain 1586–1906: A Colony So Fertile* (Oxford: Oxford University Press, 2008)

Hodges, James, *The Rights and Interests of the Two British Monarchies Inquir'd Into, and Clear'd; With a Special Respect to an United Or Separate State. Treatise I* (London, 1703)

——, *The Rights and Interests of the Two British Monarchies: With a Special Respect to an United or Separate State. Treatise III* (London, 1706)

Hodgson, John, *Memoirs of the Lives of Thomas Gibson, M.D.: Jonathan Harle, M.D.; John Horsley, M.A., F.R.S.; William Turner, M.D.* (Newcastle, 1831)

Hodson, Yolande, 'William Roy and the Military Survey of Scotland', in *The Great Map: The Military Survey of Scotland 1747–1755* (Edinburgh: Birlinn, 2007), pp. 7–23

Hoffmann, Birgitta, 'Tacitus, Agricola and the Role of Literature in the Archaeology of the First Century AD', in *Archaeology and Ancient History: Breaking Down the Boundaries*, ed. by Eberhard W. Sauer (London: Routledge, 2004), pp. 151–65

Horsley, John, *Britannia Romana: or, The Roman Antiquities of Britain* (London, 1732)

Hoselitz, Virginia, *Imagining Roman Britain: Victorian Responses to a Roman Past* (Woodbridge; Rochester, NY: Royal Historical Society/The Boydell Press, 2007)

Houghton, L. B. T., 'Lucan in the Highlands: James Philp's Grameid and the Traditions of Ancient Epic', in *Neo-Latin Poetry in the British Isles*, ed. by L. B. T. Houghton and Gesine Manuwald (London: Bristol Classical Press, 2012), pp. 190–207

Hullmandel, Charles Joseph, *Britannia Delineata: Comprising Views of the Antiquities, Remarkable Buildings, and Picturesque Scenery of Great Britain: Kent* (London: Rodwell & Martin, 1822)

Hume, David, *The History of England: From the Invasion of Julius Caesar to the Revolution in 1688*, Volume 1 (London, 1767)

——, *The Letters of David Hume*, Volume 2, ed. by J. Y. T. Greig (Oxford: Clarendon Press, 1932)

Innes, Thomas, *A Critical Essay on the Ancient Inhabitants of the Northern Parts of Britain, or Scotland*, Volume 1 (London, 1729)

Johnson, Samuel, *A Journey to the Western Islands of Scotland* (London, 1785)

Keppie, Lawrence, 'John Horsley and the Britannia Romana (1732): The Road to Publication', *Archaeologia Aeliana*, 5, 42 (2013), pp. 1–34

——, *Roman Inscribed and Sculptured Stones in the Hunterian Museum, University of Glasgow* (London: Society for the Promotion of Roman Studies, 1998)

——, *The Antiquarian Rediscovery of the Antonine Wall* (Edinburgh: Society of Antiquaries of Scotland, 2012)

——, 'The French Cartographer and the Clan Chief: Archaeological Fieldwork in Perthshire, 1763', *Proceedings of the Society of Antiquaries of Scotland*, 145 (2015), pp. 401–25

Kidd, Colin, *Subverting Scotland's Past: Scottish Whig Historians and the Creation of an Anglo-British Identity, 1689–c.1830* (Cambridge: Cambridge University Press, 1993)

——, 'The Canon of Patriotic Landmarks in Scottish History', *Scotlands*, 1 (1994), pp. 1–17

——, 'The Ideological Uses of the Picts', in *Scottish History: The Power of the Past*, ed. by Richard J. Finlay and Edward J. Cowan (Edinburgh: Edinburgh University Press, 2002), pp. 169–90

——, '"The Strange Death of Scottish History" Revisited: Constructions of the Past in Scotland, c.1790–1914', *The Scottish Historical Review*, 76,1.201 (1997), pp. 86–102

Kinghorn, Alexander Manson, 'Biographical and Critical Introduction', in *The Works of Allan Ramsay*, Volume 4 (Edinburgh: The Scottish Text Society, 1970), pp. 1–170

Kinghorn, Alexander Manson, and Alexander Law, 'Allan Ramsay and Literary Life in the First Half of the Eighteenth Century', in *The History of Scottish Literature, Volume 2 1660–1800*, ed. by Andrew Hook (Aberdeen: Aberdeen University Press, 1987), pp. 65–78

Knox, John, *A View of the British Empire: More Especially Scotland; with Some Proposals for the Improvement of That Country, the Extension of Its Fisheries, and the Relief of the People* (London, 1785)

Krebs, Christopher B., *A Most Dangerous Book: Tacitus's Germania from the Roman Empire to the Third Reich* (New York; London: W. W. Norton, 2011)

Laing, Malcolm, *The History of Scotland*, Volume 2 (London; Edinburgh, 1800)

Law, Alexander, *Education in Edinburgh in the Eighteenth Century* (London: University of London Press, 1965)
Levine, Joseph M., *Dr Woodward's Shield: History, Science, and Satire in Augustan England* (Berkeley: University of California Press, 1977)
Livy, *Rome's Italian Wars: Books 6–10*, trans. by John C. Yardley (Oxford: Oxford University Press, 2000)
———, *The Dawn of the Roman Empire: Books 31–40*, trans. by John C. Yardley (Oxford: Oxford University Press, 2000)
Lowenthal, David, *The Past Is a Foreign Country* (Cambridge: Cambridge University Press, 1985)
Lukis, W. C., ed., *The Family Memoirs of the Rev. William Stukeley, M.D. and the Antiquarian and Other Correspondence of William Stukeley, Roger and Samuel Gale*, Volume 1 (Durham: Published for the Surtees Society by Andrews & Co., 1882)
———, ed., *The Family Memoirs of the Rev. William Stukeley, M.D. and the Antiquarian and Other Correspondence of William Stukeley, Roger and Samuel Gale*, Volume 2 (Durham: Published for the Surtees Society by Andrews & Co., 1883)
———, ed., *The Family Memoirs of the Rev. William Stukeley, M.D. and the Antiquarian and Other Correspondence of William Stukeley, Roger and Samuel Gale*, Volume 3 (Durham: Published for the Surtees Society by Andrews & Co., 1887)
Lumisden, Andrew, *Remarks on the Antiquities of Rome and its Environs: Being a Classical and Topographical Survey of the Ruins of That Celebrated City* (London, 1797)
MacDonald, George, 'General William Roy and His "Military Antiquities of the Romans in North Britain"', *Archaeologia*, 68 (1917), pp. 161–228
———, 'John Horsley, Scholar and Gentleman', *Archaeologia Aeliana*, 4, 10 (1933), pp. 1–57
———, 'John Horsley', *The Journal of Roman Studies*, 22.2 (1932), pp. 161–4
Macdonald, James, 'The Origin and Growth of the Tradition, "Ecce Tiber! Ecce Campus Martius!" As Applied to the Tay and the Inches of Perth', *Proceedings of the Society of Antiquaries of Scotland*, 33 (1899), pp. 116–28
———, *Tituli Hunteriani: An Account of the Roman Stones in the Hunterian Museum, University of Glasgow* (Glasgow: T. & R. Annan & Sons, 1897)
Macmillan, Duncan, '"Truly National Designs": Runciman's Scottish Themes at Penicuik', *Art History*, 1.1 (1978), pp. 90–8
Macpherson, David, *Geographical Illustrations of Scottish History, Containing the Names of Places Mentioned in Chronicles, Histories, Records, &c.* (London, 1796)
Macpherson, James, *An Introduction to the History of Great Britain and Ireland* (London, 1771)
———, *Fingal, An Ancient Epic Poem, in Six Books: Together with Several Other Poems, Composed by Ossian the Son of Fingal* (London, 1762)

——, *Fragments of Ancient Poetry, Collected in the Highlands of Scotland, and Translated from the Galic or Erse Language* (Edinburgh, 1760)

——, *The Works of Ossian, the Son of Fingal*, Volume 2 (London, 1765)

Macpherson, John, *Critical Dissertations on the Origin, Antiquities, Language, Government, Manners and Religion of the Ancient Caledonians, Their Posterity the Picts, and the British and Irish Scots* (London, 1768)

Maitland, William, *The History and Antiquities of Scotland from the Earliest Account to the Death of James I*, Volume 1 (London, 1757)

——, *The History of Edinburgh, From Its Foundation to the Present Time* (Edinburgh, 1753)

Manning, Susan, 'Antiquarianism, the Scottish Science of Man, and the Emergence of Modern Disciplinarity', in *Scotland and the Borders of Romanticism*, ed. by Leith Davis, Ian Duncan, and Janet Sorensen (Cambridge: Cambridge University Press, 2004), pp. 57–76

Mason, Roger A., 'Civil Society and the Celts: Hector Boece, George Buchanan and the Ancient Scottish Past', in *Scottish History, the Power of the Past*, ed. by Richard J. Finlay and Edward J. Cowan (Edinburgh: Edinburgh University Press, 2002), pp. 95–119

Maule, Henry, 'The History of the Picts', in *Miscellanea Pictica* (Glasgow: D. Webster, 1818), pp. 9–60

Maxwell, Gordon S., *A Battle Lost: Romans and Caledonians at Mons Graupius* (Edinburgh: Edinburgh University Press, 1990)

McGinnis, Paul J., and Arthur H. Williamson, 'Introduction', in *George Buchanan: The Political Poetry* (Edinburgh: Scottish History Society, 1995), pp. 1–42

McKean, Thomas A., 'The Fieldwork Legacy of James Macpherson', *The Journal of American Folklore*, 114.454 (2001), pp. 447–63

Mellor, Ronald, 'Introduction', in *Tacitus: The Classical Heritage*, ed. by Ronald Mellor (New York; London: Garland, 1995), pp. i–liv

Melville, Robert, *A Critical Inquiry into the Constitution of the Roman Legion. With Some Observations on the Military Art of the Romans, Compared with That of the Moderns* (Edinburgh, 1773)

Mencke, Johann Burchard, *De Charlataneria Eruditorum Declamationes Duae* (Amsterdam, 1715)

Mercer, Thomas, *Poems: By the Author of The Sentimental Sailor* (Edinburgh, 1774)

Mitchell, Arthur, ed., *Geographical Collections Relating to Scotland*, Volume 2 (Edinburgh: T. and A. Constable, 1907)

Mitchell, Sebastian, 'Landscape and the Sense of Place in the Poems of Ossian', in *The International Companion to James Macpherson and the Poems of Ossian*, ed. by Dafydd Moore (Glasgow: Scottish Literature International, 2017), pp. 65–75

Mothersole, Jessie, *In Roman Scotland* (London: The Bodley Head, 1927)

Mudie, Robert, *The Modern Athens: A Dissection and Demonstration of Men and Things in the Scotch Capital* (London: Knight and Lacey, 1825)

Murray, David, *Museums: Their History and Their Use*, Volume 1 (London: Routledge/Thoemmes Press, 1996)

Neale, John Preston, *Views of the Seats of Noblemen and Gentlemen, in England, Wales, Scotland, and Ireland*, Volume 2 (London: Sherwood, Jones and Co., 1825)

Nichols, John, ed., *Bibliotheca Topographica Britannica, Volume 3, No II. Reliquae Galeanae: or, Miscellaneous Pieces by the Late Learned Brothers Roger and Samuel Gale* (London, 1781)

———, ed., *Bibliotheca Topographica Britannica, Volume 5, No. XXXVI* (London, 1786)

Nicolson, William, *The Scottish Historical Library* (London, 1702)

Nimmo, William, *A General History of Stirlingshire* (Edinburgh, 1777)

Nodier, Charles, *Promenade from Dieppe to the Mountains of Scotland* (Edinburgh; London: W. Blackwood; T. Cadell, 1822)

O'Donoghue, Yolande, *William Roy, 1726–1790: Pioneer of the Ordnance Survey* (London: British Museum Publications Ltd, 1977)

Ouston, Hugh, 'York in Edinburgh: James VII and the Patronage of Learning in Scotland 1673–1688', in *New Perspectives on the Politics and Culture of Early Modern Scotland*, ed. by John Dwyer, Roger A. Mason, and Alexander Murdoch (Edinburgh: John Donald, 1982), pp. 133–55

———, 'Cultural Life from the Restoration to the Union', in *The History of Scottish Literature, Volume 2 1660–1800*, ed. by Andrew Hook (Aberdeen: Aberdeen University Press, 1987), pp. 11–30

Paget Hett, Francis, ed., *The Memoirs of Sir Robert Sibbald (1641–1722)* (London: Oxford University Press, 1932)

Parry, Graham, *The Trophies of Time: English Antiquarians of the Seventeenth Century* (Oxford: Oxford University Press, 2007)

Peacham, Henry, *The Compleat Gentleman* (London, 1634)

Pennant, Thomas, *A Tour in Scotland, and Voyage to the Hebrides, MDCCLXXII, Part I* (London, 1776)

———, *A Tour in Scotland, MDCCLXXII, Part II* (London, 1776)

Philip, James, *The Grameid: An Heroic Poem Descriptive of the Campaign of Viscount Dundee in 1689 and Other Pieces*, trans. by Alexander. Murdoch (Edinburgh: Scottish History Society, 1888)

Pichot, Amédée, *Historical and Literary Tour of a Foreigner in England and Scotland*, Volume 2 (London: Saunders & Otley, 1825)

Piggott, Stuart, *Ancient Britons and the Antiquarian Imagination: Ideas from the Renaissance to the Regency* (London: Thames and Hudson, 1989)

———, *William Stukeley, An Eighteenth-Century Antiquary* (London: Thames and Hudson, 1985)

Pinkerton, John, *An Enquiry into the History of Scotland Preceding the Reign of Malcolm III*, Volume 1 (London, 1789)

Pittock, Murray, 'Alexander Robertson of Struan', in *Oxford Dictionary of National Biography*, Volume 47 (Oxford: Oxford University Press, 2004), pp. 201–3.

———, *Inventing and Resisting Britain: Cultural Identities in Britain and Ireland, 1685–1789* (Basingstoke: Macmillan Press, 1997)

―――, *Scottish Nationality* (Basingstoke: Palgrave, 2001)
Pitts, Lynn F., and J. K. St Joseph, *Inchtuthil: The Roman Legionary Fortress* (London: Society for the Promotion of Roman Studies, 1985)
Plank, Geoffrey Gilbert, *Rebellion and Savagery: The Jacobite Rising of 1745 and the British Empire* (Philadelphia: University of Pennsylvania Press, 2006)
Poems in English and Latin, on the Archers, and Royal Company of Archers (Edinburgh, 1726)
Pointer, John, *Britannia Romana, or, Roman Antiquities in Britain Viz. Coins, Camps, and Publick Roads* (Oxford, 1724)
Poleni, Giovanni, *Utriusque Thesauri Antiquitatum Romanarum Graecarumque Nova Supplementa*, Volume 3 (Venice, 1737)
Polybius, *The Histories*, Volume 3, ed. by Frank W. Walbank and Christian Habicht, trans. by William R. Paton (Cambridge, MA; London: Harvard University Press, 2011)
Ramsay, Allan, *A Scots Ode, to the British Antiquarians* (Edinburgh, 1726)
―――, *Poems* (Edinburgh, 1720)
―――, *Tartana: or The Plaid* (Edinburgh, 1718)
―――, ed., *The Ever Green, Being a Collection of Scots Poems, Wrote by the Ingenious Before 1600*, Volume 1 (Edinburgh, 1724)
―――, *The Works of Allan Ramsay*, Volume 3, ed. by Alexander Manson Kinghorn and Alexander Law (Edinburgh: The Scottish Text Society, 1961)
Renan, Ernest, *Qu'est-ce qu'une nation? Conférence faite en Sorbonne, le 11 mars 1882* (Paris: Lévy, 1882)
Robertson of Struan, Alexander, *Poems, on Various Subjects and Occasions, by the Honourable Alexander Robertson of Struan, Esq.* (Edinburgh, 1752)
Robertson, William, *The History of Scotland, During the Reign of Queen Mary and King James VI . . . With a Review of the Scotch History Previous to That Period*, Volume 1 (London, 1759)
de Rossi, Filippo, *Ritratto di Roma Antica* (Rome, 1689)
Roy, William, 'An Account of the Measurement of a Base on Hounslow Heath', *The Philosophical Transactions of the Royal Society*, 75 (1785), pp. 385–480
―――, *The Military Antiquities of the Romans in Britain* (London, 1793)
Russell, Miles, and Harry Manley, 'Trajan Places: Establishing Identity and Context for the Bosham and Hawkshaw Heads', *Britannia*, 46 (2015), pp. 151–69
Sailor, Dylan, 'The Agricola', in *A Companion to Tacitus*, ed. by Victoria Emma Pagán (Chichester: Wiley-Blackwell, 2012), pp. 23–44
Salmon, Nathaniel, *A New Survey of England* (London, 1728)
Scarth, Harry M., *Roman Britain* (London: Society for Promoting Christian Knowledge, 1883)
Schaps, David, 'The Found and Lost Manuscripts of Tacitus' Agricola', *Classical Philology*, 74.1 (1979), pp. 28–42
Scott, Sarah, 'Britain in the Classical World: Samuel Lysons and the Art of Roman Britain, 1780-1820', *Classical Receptions Journal*, 6.2 (2014), pp. 294–337
Scott, Walter, *The Antiquary* (Oxford: Oxford University Press, 2009)

——, *The History of Scotland*, Volume 1 (London: Longman, Rees, Orme, Brown, & Green, 1830)
Shaw, Lachlan, *The History of the Province of Moray* (Edinburgh, 1775)
Shaw, William, *An Enquiry into the Authenticity of the Poems Ascribed to Ossian* (London, 1781)
Sibbald, Robert, *An Account of the Scotish Atlas, or, The Description of Scotland Ancient & Modern* (Edinburgh, 1683)
——, *Commentarius in Julii Agricolae Expeditiones 3. 4. 5. 6. 7. in Vita Ejus, per Cornelium Tacitum Generum Ejus, Descriptas; et in Boreali Britanniae Parte, Quae Scotia Dicitur, Gestas* (Edinburgh, 1711)
——, *Conjectures Concerning the Roman Ports, Colonies, and Forts, in the Firths, Taken from Their Vestigies and the Antiquities, Found Near Them* (Edinburgh, 1711)
——, *Historical Inquiries, Concerning the Roman Monuments and Antiquities in the North-Part of Britain Called Scotland* (Edinburgh, 1707)
——, *Memoirs of the Royal College of Physicians at Edinburgh* (Edinburgh: T. G. Stevenson, 1837)
——, *Nuncius Scoto-Britannus, sive, Admonitio de Atlante Scotico seu Descriptione Scotiae Antiquae et Modernae* (Edinburgh, 1683)
——, *Scotia Illustrata, sive, Prodromus Historiae Naturalis* (Edinburgh, 1684)
——, *Series Rerum a Romanis Post Avocatum Agricolam in Britannia Boreali Gestarum* (Edinburgh, 1711)
——, *The History, Ancient and Modern, of the Sheriffdoms of Fife and Kinross* (Edinburgh, 1710)
——, *The History, Ancient and Modern, of the Sheriffdoms of Linlithgow and Stirling* (Edinburgh, 1710)
——, *The Liberty and Independency of the Kingdom and Church of Scotland Asserted from Antient Records* (Edinburgh, 1702)
Simpson, A. D. C., 'Sir Robert Sibbald – The Founder of the College', in *Proceedings of the Royal College of Physicians of Edinburgh Tercentenary Congress 1981*, ed. by Reginald Passmore (Edinburgh: Royal College of Physicians of Edinburgh, 1982), pp. 59–91
Sinclair, John, *The Statistical Account of Scotland*, Volume 1 (Edinburgh, 1791)
——, *The Statistical Account of Scotland*, Volume 2 (Edinburgh, 1792)
——, *The Statistical Account of Scotland*, Volume 13 (Edinburgh, 1794)
——, *The Statistical Account of Scotland*, Volume 18 (Edinburgh, 1796)
——, *The Statistical Account of Scotland*, Volume 19 (Edinburgh, 1797)
Slezer, John, *Theatrum Scotiae* (London, 1693)
Small, Andrew, *Interesting Roman Antiquities Recently Discovered in Fife Ascertaining the Site of the Great Battle Fought Betwixt Agricola and Galgacus; with the Discovery of the Position of Five Roman Towns, and of the Site and Names of Upwards of Seventy Roman Forts* (Edinburgh, 1823)
Smellie, William, *Account of the Institution and Progress of the Society of the Antiquaries of Scotland* (Edinburgh, 1782)

Smiles, Sam, *The Image of Antiquity: Ancient Britain and the Romantic Imagination* (New Haven: Published for the Paul Mellon Centre for Studies in British Art by Yale University Press, 1994)

Smith, John, *Galic Antiquities: Consisting of a History of the Druids, Particularly of Those of Caledonia* (Edinburgh, 1780)

Somner, William, *A Treatise of the Roman Ports and Forts in Kent* (Oxford, 1693)

Sponberg Pedley, Mary, *The Commerce of Cartography: Making and Marketing Maps in Eighteenth-Century France and England* (Chicago: University of Chicago Press, 2005)

Stafford, Fiona, *The Sublime Savage: A Study of James Macpherson and the Poems of Ossian* (Edinburgh: Edinburgh University Press, 1988)

Stafford, Fiona, and Howard Gaskill, 'Editors' Preface', in *From Gaelic to Romantic: Ossianic Translations* (Amsterdam: Rodopi, 1998), pp. xi–xiv

Stelten, Leo F., 'Introduction', in *Vegetius: Epitoma Rei Militaris* (New York: Peter Lang, 1990), pp. xiii–xxi

Stevenson, R. B. K., 'The Museum, Its Beginnings and Its Development', in *The Scottish Antiquarian Tradition*, ed. by Alan S. Bell (Edinburgh: John Donald, 1981), pp. 31–85

Stuart, John, 'Notice of Letters Addressed to Captain Shand, R.A., by Professor Thorkelin and General Robert Melville, on Roman Antiquities in the North of Scotland, 1788–1790', *The Proceedings of the Society of Antiquaries of Scotland*, 7 (1866), pp. 26–34

Stuart, Robert, *Caledonia Romana: A Descriptive Account of the Roman Antiquities of Scotland* (Edinburgh: Sutherland and Knox, 1852)

Stukeley, William, *An Account of a Roman Temple, and Other Antiquities, Near Graham's Dike in Scotland* (London, 1720)

———, *An Account of Richard of Cirencester, Monk of Westminster, and of His Works* (London, 1757)

———, *Itinerarium Curiosum: or, An Account of the Antiquities, and Remarkable Curiosities in Nature or Art, Observed in Travels Through Great Britain* (London, 1776)

———, *Of the Roman Amphitheater at Dorchester* (London, 1723)

———, *The Commentarys, Diary, & Common-Place Book & Selected Letters of William Stukeley.* (London: Doppler Press, 1980)

———, *The Medallic History of Marcus Aurelius Valerius Carausius, Emperor in Brittain*, Volume 1 (London, 1757)

Swann, Marjorie, *Curiosities and Texts: The Culture of Collecting in Early Modern England* (Philadelphia: University of Pennsylvania Press, 2001)

Sweet, Rosemary, *Antiquaries: The Discovery of the Past in Eighteenth-Century Britain* (London: Hambledon and London, 2004)

———, *Cities and the Grand Tour: The British in Italy, c.1690–1820* (Cambridge: Cambridge University Press, 2012)

Tacitus, Cornelius, *Agricola, Germania, Dialogus*, trans. by Maurice Hutton and William Peterson (Cambridge, MA: Harvard University Press, 2006)

―――, *The Annals, Books IV–XII*, trans. by John Jackson (London: William Heinemann, 1956)

―――, *The Histories, Books I–III*, trans. by Clifford Herschel Moore (London: William Heinemann, 1968)

The Annual Register, or a View of the History, Politicks and Literature of the Year 1807 (London: W. Otridge & Son, 1809)

The Bee, or Literary Weekly Intelligencer, Volume 4 (Edinburgh, 1791)

The Bee, or Literary Weekly Intelligencer, Volume 6 (Edinburgh, 1791)

The Eclectic Review, Volume 21 (London, 1824)

The Edinburgh Magazine and Review, Volume 1 (Edinburgh, 1774)

The Gentleman's Magazine and Historical Chronicle for the Year MDCCXC, Volume 60, Part 2 (London, 1790)

The Traveller's Guide: or, A Topographical Description of Scotland, and of the Islands Belonging To It (Edinburgh, 1798)

The Trimontium Trumpet, Number 32 (The Trimontium Trust, 2018)

Thomas, Sophie, *Romanticism and Visuality: Fragments, History, Spectacle* (New York; London: Routledge, 2008)

du Toit, Alexander, 'George Chalmers', in *The Oxford Dictionary of National Biography*, Volume 10 (Oxford: Oxford University Press, 2004), pp. 870–1

―――, 'Patrick Abercromby', in *The Oxford Dictionary of National Biography*, Volume 1 (Oxford: Oxford University Press, 2004), p. 89

Toland, John, *A Collection of Several Pieces of John Toland*, Volume 1 (London, 1726)

Turner, Frank M., *The Greek Heritage in Victorian Britain* (New Haven: Yale University Press, 1981)

―――, 'Why the Greeks and Not the Romans in Victorian Britain', in *Rediscovering Hellenism: The Hellenic Inheritance and the English Imagination*, ed. by G. W. Clarke (Cambridge: Cambridge University Press, 1989), pp. 61–81

Turnock, David, *The Historical Geography of Scotland Since 1707: Geographical Aspects of Modernisation* (Cambridge: Cambridge University Press, 1982)

Vance, Norman, *The Victorians and Ancient Rome* (Oxford: Blackwell Publishers, 1997)

Vance, Norman, and Jennifer Wallace, 'Introduction', in *The Oxford History of Classical Reception in English Literature*, Volume 4 (Oxford: Oxford University Press, 2015), pp. 1–27

Walker, Marshall, *Scottish Literature Since 1707* (London; New York: Longman, 1996)

Walpole, Horace, *Private Correspondence of Horace Walpole, Earl of Orford*, Volume 4 (London: Rodwell and Martin, 1820)

Webster, D., ed., *Miscellanea Pictica* (Glasgow, 1818)

Wilson, Daniel, *The Archaeology and Prehistoric Annals of Scotland* (Edinburgh: Sutherland and Knox, 1851)

Withers, Charles W. J., *Geography, Science, and National Identity: Scotland since 1520* (Cambridge: Cambridge University Press, 2001)

———, 'How Scotland Came to Know Itself: Geography, National Identity and the Making of a Nation', *Journal of Historical Geography*, 21.4 (1995), pp. 371–97

———, 'William Roy's World: Maps and Mapping in the Age of Enlightenment', in *The Great Map: The Military Survey of Scotland 1747–1755* (Edinburgh: Birlinn, 2007), pp. 37–46

Wodrow, Robert, *Analecta, or Materials for a History of Remarkable Providences; Mostly Relating to Scotch Ministers and Christians*, Volume 3 (Edinburgh: The Maitland Club, 1842)

Wood, John Philip, *Antient and Modern State of the Parish of Cramond* (Edinburgh, 1794)

Woolliscroft, D. J., and Birgitta Hoffmann, *Rome's First Frontier: The Flavian Occupation of Northern Scotland* (Stroud: Tempus, 2006)

Wright, Thomas, *The Celt, the Roman, and the Saxon: A History of the Early Inhabitants of Britain, Down to the Conversion of the Anglo-Saxons to Christianity* (London: Arthur Hall, Virtue & Co., 1852)

Index

References to images are in *italics*

Abercrombie, William, 23
Abercromby, Patrick, 105, 139, 146
   The Martial Achievements of the Scots Nation, 58–9, 131
Acts of Union (1707), 5, 54, 55–6, 72, 112
   and Clerk, 37
   and Sibbald, 25–6
Adair, John, 22, 92
Adam, Alexander
   Roman Antiquities, 8
Adamson, Henry
   The Muses Threnodie, 143, 144
Advocates Library (Edinburgh), 21, 95–6, 108
Agricola, Gnaeus Julius 19, 21, 26, 59, 131, 134–41
   and Buchan, 182
   and Clerk, 43
   and Gordon, 61
   and Highlanders, 113
   and Horsley, 83
   and Agricolamania, 141–6
   and Melville, 116–17, 120
   and Roy, 121
   and Stukeley, 76
Agricola (Tacitus), 2–3, 7, 90, 145, 179
   and Abercromby, 58
   and Caledonia, 131–2
   and Chalmers, 171–2
   and Gordon, 41
   and Melville, 116–17
   and Ossian, 160, 161–2
   and rediscovery, 132–4
   and Sibbald, 17, 18, 23–4, 28
Ainslie, John
   Scotland, 104
Allan, David, 7
altars, 91, 92–3, 94–5, 96, 97, 153–4
Althamer, Andreas, 133
ancient Rome *see* Roman Empire
Anderson, James, 40
Anderson, John, 6, 95, 99, 115, 123, 149
   and Antonine Wall, 105
Angers (France), 17

Angus, 21, 175
Annandale, 120
Anne of Great Britain, Queen, 66
Antiquarian Society of Perth, 126, 173, 180
antiquarianism, 18, 22, 23–5
   and Clerk, 33, 36–7, 38–9, 41–3
   and eighteenth century, 169–73
   and England, 71–2
   and Gordon, 39–41
   and nineteenth century, 189–92
   and regional, 173–6
   and Stukeley, 74–5
   see also antiquities
antiquities, 21, 90–2, 119–25, 126–7
   and collections, 92–6
   and identification, 99–100, 104
   see also altars; coinage; distance slabs; sculpture; swords
Antonine Itinerary, 150
Antonine Wall, 11, 20–1, 22, 24, 105, 199
   and *Agricola*, 132
   and archaeology, 198
   and Chalmers, 172
   and Clerk, 38
   and distance slabs, *82*, 91, 97, 98, 115
   and Gordon, *60*
   and Highlanders, 115
   and Horsley, *82*, 83
   and inscriptions, 91, 97
   and Keppie, 189–90
   and maps, 104
   and Ossian, 161
   and Pennant, 183
   and poetry, 180
   and Roy, 120, 123
   and Stukeley, 76–7
Antoninus Pius, Emperor, 20, 76, 172
archaeology, 20, 91–2, 198
archery, 66, 67
architecture, 46, 47–8, 192
Ardoch Fort, 38, 92, *122*, 135, 183
   and maps, 104–5

Argyll, John Campbell, 2nd Duke of, 139
artefacts *see* antiquities
Arthur's O'on, 19, 21, 91, 105–7, 108
   and Agricola, 135, 140
   and Bertram, 151
   and Pennant, 183
   and Stukeley, 71, 76, 77, 79
Atticus, Aulus, 144, 176
Ayres, Philip, 6

Bacon, Francis
   A Brief Discourse of the Happy Union in the Kingdoms of Scotland and England, 38
Balfour, Andrew, 21, 95
Balfour, James, 21, 57
Balmuildy, 83
Balvaird, David Murray, 2nd Lord, 9
Bar Hill Fort, *60*, 91
Barbié du Bocage, Alexandre
   L'Écosse avec ses Isles, 104
Barclay, Robert, 141
Barclay, William, 134
Baron, the *see* Clerk of Penicuik, Sir John
Barra Hill, 126–7
Batoni, Pompeo, 9
Battledykes, 117
Baxter, William, 97
   Glossarium Antiquitatum Britannicarum, 77, 78, 164
Beattie, James, 7–8
Bede, 2, 77
   Historia Ecclesiastica Gentis Anglorum, 24
Bellenden, John, 2
Bellin, Jacques Nicolas
   Carte Réduite des Isles Britannique, 104
Benario, Herbert, 139
Bertha, 144
Bertram, Charles Julius, 150–3, 163–5
Bibliotheca Topographica Britannica, 36
Blackwell, Thomas, 42, 80, 91, 93–4, 159
   An Enquiry into the Life and Writings of Homer, 156
Blaeu, Joan
   Atlas of Scotland, 104
Blair, Hugh, 156–7, 157, 159, 181
Blairgowrie, 175
Boece, Hector, 7, 53, 57, 133
   Historia Gentis Scotorum, 2–3, 58–9
   and locations, 175, 176
   and Ossian, 161, 163
Boerhaave, Herman, 39, 47, 94
Bonne, Rigobert, 104
Bonnie Prince Charlie *see* Charles Edward Stuart
Borgia, Rodrigo and Cesare, 42
Boswell, James, 29, 132
Boudica, 53, 59, 197
Bowen, Emanuel
   Map of North Britain, 105
Bower, Walter, 2
Boyd Haycock, David, 85
Boyse, Samuel, 140–1
Bracciolini, Gian Francesco Poggio, 133
Brigantia, 80, 100, *101*–3, 104
Brion de la Tour, Louis
   L'Écosse, 104

Britain *see* Great Britain
Britannia Delineata, 193
British Empire, 198
Britton, John
   Modern Athens!, 192
Brown, Iain Gordon, 33, 40, 41, 54, 192
Brown, Keith, 54
Bruce, Sir Michael, 106–7, 151
Bruce, Robert the, 197, 198, 199
Brutus, 55
Buchan, David Steuart Erskine, 11th Earl of, 96, 141, 175, 181–2
Buchanan, David, 24
Buchanan, George, 7, 20, 58–9, 161, 176
   and *Agricola*, 133–4
   and Arthur's O'on, 105, 106
   Rerum Scoticarum Historia (The History of Scotland), 2, 3–4, 24, 53
Buchanan, John (author)
   A Defence of the Scots Highlanders, 179
Buchanan, John (banker/antiquarian), 190
Buchner, August, 24
Burn, Richard, 93, 97
Burnswark, 38, 183
Burt, Edmund, 115
Burton, John Hill, 165
   The History of Scotland From Agricola's Invasion to the Revolution of 1688, 191–2
Burton, William, 136

Cadder, 83
Caesar, Julius, 2, 37, 57, 74–5, 123, 164
   De Bello Gallico, 114
Caithness, 21
Caledonia, 13, 127–8, 164–5, 194–9
   and Agricola, Gnaeus Julius, 134–41
   and *Agricola* (Tacitus), 131–2, 133–4, 145–6
   and Buchan, 181–2
   and Clerk, 33–4, 43–6
   and *De Situ Britanniae*, 151–5
   and eighteenth century, 169–73
   and England, 67–9, 71–2, 85–7, 194
   and Gaelic poetry, 149–50
   and Gordon, 40–2, 61, 62–3
   and Horsley, 81, 83–4
   and literature, 63–7
   and Melville, 115–16
   and militarism, 112–13
   and monuments, 104–8
   and nineteenth century, 189–92
   and Ossian, 155–6, 157–63, 176–80
   and resistance, 55–6
   and Sibbald, 18–25, 26–7, 28–9
   and Stukeley, 75–7, 78–9
   see also antiquities; Picts
Calgacus (Galgacus), 41, 44–5, 141, 179, 197–8, 199
   and Abercromby, 59, 139
   and *Agricola*, 139, 145
   and Boece, 133
   and Buchan, 182
   and Gordon, 42, 61, 139, 140
Camden, William, 92, 97, 113, 164
   Britannia, 18, 19, 24, 39
Camelon, 19, 20, 57–8, 77, 79

Index

and Agricola, 135, 140, 142
and Burton, 192
and Chalmers, 172
and Horsley, 83
and Roy, 124
see also Arthur's O'on
Cammo, 46–7
Cant, James, 144
Caracalla (Antoninus), Emperor, 23, 83, 158, 159, 160, 162
Caratacus (Caratak), 53, 59
Carausius, Emperor, 20, 21, 76, 79
and Ossian, 158, 160, 162–3
Cardonnel, Adam de, 170
Picturesque Antiquities of Scotland, 184
Carriden House, 92, 96, 97
Casaubon, Isaac, 23
Casley, David, 152
Castell, Robert
Villas of the Ancients, 46
Castle Cary, 92–3
Catholicism, 25, 61–2, 94, 134
Catter Mellie, 175
Cawder House, 92
Cay, Robert, 83
Chalmers, George, 176, 195
Caledonia, 170–3
Chamberlayne, John
Magnae Britanniae Notitia, 113
Charles II of Great Britain, King, 17, 27, 54
Charles Edward Stuart (Bonnie Prince Charlie), 65, 112, 198
Chatterton, Thomas, 163
Christianity, 1, 5, 12, 62, 75, 78; *see also* Catholicism; Church of Rome
Church of Rome, 54, 61, 94
Cicero, 7
civilisation, 19, 27–8
Clapham, John, 136
Clark, James
Scotland's Speech to her Sons, 56
Clark, John, 157
Claudian, 23
Cleghorn, 120
Clerk, George, 120
Clerk, Sir James, 94, 107, 115–16, 182–3
Clerk of Eldin, John, 116
Clerk of Penicuik, Sir John, 33–9, 43–6, 52, 86, 143, 195
and Agricola, 137, *138*, 139, 140–1
and antiquities, 91, 92, 93–4, 99, 100, *101–3*, 104
and Arthur's O'on, 105–6
The Country Seat, 46, 141
Dissertatio de Monumentis Quibusdam Romanis, in Boreali Magnae Britanniae Parte, Detectis Anno 1731, 39
Dissertatio de Stylis Veterum, et Diversis Chartarum Generibus, 39
Enquiry into the Roman Stylus, 39
and Gordon, 41–3, 61, 63
and Highlanders, 113
History of the Union, 37, 45
and Horace, 36, 123
and Horsley, 80, 81, 83, 85

and inscriptions, 96, 97
A Letter to a Friend Giving an Account of How the Treaty of Union Has Been Received Here, 37
and Ramsay, 65
and Romanisation, 46–8
Clerk, Matthew, 116
Clyde River, 19, 20, 21
Codex Hersfeldensis, 132–3
coinage, 21, 90, 92, 95, 96, 108
Coleman, James, 185
Remembering the Past in Nineteenth-Century Scotland, 197
Collingwood, R. G., 85
Collingwood Bruce, John
The Roman Wall, 194
Constable, Thomas, 175
Constantine the Great, Emperor, 76
Coote, Henry Charles
The Romans of Britain, 193–4
Corsica, 68
Corstorphine, 25
Coupar Angus, 175
Cramond, 46, 92, 142, 172, 175
Crawford, Matthew, 80, 94
Culloden, Battle of, 112, 114
Cumberland, Duke of, 114
Cumbernauld House, 92
Cumean Sibyl, 47
Curle, James, 198
Czartoryska, Princess Izabela, 99

Dalginross, 173, 174–5
Darien Scheme, 5, 27
Davidson, Neil, 6
De Situ Britanniae, 79, 150–5, 163–4, 165, 169, 195, 196
and Burton, 192
and Chalmers, 172
and Roy, 120, 121, 123, 124
De Wet, Jacob, 54
Defoe, Daniel, 37, 55, 95, 113
The History of the Union of Great Britain, 43
Dempster, Thomas, 134
Diana of Ephesus, 100
Dibdin, Thomas Frognall, 85
Dick, Sir Alexander, 96
Dio, Cassius, 23, 37, 132
Roman History, 58, 114, 150
distance slabs, *82*, 91, 92, 97, 98, 99, 115
Dorret, James
General Map of Scotland, 104–5
Douglas, Gavin, 7
Dow, Daniel
Ossian's Hall, 183
druids, 47, 74, 183
Drummond, David, 24
Drummond, William, 7
Drustus, King, 57
Du Toit, Alexander, 173
Dulacq, Joseph
Théorie Nouvelle sur le Mécanisme de l'Artillerie, 123
Duncan, Douglas, 37
Duncan, William

The Commentaries of Caesar Translated into English, 9, 123
Dundas, David, 119
Dundas, Thomas, 9
Duntocher Fort, 92

earthworks, 90, 104–5, 124, 173–4
East Lothian, 20, 23, 24, 40
Edinburgh, 46, 192, 198
Edinburgh University, 95
education, 7–8, 17
Egypt, 4
Egyptian Society, 42
Elegye Upon the Never Enough to be Lamented Decease of that Antient Illustrious and Venerable Lady Princess Scocia, An (anon), 56
Elphinstone, John
  New & Correct Map of North Britain, 104
England, 1, 5, 17, 48, 120–1
  and Caledonia, 67–9, 85–7
  and Roman Empire, 2, 12, 53, 192–4
  see also Acts of Union; Horsley, John; Stukeley, William
Enlightenment, 29, 113, 125, 168–9
Ennius, 64
Epictetus, 18
Equites Romani, 38, 42, 137
etymology, 20, 24–5, 174, 175
Eugene, King, 58

famine, 5, 27
Fendoch, 173
Fergus I of the Scots, King, 56
Fergus II of the Scots, King, 57–8
Ferguson, Adam, 157, 158, 168
Ferguson, William, 1, 5
Fergusson, Robert
  Elegy, On the Death of Scots Music, 179–80
Fife, 17, 23, 27, 136–7, 141, 176
Florus, 7
folklore, 22, 126, 141, 174, 175
Forbes, Duncan, 115
Forbes, Sir William, 9
Forbes of Disblair, William
  The True Scots Genius Reviving, 56
Fordun, John of, 2, 57, 106, 161, 163
  Chronica Gentis Scotorum, 24
forgeries, 163
Fort Augustus, 119
Fort George, 114
Forth, Firth of, 19, 20, 21, 169–70
Forth and Clyde Canal, 95
Forth/Clyde isthmus, 11, 19, 26, 113, 137, 154, 160; *see also* Clyde River; Forth, Firth of
France, 7, 12, 17, 197
Fraser, James, 199
Fulvius, Andreas
  Antichità di Roma con Figure, 24

Gaelic, 19, 114, 142–3, 149–50
Gaels *see* Highlands
Gale, Roger, 36, 38, 39, 41, 44–5, 47
  and antiquities, 92
  and Arthur's O'on, 106
  and Horsley, 80, 81, 83
  and Maitland, 143
  and Scotland, 85–6
  and Stukeley, 74, 77, 84
Gale, Samuel, 78
Galgacus *see* Calgacus
Gaskill, Howard, 185
Geoffrey of Monmouth, 1, 55
  Historia Regum Britanniae, 163
George IV of Great Britain, King, 9, 185
Gericke, Crispin, 92
Germany, 4, 12, 133, 197
Gibbon, Edward, 162, 178–9
Gibbons, Luke, 181
Gibson, Edmund, 78
  Britannia, 18, 21, 26
Gildas, 2, 153
Gillies, John, 192
Gilmorehill (Glasgow), 190
Glasgow University, 22, 95, 98, 99, 183, 190
Glen, James, 93
Glenmailen, 126, 173
Glorious Revolution (1689–90), 27
Gordon, Alexander, 29, 79, 154, 170, 195
  Additions and Corrections, By Way of Supplement, to the Itinerarium Septentrionale, 42, 62–3, 80
  and antiquities, 91, 92, 93, 94, 100
  and Arthur's O'on, 105, 106
  and Caledonia, 39–43, 149
  and Clerk, 33
  and earthworks, 124
  and Highlanders, 113
  and inscriptions, 96–7
  and Melville, 117
  and Mons Graupius, 141, 174
  and sculpture, 98
  see also Itinerarium Septentrionale
Gordon, Thomas
  The Works of Tacitus, 138–9
Gordon of Fyvie, William, 9, *10*
Gordon of Straloch, Robert, 11, 24
Gough, Richard, 39, 107
  Britannia, 114, 144
Graevius, Johann
  Thesaurus Antiquitatum Romanarum, 96
Grafton, Anthony, 163
Graham of Claverhouse, John, 64
Grand Tour, 8–9, 35–6, 118
Grant of Boharn, Rev. George, 178
Grassy Walls, 173
Gravina, Giovanni Vincenzo
  De Romano Imperio, 37
Great Britain, 5, 127–8, 168–9; *see also* England; Scotland
Greece, 192
Gregory, David, 8
Grenier, Katherine Haldane, 183
Gronovius, Abraham, 39, 94, 96
Gronovius, Jacobus, 35
Groom, Nick, 163
Grose, Francis
  Antiquities of Scotland, 183–4
Grotius, Hugo, 37

Index

Gruter, Jan, 92
Gryme, 2
Grymisdyke, 2
Guischardt, Karl Gottlieb
   Mémoires Militaires sure les Grecs et les Romains, 123
Gullane, 24–5

Hadrian, Emperor, 20, 23, 83, 162
Hadrian's Wall, 38, 40, 43, 44, 86
   and Hanoverians, 127
   and Horsley, 80, 83
   and Sibbald, 20, 23
   and Stukeley, 68, 75, 77
   and tourism, 194
Hall of Dunglass, Sir James, 9
Hamilton, Douglas, 8th Duke of, 9
Hamilton, Thomas, 192
Hamilton, William, 80
Hampton, James
   The General History of Polybius, 123
Hanoverians, 66, 112, 113–15, 115, 127
Haverfield, Francis, 85
   The Romanization of Roman Britain, 194
'Hawkshaw Head', 104
Haywood, Ian, 159–60
Hearne, Thomas, 84
Henry, Robert
   The History of Great Britain, 99, 158
Hermann (Arminius), 12, 197
Herodian, 23, 132
Hertford, Earl of, 38, 44
hieroglyphics, 42
Highlands, 4, 6, 27–8, 118–19
   and Agricola, 142–3
   and barbarity, 114–15, 127
   and Jacobites, 112, 113–15
   and poetry, 155
   and tourism, 184, 185
   see also Gaelic; Ossian
Hingley, Richard, 114, 115, 193, 194, 198
   The Recovery of Roman Britain, 189
History of the Picts, The (anon), 57–8
Hodges, James, 55–6
Hodgson, John, 85
Hole, William Brassey, 198
Home, John, 155
Homer, 156, 160
Horace, 36, 38, 41, 48, 65, 66, 150, 158, 179
Horsley, John, 33, 39, 62, 149, 170
   and antiquities, 92, 95
   and Arthur's O'on, 106
   and Bertram, 152, 154
   Britannia Romana, 68–9, 71–2, 79–81, *82*, 83–5, 123
   and inscriptions, 97
   and Melville, 117
   and Mons Graupius, 141–2
   and sculpture, 98
Hoselitz, Virginia, 193
Hume, David, 12
   History of England, 169
Hume of Godscroft, David, 7
Hunter, Dr William, 190

Hunterian Museum (Glasgow), 190

illustration, 100, *102–3*
Inchtuhil, 142, 173
Inglis, Sir John, 46, 92
Ingliston, 20, 21
Innes, Father Thomas
   A Critical Essay on the Ancient Inhabitants of the Northern Parts of Britain, or Scotland, 61–2, 63
inscriptions, 20–1, 22, 90, 91, 92, 96–7
   and Clerk, 93
   and Glasgow, 95, 190
   and militarism, 114
institutional collections, 95–6
Inveresk, 9, 170
Ireland, 62, 113; *see also* Ossian
Ireland, William Henry, 163
Irvine, Christopher, 24
Italy, 8–9, 24, 35–6, 62, 106, 133
   and sculpture, 90, 98, 99, 104, 183
   and Stukeley, 77–8
Itinerarium Septentrionale (Gordon), 39–40, 41–2, 59, 61, 68
   and Agricola, 134, 139–40
   and Burton, 192
   and Clerk, 94
   and Horsley, 80
   and Nimmo, 178
   and Stukeley, 79

Jacobites, 54, 119, 199
   and poetry, 63, 64, 65, 67
   and rebellions, 5, 9, 112, 113–14
James IV of Scotland, King, 58
James V of Scotland, King, 2
Jelfe, Andrew, 77
Johnson, Maurice, 74
Johnson, Samuel, 12, 132, 157
   Journey to the Western Isles of Scotland, 185
Johnston, Arthur, 139
Julia Domna, Empress, 100
Julius Hoss *see* Arthur's O'on
Jurin, James, 77
Juvenal, 19, 179

Kames, Lord, 158
Keithock, 117
Keppie, Lawrence, 95, 183
   The Antiquarian Rediscovery of the Antonine Wall, 189–90
Kidd, Colin, 57, 159, 198
Killiecrankie, Battle of, 64
Kirkbuddo, 117
Knox, John, 92
Krebs, Christopher
   A Most Dangerous Book, 12, 133

Laing, Malcolm
   The History of Scotland, 162
Lassels, Richard
   The Voyage of Italy, 9
Latin, 7–8, 37, 141
   and Gaelic, 142–3

and poetry, 63–4
and Sibbald, 17, 18, 19
and Tacitus, 132
Lee, Thomas Ashe, 114–15
Leiden (Netherlands), 8, 17, 35, 96
Leighton, Robert, 25
Lenzie, 175
Leslie, Bishop John, 61
Lhuyd, Edward, 21, 77, 92–3, 98
Linlithgow, 21, 76, 96, 97, 136, 172
Lintrose, 117
Lipsius, Justus, 134
   De Militia Romana, 116
Livy (Titus Livius), 7, 24, 123
Lock, Daniel, 78
Lollius Urbicus, 76, 91, 98, 198
Lomond Hills, 176
London, 17
Lowenthal, David
   The Past is a Foreign Country, 195, 196
Lowlands, 6, 27–8, 113, 149
Lucan, 64, 158
Lumisden, Andrew, 106
Lumsdaine of Innergelly, Robert, 100
Lupus, Virius, 162
Lysons, Samuel, 193

McDiarmid, Rev., 174–5
MacDonald, George, 85, 198
MacDonald, James, 143–4
MacLaurin, John, 44
McOmie, John, 173, *174*
Macpherson, David, 142
Macpherson, James, 155–65, 176–80, 195
   An Introduction to the History of Great Britain and Ireland, 161–2
Macpherson of Sleat, John
   Critical Dissertations on the Origin, Antiquities, Language, Government, Manners and Religion of the Ancient Caledonians, 177
Macrae, James, 62–3
McRonald, Theodore, 173
Maffie, Francesco Scipione, 42
Maitland, Charles, 95
Maitland, William, 93, 100
   The History and Antiquities of Scotland, 142–3
Major, John, 61
Manning, Susan, 168, 169
maps, 104–5, 119, 121, 124–5, 150
marble, 9, 38, 90, 94, 98, 104
Marcellinus, Ammianus, 23
Mark, George, 81
Mary Stuart (Mary Queen of Scots), 4, 53, 161, 198, 199
Masters, Robert, 84
Maule of Melgum, Henry, 57
Mavisbank, 47, 93–4
Mayor, J. E. B., 155
Meikleour (Cleaven Dyke), 173, *174*
Melville, Robert, 115–18, 120, 121, 124, 127, 195
   and Agricola, 137–8
   and Bertram, 154
   A Critical Enquiry into the Constitution of the Roman Legion, 117

and Shand, 126
Mercer, Thomas
   Arthur's Seat, 180
Middleby (Birrens), 38, 46, 91, 142, 183
   and antiquities, 92, 94
militarism, 9, 83–4, 112–13, 198–9
   and Romans, 114, 116–17
   and Roy, 119–25, 123–4
Milne, Alexander, 92
monarchy, 53–4, 62
Mons Graupius (Mons Grampius), battle of, 61, 117, 141–2, 162
   and *Agricola*, 132, 133, 135, 139–40
   and location, 174–5, 176, 191–2, 199
Montesquieu, 99
Montrose, Marquess of, 95, 98
monuments, 104–8
Moray, 21, 172
Mothersole, Jessie
   In Roman Scotland, 199
Mudie, Robert
   The Modern Athens, 192
Mugdock Castle, 98

Napoleon Bonaparte, 184–5
Nennius, 153, 162–3
   Historia Brittonum, 24
neo-Stoicism, 7
Nepos, Cornelius, 7
Netherbow (Edinburgh), 100
Netherlands, 7, 8, 17, 35, 96
Newstead, 96, 199
Newton, Isaac, 73
Nichols, John, 36, 84
Nicolson, William, 22, 134
   The Scottish Historical Library, 135
Nimmo, William
   A General History of Stirlingshire, 177–8
Nodier, Charles
   Promenade de Dieppe aux Montagnes d'Écosse, 185
Normans, 2
Notitia Dignitatum, 150
Notitia Imperii Occidentalis, 23
numismatics *see* coinage

Old Meldrum (Barra Hill), 126–7
Orrea (Burntisland), 20
Ossian, 155–63, 164, 165, 169, 183, 195, 196
   and Chalmers, 172
   Comala, 158, 160–1
   Fingal, 155, 157, 158, 159, 160, 199
   Fragments of Ancient Poetry, 155, 158, 159
   and influence, 176–80, 181
   Temora, 160
   and tourism, 184–5
   The War of Caros, 158, 160
Ouston, Hugh, 28
Ovid, 7

'pamphlet wars', 55–6
Pantheon (Rome), 77, 106
Paris, 2, 17, 23, 61, 104, 134
Parthia, 4

Patin, Charles
  Imperatorum Romanorum Numismata, 21
Paton, George, 39, 107
patriotism, 1–2, 7, 195, 197–9
  and Clerk, 43–4
  and Germany, 133
  and Gordon, 59
  and Union, 55–6
Patrizi, Francesco, 116
Peacham, Henry, 97–8
Pedley Sponberg, Mary, 125
Pembroke, Earl of, 38, 40, 73, 104
Penicuik House, 47–8, 80, 93–4, 107, 115, 182–3, 184
Pennant, Thomas, 84, 98, 183, 114
  A Tour in Scotland, 143–4
Perizonius, 35
Perth, 143–4, 180
Perth, Earl of, 95
Perthshire, 173–4
Philosophical Society of Edinburgh, 43
philosophy, 18
Philp, James
  The Grameid, 63, 66–7
Pichot, Amédée
  Historical and Literary Tour of a Foreigner in England and Scotland, 193
Picts, 57–9, 61
Piggott, Stuart, 77, 84
Pinkerton, John, 131, 133, 142, 155, 162
piracy, 62–3
Pitcairn, Archibald, 26
Pittock, Murray, 6, 55, 177
Playfair, James, 142, 175
Playfair, William Henry, 192
Pliny, 7, 47, 48, 57
Poems in English and Latin, on the Archers, and Royal Company of Archers, 67
poetry, 13, 63–7, 143, 149–50, 179–80; *see also* Ossian
Pointer, John
  Britannia Romana, 86
Poleni, Giovanni
  Utriusque Thesauri Antiquitatum Romanarum Graecarumque Nova Supplementa, 39
politics, 36, 65; *see also* Whigs
Polybius, 123
Pont, Timothy, 11, 24, 105, 124
Pope, Alexander, 156
Primitivism, 177, 196
private collections, 92–4
propaganda, 13
Ptolemy map, 150
Puységur, Jacques François de Chastenet de
  Art de la Guerre, 123

Ramsay, Allan, 45, 64–7, 179
  The Archers March, 66
  Epistle to a Friend at Florence, in His Way to Rome, 66
  The Ever Green, 65
  On Seeing the Archers Diverting Themselves at the Buts and Rovers, 65–6
  Tartana: or the Plaid, 65

  To the Phiz, 66
  The Vision, 65
Ravenna Cosmography, 150
Regal Union (1603), 5
Reichel, Servaz, 92
reliefs, 99, 100
Renaissance, 2
Renan, Ernest, 6
Richard of Cirencester, 152–5, 169
Richborough (Kent), 74
Ritratto di Roma Antica con Figure, 24
Robertson, William, 158
  The History of Scotland, 5
Robertson of Ladykirk, Roger, 9
Robertson of Struan, Alexander, 67
Rochette, Louis de la, 99, 105, 142, 144, 177
Roman Empire, 2, 4, 62
  and Clerk, 33, 36–9, 182–3
  and England, 68–9, 192–4
  and Gordon, 61
  and Horsley, 80–1
  and militarism, 112–13, 114, 116–17
  and Ossian, 158–63
  and Picts, 57–9
  and poetry, 64, 66–7
  and Scotland, 6–9, 11–13, 57–9
  and Sibbald, 15–16, 17–18
  and Stukeley, 74–7, 84
  see also Agricola, Gnaeus Julius; Caledonia
Rome *see* Italy; Roman Empire
Ross, Andrew, 8
Rossi, Filipo, 24
Roy, William, 105, 150, 174, 195
  and Agricola, 137–8
  and Bertram, 154–5
  and Burton, 192
  and Chalmers, 170
  The Military Antiquities of the Romans in Britain, 118–25, 126, 127–8, 189
  and Ossian, 157
Royal Company of Archers, 65–6, 67
Royal Society (London), 28, 38, 39, 73, 77, 113, 121
Ruddiman, Thomas, 96, 170
  Rudiments of the Latin Tongue, 7
Runciman, Alexander, 183

Sailor, Dylan, 145
Sallust, 7
Salmon, Nathaniel, 86
Saumaise, Claude, 23
Saxons, 2
Scaliger, Joseph Justus, 4, 56, 92, 96
Scarth, Harry
  Roman Britain, 194
Scipio, 64
Scota, 2, 56
Scotland, 1–5, 62, 168–9
  and Clerk, 46–8
  and historiography, 112–13
  and history, 5–6, 180–2
  and patriotism, 197–9
  and resistance, 52–5, 57–9
  and Roman Empire, 6–9, 11–13
  and romanticism, 185–6

and Sibbald, 15–16, 25–8
and tourism, 183–5
see also Caledonia; Highlands; Lowlands
Scott, James, 144
Scott, Sarah, 193
Scott, Sir Walter, 176, 181, 185
  The Antiquary, 108, 144–5
Scott of Scotstarvit, Sir John, 7
sculpture, 90, 92, 94, 97–9, 100, *101–3*, 104
Seneca, 18
Severus Septimius, Emperor, 20, 23, 83, 100, 135, 162
  and Arthur's O'on, 106
  and militarism, 114
Shakespeare, William, 163
Shand, Alexander, 126–7, 137–8, 174
Shaw, Lachlan, 114
  The History of the Province of Moray, 169–70
Shaw, William, 162
  An Enquiry into the Authenticity of the Poems Ascribed to Ossian, 157, 158
Shirva, 91, 92, 98, 99
Sibbald, Sir Robert, 5, 15–18, 52, 175, 195
  and *Agricola*, 134–7, 141
  and antiquities, 91, 92, 95–6, 100
  and Antonine Itinerary, 150
  and Arthur's O'on, 106
  and Buchanan, 53
  and Carausius, 163
  and Chalmers, 170
  and Clerk, 39, 44
  Commentarius in Julii Agricolae Expeditiones, 15, 21, 137
  Conjectures Concerning the Roman Ports, Colonies, and Forts, in the Firths, 15, 24, 28, 169
  Description of the Isles of Orkney and Zetland, 17
  Directions for his Honoured Friend Mr Llwyd How to Trace and Remarke the Vestiges of the Roman Wall Betwixt Forth and Clyde, 21
  Disputatio Medica de Variis Tabis Speciebus, 17
  and Highlanders, 113
  Historical Inquiries, Concerning the Roman Monuments and Antiquities in the North Part of Britain Called Scotland, 15, 19, 23, 26, 27, 28, 40, 78, 134, 135
  History, Ancient and Modern, of the Sheriffdoms of Fife and Kinross, 17
  and influences, 25–8
  and legacy, 28–9
  The Liberty and Independency of the Kingdom and Church of Scotland, 25
  and maps, 125
  and Melville, 117
  and Roman Scotland, 18–25
  Scotish Atlas, 17, 22, 26, 28
  and Stoicism, 123
  and Stukeley, 78
Sinclair, Sir John, 175
Slezer, John
  Theatrum Scotiae, 25
Sloane, Sir Hans, 25, 28, 73, 135, 137
Small, Andrew
  Interesting Roman Antiquities Recently Discovered in Fife, 176, 189

Smellie, William, 96
Smith, George, 127
Smith, John
  Galic Antiquities, 178
Society for the Encouragement of Learning (London), 42
Society of Antiquaries of London, 38, 42, 44, 72
  and Bertram, 163
  and Roy, 121
  and Stukeley, 73
Society of Antiquaries of Scotland, 96, 104, 173, 175, 176, 178
Solinus, 18
Solway Firth, 20
Somner, William
  A Treatise on the Roman Ports and Forts in Kent, 24
sovereignty, 54
Stafford, Fiona, 158, 185
Stair, James Dalrymple, Viscount, 54
  The Institutions of the Law of Scotland, 53
Statistical Account of Scotland, The, 144, 175, 176
Stirlingshire, 177–8
Stonehaven, 175
stones *see* distance slabs; inscriptions
Strabo, 37, 57
Strachey, John, 79, 85
Stuart, House of, 64, 66, 112, 113–14; *see also* Charles Edward Stuart; Mary Stuart
Stuart, Robert, 108
  Caledonia Romana, 190–1
Stukeley, William, 72–3, 84, 164, 195
  An Account of a Roman Temple, and Other Antiquities, Near Graham's Dike in Scotland, 40, 71, 74, 75, 76–7, 78–9
  An Account of Richard of Cirencester, 74
  and Agricola, 137
  and Arthur's O'on, 106–7
  and Caledonia, 149
  and Clerk, 38, 45–6
  and *De Situ Britanniae*, 150–4
  A Description of a Roman Pavement Found Near Grantham in Lincolnshire, 74
  and Horsley, 83, 85
  and inscriptions, 97
  Iter Boreale, 68
  Itinerarium Curiosum, 74
  The Medallic History of Marcus Aurelius Valerius Carausius, 74
  Of the Roman Amphitheater at Dorchester, 74
  and Ossian, 157
  and sculpture, 98
Suetonius, 7, 37
  De Grammaticis et Rhetoribus, 133
Sutherland, James, 21, 95
Sweet, Rosemary, 9, 86
swords, 40, 66, 96, 115–16

Tables of Ptolemy, 23
Tabula Peutingeriana (*Peutengerian Tables*), 23, 150
Tacitus, 61, 37, 44–5, 74, 164, 174–5
  Annals, 59
  Dialogus de Oratoribus, 133

Germania, 7, 12, 133
  see also *Agricola* (Tacitus)
tartan, 65, 185
Tay River, 83, 114, 117, 135, 142, 143–4
Theodosius, 76
Thetargus, King, 57
Thomas, Sophie, 197
Thorkelin, Grimur, 121, 126
Thule, 19, 26
Toland, John, 58
tourism, 183–4, 193, 194; *see also* Grand Tour
Traveller's Guide or, a Topographical Description of Scotland, The (anon), 178
tribes, 19, 20
Turnberry, 23
Tweeddale, 104
Tyne River, 20

Union *see* Acts of Union
Urry, John, 92

Van Boxhorn, Marcus Zuerius, 24
Vaugondy, Gilles Robert de, 104
Vegetius
  Epitoma Rei Militaris, 123
Vercingetorix, 197
Vikings, 2, 53
villas, 46, 47, 48, 172
Virgil, 64, 158
  Aeneid, 7, 154, 156–7

Wade, General, 114
Walker, Marshall, 65
Wallace, William, 197, 198, 199
Walpole, Horace, 1
Wanley, Humfry, 72
Warburton, John, 80, 127
  Vallum Romanum, 123
Ward, John, 97
Wars of Independence, 1, 55, 65
Watson, Lt-Col David, 118–19
weapons, 21, 96; *see also* swords
Wedderburn, James, 170
Wex, Karl, 155
Whigs, 38, 65, 127, 137, 138
Whitaker, John, 84
William III (of Orange) of England, King, 64
Williams, Hugh William, 192
Wilson, Sir Daniel, 108
  The Archaeology and Prehistoric Annals of Scotland, 191
Winchelsea, Earl of, 38, 73
Withers, Charles, 17, 125
Wodrow, Robert, 22, 25, 62, 95
Wood, John, 175
Woodward, B. B., 155
Woodward, Dr, 38
Wright, Thomas
  The Celt, the Roman and the Saxon, 194

Xiphilinus, 114

EU representative:
Easy Access System Europe
Mustamäe tee 50, 10621 Tallinn, Estonia
Gpsr.requests@easproject.com

www.ingramcontent.com/pod-product-compliance
Lightning Source LLC
Chambersburg PA
CBHW070349240426
43671CB00013BA/2447